MW01535386

HARD PRESS
NET

ISBN: 9781314641738

Published by:
HardPress Publishing
8345 NW 66TH ST #2561
MIAMI FL 33166-2626

Email: info@hardpress.net
Web: http://www.hardpress.net

THE LIBRARY
OF
THE UNIVERSITY
OF CALIFORNIA
LOS ANGELES

CHAS. E. LAURIAT CO.
IMPORTERS & BOOKSELLERS
385 Wash'n St. Boston

ACROSS WIDEST AFRICA

A. Henry Savage Landor.   Adem, the faithful Somali.

ACROSS WIDEST AFRICA

AN ACCOUNT OF THE COUNTRY AND PEOPLE
OF EASTERN, CENTRAL AND WESTERN AFRICA
AS SEEN DURING A TWELVE MONTHS' JOURNEY
FROM DJIBUTI TO CAPE VERDE   ❧   ❧   ❧

BY

A. HENRY SAVAGE LANDOR

AUTHOR OF

"In the Forbidden Land," "Tibet and Nepal," "China and
the Allies," "Across Coveted Lands," &c.

*Illustrated by 160 Half-tone Reproductions of Photographs and a
Map of the Route*

Volume I

LONDON

HURST AND BLACKETT LTD.

182, HIGH HOLBORN, W.C.

1907

All rights reserved

THE
CHAPEL
RIVER
PRESS

KINGSTON
SURREY

DT
351
L23a
v. 1

BY GRACIOUS PERMISSION

I

DEDICATE THIS WORK

TO

HIS MAJESTY VICTOR EMMANUEL III.

KING OF ITALY

1928903

PREFACE.

THE journey across widest Africa described in this book was over 8,500 miles in length, and occupied 364 days. Pleasure was its sole object. No white person accompanied the Author, who bore the entire cost of the expedition.

In the transliteration of native names, the local sound has with a few unavoidable exceptions been given, the vowels to be pronounced as in Italian.

A. HENRY SAVAGE LANDOR.

CONTENTS OF VOLUME I.

CONTENTS

LIST OF ILLUSTRATIONS TO VOLUME I.

LIST OF ILLUSTRATIONS XV

ACROSS WIDEST AFRICA

———◆———

CHAPTER I.

" Oh, sir, I am a worm, such a worm ! " . . . . was the exclamation of a tall, pleasant-looking Armenian, whom I met on my arrival in Djibuti, and who heartily grasped my hand. . . . "And," he added, " I represent . . . ." Here he quoted the name of a notorious but not very notable London halfpenny newspaper.

It had required no effort on my part to believe that the two statements—usually in the inverted order—went together, but for curiosity's sake I meekly begged to inquire of my interlocutor :

" What sort of a worm are you ? "

"Oh, sir . . . . such a worm, such a worm!" And with the delightful hesitation of stammering people, as well as much muscular straining of the neck, he eventually burst out : " I mean . . . . a . . . . a . . . . a book-worm ! And . . . . you write books . . . . and . . . . I am such—such a worm."

I must confess that one of the principal reasons that had taken me to Africa was to get away from people and books, book-talk, reporters and newspapers. To find myself on landing confronted with an interviewer was a most unexpected surprise—almost a grief. Interviews are a nuisance at all times, but with the thermometer registering 110° in the shade, the Djibuti hotel a little worse than the accommodation one provides for dogs, and the food—oh, the food ! . . . . hardly deserving such a name, this was, indeed, a severe trial.

I am superstitious and get more and more superstitious every day. All people are superstitious more or less, but will not own it. I do.

I am a firm believer in good and evil omens, and though omens seldom come true I cannot help going on believing in them. Before I started, and at the beginning of this particular journey, all the omens were bad.

Having one day taken it into my head to go across Africa—I was in London at the time—I proceeded to the Charing Cross railway station to inquire at what time the continental train would leave the next morning. Having received the required information, I was proceeding to walk out of the station when the roof came down with great *fracas*. On leaving my flat to drive to the station *en route* for Marseilles a funeral crossed my road—another sign of bad luck.

Needless to say, the passage across the Channel was fearful, and the crossing of the Mediterranean Sea from Marseilles to Port Said worse still. Deck-houses were washed away, skylights smashed by the waves, the saloon and cabins flooded, and we were two days late in reaching our destination owing to the force of the gale encountered.

After I had set foot on *terra firma* again at Port Said, and when I was driving in a cab to the railway station in order to proceed by train to Cairo, the conveyance, overladen with luggage, with dragomans and porters standing on the steps, sitting on the box and clinging behind, three wheels out of four of the vehicle suddenly gave way in ploughing through the heavy sand, and further progress was temporarily suspended. In a moment, however, dozens of men ran up to help, the baggage was conveyed to the station upon men's heads, and Cairo was safely reached.

A few days were quite sufficient to settle all the last details for my transcontinental journey. At the British Agency, Lord Cromer, Mr. Boyle, and Mr. Cecil Higgins showed me unbounded civility, and did all in their power to give me what official help they could. In the Sudan Government, Captain R. Owen furnished me with much lucid information regarding some of the country under British rule that I should have to cross, and I am greatly indebted to him and to Colonel Watson, A.D.C. to the Khedive, as well as to the officers in the Citadel, for a great deal of thoughtful kindness shown me.

Having accomplished all I wished to do in Cairo, having purchased more rifles for my men and more tents, I again returned to Port Said and embarked on a Messagerie boat, the *Oxus*, plying to French Somaliland.

I disembarked at Djibuti on January 5th, 1906. Djibuti was gaily decorated owing to the arrival in the harbour of some Russian warships which had been interned in the Philippine Islands during the Russian and Japanese war, and one or two English war vessels were also in the harbour. Those who have visited Djibuti remember and speak of it as the most odious place they have ever seen. For my part, I have seen places as odious as Djibuti, but never one more odious. It has all the drawbacks of a sprouting civilization, and, with the exception of a few highly-respectable French officials and a few merchants, the white people one meets are not quite so attractive as they might be.

The Governor's palace is quite imposing, although somewhat out of proportion to the size of the town. Attempts have been made to make streets at right angles, and there is even a square, with a well-patronized *café*. There is a saying in France among Colonials that the only vegetation of Djibuti consists of three cast-iron trees in this particular square, but when I was in Djibuti even that much " vegetation " had disappeared, if ever it had been there at all.

The town is built upon a barren plain divided into two sections connected by a road reclaimed from the sea. The French Governor most kindly offered every possible assistance, should I need it, and I had the pleasure of meeting one or two of the principal traders in the place. Mr. Kevorkhoff, a Russian Armenian, who has made a considerable fortune in the country, seemed to have a store well-fitted for colonial purposes, his trade being mostly, I think, in Abyssinian imports and exports, firearms for the Negus' people and provisions for Europeans. In the afternoon he drove me some miles out of the town to show me the public garden, the pride of the Djibuti residents. The pride was greater than the garden. Many plants were shown me which will some day grow, I suppose, and no doubt if people keep on pouring water upon them, in future times far removed there will be a few acres of luxuriant vegetation. If not, it will not be for the lack of interest, expense and trouble bestowed by the residents in their endeavour to satisfy the craving for a little verdure in so barren and hot a region.

France annexed this portion of the Somali coast as long ago as 1858, but the town of Djibuti itself only dates from 1896, when the Governor's residence was removed from Obock on the north side of the entrance to the Gulf of Toudjourrah.

The trade of the place is mostly a transit trade. Besides Mr. Kevorkhoff, there are a number of French, Italian and Greek traders, some quite successful in a comparatively small way, others not quite so successful. The chief profit, I believe, is made by importing arms and Gras cartridges into Abyssinia, as well as exporting coffee of most delicious quality, ivory and rubber from that country.

There are few places where the hours pass more slowly than at Djibuti. I am one of those persons who can live quite happily on almost nothing so long as that " almost nothing " is good, but I abhor pompous bad- ness. Hence, some miserable hours were those spent in the capital of French Somaliland. No doubt it may impress some people to see the hotel proprietor parade about with decorations on his chest for services rendered or not to some country or other ; and perhaps it satisfies some people to hear this grand person shout and order servants about—orders which were never obeyed. Per- haps some people are even proud to put up in one of the filthy rooms of the hotel belonging to so distinguished a personage. After inspecting every room in the place, I eventually hired the only one in which it was possible to live. A dingy double chamber, with a stinking carpet, two or three beds with dubious-looking linen, a washing basin . . . . Brr ! . . . . if one were given

to slight exaggeration one might propose to make it the
basis of a profitable grease factory. And the towels
. . . . good gracious me! . . . . when had they last
been to the laundry ?

"And for all this, how much, if you please ? " I
meekly inquired.

"About one louis a day with little extras ; " extras
which came to two louis when the bill arrived.

It was not possible to remain in the room during the
day, so notwithstanding the sun, which is indeed scorch-
ing at Djibuti, I went out for a walk. The sight of a
harbour is always interesting. In the Djibuti anchor-
age there is plenty of life. French steamers on their
way to Madagascar and the Far East generally call here,
and also many warships, English, French and Russian.
The lateen sails of Arab boats, which were numerous in
the harbour, always add picturesqueness to a seascape.
These boats are wonders of naval construction, with
their admirable lines for speed and rough seafaring.

Still, one could not look at the harbour the whole day
or walk about the town, three minutes being the longest
time one can occupy in travelling across its length and
about two minutes across its width. The sand in which
one sank was burning, and radiated the torrid rays of
the sun. The streets were deserted, except for a pariah
dog or two drowsily sleeping in what little shade they
got inside a doorway ; for towards noon when the sun
is on the meridian, the shadow is directly under one's
person, and vertical walls give no shadow at all. If by
chance one of these dogs got up and barked at the
unusual sight of a stranger wandering about in the
middle of the day, one immediately heard female voices
of Greek and Italian nationalities call out words of

endearment from balconies and doorways. These were the only people who were awake—people like that always are—but all the others were asleep, fast asleep, with all the light shut out of their houses by screens and by the large verandahs surrounding the houses. It is only towards the evening that the good people begin to wake up again.

The houses in the European settlement were not much to look at, but they were practically built to suit the climate, with its hot winds and torrid but healthy heat. There were no glass panes to the windows, and the Indian punkah had been generally adopted in order to make life possible in the rooms. The moment one entered a house one felt quite stifled.

There was an ice factory in Djibuti, a great boon to the residents when it worked, but it had a way of stopping when it was most needed.

More interesting than the foreign settlement was certainly the native town. There were three main agglomerations of huts, of which Djibuti was the principal, then Bunder and Djedid, as well as another, Boulers, on the way to Zeila in British Somaliland. These agglomerations aroused more pity than interest. They consisted of a lot of miserable shanties erected anyhow, with putrid beams, rotten mats, and pieces of canvas ; some only had thatched roofs. A mortar and pestle here and there, some calabashes and a few pots and pans strewn about the ground—that was all. None of these buildings were of a permanent nature, but seemed put up for temporary residences. In fact, the population of Djibuti was not a fixed population, but we find that many neighbouring tribes, such as the Somali, Haberual, the Issa, and the Gadabursi, as well as Danakil, come here occasionally to trade. Then many Galla come over for the same purpose, and even Sudanese and Swahilis can be seen in Djibuti, as well as many Arabs and people from Aden and the Arabian coast.

Enterprising Hindu merchants have also found their way to French Somaliland as well as to Abyssinia, and they manage to get on well. They are very saving and sober ; contented with comparatively small profits ; and fully understanding the requirements of the natives, they manage to do business successfully with a small capital on the same lines as the Greeks and the Armenians, where French and English merchants could not run a business at a profit.

Of course, especially since the railway was opened, Djibuti has become one of the chief outlets of Abyssinian trade. One often sees in the market-place Abyssinians in their characteristic trousers and a scarf draped over the shoulder. One is struck at once with the fact that although the origin of their race was evidently Semitic—as is clearly shown in the purer types—in the majority of cases strong negroid influences can be detected.

The most attractive of all the people in French Somaliland are possibly the Somali. They are quite of a superior type to any I found on my journey across Africa from east to west, except the Senegalese on the West Coast. Although not superior in intelligence, they are superior to the Senegalese in physical appearance. They are tall, thin and well-proportioned, with well-chiselled limbs and features, a good arched nose, with rather finely-modelled nostrils, and the lips, although developed, are not so offensively full as with most of the negro tribes of the central zone of Africa. Their skin is of a smooth, delicate texture, with no superabundance of oily excretion, as in most negroid races, and their active life gives them a wiry, supple appearance quite devoid of extra flesh. They are of a nervous temperament, extremely sober and moral—when not demoralized by European ways—dignified and faithful in a high degree to their leaders. There is no bravado about them, but they are somewhat cruel by nature. They can endure hardships silently and stand impassive in case of danger. They are excellent walkers and camel-men, and many of them make first-class *shikaris*. In their normal condition they are nomad shepherds. One of their chief as well as most remunerative amusements consists in raiding neighbouring tribes, and in this they show great cunning.

As far as I could judge, the Somali seemed quite happy under French rule. We shall see that of the great number of men I employed during my journey across Africa, it was only a Somali—a French Somali—who remained faithful to the very end, notwithstanding the severe hardships and sufferings which he had to endure.

CHAPTER II.

BEFORE the construction of the railway the most frequented route from Djibuti to Adis-Ababa was across the Somali desert *via* Gueldessa-Harrar-Tchertcher as far as the Hawash river, then by the escarpment up to the plateau on which the Abyssinian capital is to be found.

There was a shorter but somewhat more dangerous route branching off at Adde Galla, when the railway was completed up to that point, across the Danakil desert, doing away with a great détour, and meeting the high trail near the foot of the escarpment. Since the railway reached its present terminus at Dire-Dawa another route has been most generally adopted, between the two others, much shorter than the one by Harrar and the Tchertcher (462 kilometres), and a great deal safer and more comfortable than the one by the desert—usually called the " Bilen route " (420 kilometres). This route is the one by Assabot, the one which I followed, some 385 kilometres in length, along fairly level country skirting the northern spurs of the Tchertcher.

These three routes, besides one much longer seldom used—named the " desert route "—which describes an immense détour near Adis-Ababa in order to avoid the steep ascent of the escarpment, have now Dire-Dawa as their centre on the east. On the west at Tadetchimalka they all meet and proceed along a common trail as far as Adis-Ababa. The long desert route is sometimes used by caravans of camels, as the humped animals have great difficulty in climbing up the steep incline between Tadetchimalka and Baltchi.

According to surveys made, the difference between the maximum and minimum elevations on the Bilen route between Dire-Dawa and Tadetchimalka is only about two thousand feet, the highest points being Dire-Dawa, which my own aneroids registered at 3,500 feet high, and the Hawash river 2,800 feet. Whereas on the Assabot route, as we shall see, the difference is somewhat greater, but not nearly so much so as upon the Harrar-Tchertcher route, where, at Uarabile, an elevation of 7,189 feet occurs, and, at Kulubi, the trail goes over a height of 8,225 feet. The next highest altitudes are at Derru and at Kunni, the lowest point of the many undulations being at Irna, where the trail descends to 1,763 metres (6,940 feet), according to Marchand's surveys.

This route is frequently chosen notwithstanding its many ups and downs and greater length, as it is cooler owing to the elevation and the vegetation all along. It has everywhere plenty of good spring-water and pastures for the animals. Supplies of food can be obtained for the men from the Galla who inhabit the country, and who are great cultivators of the land.

The Bilen desert route is dry and extremely hot; in one portion water must be carried for a considerable distance—some two days' hard marching—and no grazing is to be found for the animals. There are, of course, no villages, and therefore no food supplies are to be obtained, while the Danakil and brigand tribes frequently take advantage of the tired condition of the animals to raid passing caravans. It was only in 1903 that a French reporter, travelling with the MacMillan expedition, Monsieur Dubois-Dessaulle, was murdered on the edge of the desert by Danakils, and his body terribly mutilated. A few days before my departure from Dire-Dawa, an Arab trader and two Abyssinians met with a similar fate. Portions of their anatomy were amputated in a primitive manner and carried away in triumph by the Danakils.

It was early in the morning that I went to the station in order to proceed up country by the small railway which has been constructed by the " Compagnie Impériale des Chemins de Fer Ethiopiens " as far as the foot of the plateau of Harrar, some 210 kilometres from the coast (or about 190 miles).

A worse-regulated concern than this railway would be difficult to imagine. Instead of making it easy for people to travel by it, everything is done to prevent travellers using it, to make them uncomfortable, and to give them every possible annoyance. The brigandage of the Danakils and other tribes who extorted money from caravans upon the road was a mere nothing when compared with the exorbitant charges which were made for travellers and their baggage to those unfortunately compelled to travel on this railway. The officials and employees made themselves quite ridiculous by their impudence and the absurd regulations they attempted to enforce, and it struck me that they were trying to do their best to ruin the railway, at least if it were intended to be a paying concern. It reminded me very much of the method of systematic obstruction which was used by the unsatisfied railway officials of Italy, and which rendered travelling most tiresome and almost impossible for some time in that beautiful country.

The same things happened at Djibuti. While the train, which ran up to Dire-Dawa only twice a week, and sometimes not so often, was ready in the station for the entire night, while passengers, who were charged as much as 186 francs (£7 9s.) first-class, 62 francs (£2 10s.) second-class (the second-class corresponding to nothing in this country, but being about the same as the fourth-class in France), the passengers were kept shut out of the station among dirty negroes, baskets of stinking fish, and packing-cases until only a few minutes before the departure of the train. Every ounce of luggage had then to be weighed and paid for, and one could not obtain change for one's money. Such valuable currency as English sovereigns and five-pound notes were refused at the ticket-office as money unknown to the officials. If a prize were to be given for the greatest confusion I have ever witnessed at the departure of a train, it should certainly be awarded to the officials of the Djibuti station. My astonishment had no bounds when I discovered at the end of the journey that none of my baggage had been lost.

Anyhow, after much blowing of whistles a start was made, and the train moved out of the station, the tiny carriages being full of German commercial travellers rigged up in most elaborate tropical costumes (as the people at home imagine explorers in Central Africa should dress), and Greek carpenters, somewhat more modestly attired. Of the three carriages of which the train was formed, the first and second were combined into one, with a luggage-van. The third-class for natives seemed by far the most comfortable compartment, as it was open all round. Natives only were allowed in this carriage for the sum of fifteen francs for the entire journey, which ought to be as much as first-class passengers should pay for their convey-ance.

The line itself was not badly laid, but the carriages were bad and kept in a shocking condition.

One went over richly-coloured red soil strewn with black volcanic rock. Immediately on starting one began to ascend, and after some two hours we proceeded between flat-topped hills of no great elevation and covered with green shrubs. Here and there flocks of goats stampeded at either side as the train puffed away. Near the numerous little stations at which we stopped were Somali sheds. Near them stood natives with spears in hand. Wise-looking camels watched the train with their customary impassiveness.

There were fifteen stations, all counted, along the entire run, at distances varying from seven to forty-seven kilometres apart, the longest runs being between Ambouli and Holl Holl (forty-five kilometres) and be-tween Ada or Adde Galla and Mello (forty-seven kilo-metres).

The line was single, with only four crossings where trains could meet. Near the Abyssinian frontier one saw signs of copper, here and there the peculiar green of sulphate of copper being noticeable on the soil's sur-face. Iron was much in evidence all along, giving a black and bluish tint to the rock and earth.

When we arrived at the frontier at Ali Sabieh, eighty-eight kilometres from Djibuti, we saw a French fort upon the hill, and at kilometre 106, at Daouenlé, where the train stopped for lunch, we came across an honest

man—painfully honest. Not an Abyssinian by any
means, but a Greek named Giorgi, gaily dressed in a
starred blue shirt and striped trousers—not unlike Uncle
Sam as we see him in pictures. He had built for himself a small shed which he used as a restaurant, and for
the large equivalent of two shillings gave you five
excellent and plentiful courses, sweets, fruit, coffee and
wine included. He never failed to tell you at the end
that if you had not had sufficient, he would be glad to
give you more.

Once we got into Abyssinia there were guards of
Abyssinian soldiers at all the stations, as well as escorts
of soldiers who were placed upon the train.

Every now and then gazelles bounded about in the
most agile and graceful fashion. The whole country
was covered with high ant-heaps. As we got higher on
the plateau we left behind on our left high, rugged and
pointed peaks, the Mounts D'Arro and Mari and the very
distant Mounts of Obenu, near Lake Killelu. The train
had some difficulty in going up the steep gradient,
especially in one or two places when the engineer and
his assistant walked in front with a bag of sand each,
scattering it upon the rails so that the wheels could
have a grip. Several times the train was brought to a
standstill because there were herds of cattle grazing
upon the line. On nearing Arraua, two stations before
reaching Dire-Dawa, the plateau lost the black and
dark-grey tones of the desert country and became
more covered with verdure, a great many trees being
scattered about among the hillocks on either side. So we
puffed along, Abyssinian soldiers presenting arms everywhere as the train steamed by, and swarms of naked
children chasing the train and keeping well up with it

for some distance, at every intermediate station where
the train did not halt.

After twelve hours' travelling, stopping here and
there to pick up bolts or screws which were tumbling
off the shaky engine—at one moment there was a talk
of stopping on the line for the whole night until some of
the pieces were recovered—we eventually arrived at Dire-
Dawa, the terminus of the line, the elevation of this
place, according to my aneroids, being 3,500 feet.

The Abyssinian governor of the town, Atto Negato,
with his soldiers, was at the station doing custom-
house officer's duty. He was most civil, and said he
would never disturb Englishmen to open their baggage,
especially as he knew I had not come to the country to
trade ; but he was not so civil to the German travellers,
whom I left struggling on the platform with their baggage
open for inspection.

There was a good hotel at Dire-Dawa kept by a Greek
gentleman, a Mr. Michaïlidis, who was also the British
Consul in the place. The hotel was beautifully clean
and well-managed, and the food quite excellent, while
the charges were indeed moderate. Mr. Michaïlidis was
quite an institution in the little town which has sprouted
at the end of the railway, and his charming politeness
towards Englishmen who treat him properly was welcome. He was ready to help travellers to make up
their caravans and to get information and assistance
for them in buying animals and obtaining men. Knowing the country so well as he does, he has special facilities
for looking after the interests of travellers. He is
very quick and intelligent, most sensible and practical,
and I think that British interests could not have been
placed in better hands at Dire-Dawa.

Danakil.   Adem, an Issa Somali.   Danakil.

Author's attendants.

Dire-Dawa is practically a French town. Some of the trade is in the hands of a few French commercial houses, but there are also a number of Indian traders—in fact, the entire bazaar is Hindu. Mahommed-Ali, the principal Hindu trader, has a well-furnished store. There are also some Greek traders. I was not much struck with the French ways of doing business in that portion of the country, which is very different indeed from the French mode of doing business in Central and Western Africa. At Dire-Dawa you find a curious set of merchants, who wish to make a fortune in a short time and who endeavour to do this by attempting to extort all they can out of you for the articles you may require. Of course, sometimes one has to put up with it, but sometimes, too, one prefers to go without rather than be robbed. I think that is one of the chief reasons why Greek and Indian traders can make money hand over fist in those countries, where French merchants go bankrupt; simply because they sell you better goods and are satisfied with a high, but still infinitely more moderate, price than French merchants. Of course, another great fault I have to find with the French merchant in Abyssinia is that he goes out there generally with a small capital and bad merchandise, and he must have quick returns or else succumb. To my mind, the Greek and Indian type of merchant will always swamp European traders who do business on a small scale, as they understand better the needs and the resources of the country and what is to be got out of the people. They are satisfied with a humble and inexpensive existence, which their European rivals cannot emulate. Far from it, the average European agent who is sent out to those countries generally craves for a life

of luxury—champagne, whisky, expensive cigars, etc.,
etc.—and the etceteras come very dear in many ways
in those countries, both for the purse and the health.
So that business does not always seem to be remunerative.

The Greeks, I noticed, who were very numerous all
over Abyssinia, have a wonderful facility for learning
languages quickly, and many of them can converse
fluently in the Galla tongue, in Harrari, the Danakil
language, Somali and Amharic. They also thoroughly
understand the ways of the natives, and they are patient
to a degree where a European would lose his temper
and use his fists or his feet freely.   So that these Greeks
and Armenians, although doing business in a small
way, seem to manage to carry away all the trade of the
country.   Also it must be said that the natives are less
suspicious of these men than they are of European
traders, in whom they never put absolute trust.   In
a way they look upon Greeks and Turks as belonging
almost to their own race.   The Armenians are not so
popular as the Greeks, and they are somewhat looked
down upon by the natives, this being, I think, merely
a racial dislike, which is difficult to explain.

In the Dire-Dawa bazaar I was told that there were
some two thousand people under British protection, viz.,
Hindus, Parsees, Somalis from Berber, Arabs from Aden
and Sudanese. The Greeks were also under British
protection, and being of a quarrelsome nature they
generally had a great many questions to settle before
the local authorities. But taking things all round, it
was a well-behaved population ; these rows were only
regarding money matters, and but seldom took the
violent form of a fight.

Scenery near Harrar. In the background can be seen a hedge of cacti.

CHAPTER III.

WHILE I was getting my caravan ready at Dire-Dawa, I took an excursion to the city of Harrar, some thirty miles off, in order to visit His Highness Ras-Makonnen, Governor-General of Harrar and its Dependencies.

There is a good wide trail between Dire-Dawa and Harrar among hills fairly well covered with trees. Dog-faced monkeys of great size can be seen in numbers playing on the sand of the river-bed, which in some portions forms the trail, and gigantic cacti, twenty to thirty feet high, grow in the more open spaces, especially near villages, where they are used extensively and efficaciously as hedges. Near a Galla village on the hillside the trail makes a great détour to the south-east, but a short cut going due south exists, and by taking this and ascending the mountain at a steeper angle the great loop of the road can be avoided.

One passes a small Galla village, with its mud-walled huts and thatched roofs and a thick fence made of brush-wood. This is about nineteen kilometres from Dire-Dawa. One soon goes over the pass, where a beautiful view is obtained of the Somali plains to the north-east and east-north-east. The Foldi mountain stands in the middle foreground before the eye reaches the plain; and the Gurgurra, as well as the small Mount

D'Arro, are to the north, with the Dire-Dawa hills in the immediate foreground. The trail goes between the Rukko and the Afrotti Mountains. As one gets to the highest point on the Karra Pass (6,700 feet), a beautiful view is to be obtained of the River Idjahanen down below, as well as a more extensive view than before of the Somali valley and the Danakil country to the south-west developing itself into a grand arc of a circle from a south-westerly to a north-westerly point. To the south is the pretty lake of Haradilli, just appearing between hillocks, as one gets over the pass. In the pretty basin in which this lake lies are some Galla villages, as, after crossing the pass, we are entirely in the Galla country.

As we proceed on the road the rugged Bara Muldatta Mountains are on our right, a short distance away. Through an avenue of cacti we come to a kraal, also fenced round with cacti—*radami*, as the Galla call this useful plant.

The Galla are great shepherds. Near their villages are a great number of goats; humped oxen, and cows with long straight horns.

The trail is much frequented, as a good deal of the trade of Harrar comes this way to the railway terminus, instead of going as formerly by caravan to Zeila in British Somaliland. We met on the trail caravans of coffee for export to Aden and exchanged salutations with the men in charge of the animals.

I was somewhat amused to find my travelling companions of the Djibuti railway stranded upon the trail, sweating all over and using the most violent words in the German tongue, they having started on the road from Dire-Dawa some hours before I did in the middle of the night. They were struggling to keep upon their animals' backs some patent saddles and harness which may have been well suited for German horses ; the elaborate military bit hung several inches under the noses of the mules instead of fitting into the mouth, the head of an Abyssinian mule being much shorter than that of a German charger. Some of their gigantic patent helmets had been blown away by the wind, and one or two of the party were now travelling with hand-kerchiefs tied round their heads.

In the basin of the lake were extensive plantations of *doorah* or *dura* (sorghum), which had just been cut and was being collected in stacks all over the valley. As I went further on, more Galla villages and farms dotted the entire hillsides. The huts had cylindrical walls of wood and cane matting, plastered over with mud and supporting conical thatched roofs. Lively groups of men threshing grain with long sticks, and singing all the while in order to keep time with their work, could be seen and heard here and there. This somewhat enlivened the monotony of the journey in the hot hours of the day.

Large kites and hawks soared gracefully in the sky overhead, and amusing incidents occurred when I got off my mule in order to photograph natives. The women particularly were extremely shy and hid their faces behind both hands, running full speed into the darkest corners of their huts, while the children were terrified and shrieked to their hearts' content when they saw a camera pointed at them.

The altitude of the lake was, according to my aneroids, 6,400 feet. As we got nearer Harrar, we met some native travellers coming from that city. On reaching a second lake, the Haramaya—a most picturesque sheet of water with hundreds of cattle grazing upon the banks—I halted for some minutes at the Abyssinian rest-house in order to have lunch.

The water of the lake, owing to the cattle which went right into it to drink, and stirred up the mud and dirt, was unfit for consumption. It was simply swarming with animal life when I took a glass of it, microbes of all kinds and shapes, visible with the naked eye, swimming round the glass.

I asked the restaurant keeper to give me some tea or coffee, or a native drink, but nothing of the sort was to be had, whereas bottles of whisky, absinthe, and even a bottle of green Chartreuse were produced, the man declaring that those, and not coffee and tea, were the liquids which white people always drank. I had the unhappy idea of trying a steak cooked in Abyssinian fashion, a lot of incisions being made in the meat in order to facilitate its cooking. I do not think I have ever regretted anything so much as trying the experiment, for over the meat rancid oil had been poured which gave the dish a disgusting odour. Famished as I was, I was unable to eat it, and for hours afterwards I had in my mouth and nose the evil taste of the first morsel which I had attempted to swallow.

To the north-east of Harrar was a table-land of considerable height, the Gunduntu Mountains, with Mount D'Arro, a flat conical peak. Over undulating, cultivated country one rose to a height of 6,650 feet on a pass, and later I crossed the last pass before reaching Harrar at an elevation of 6,500 feet.

I now met hundreds of Galla upon the trail, the women with a double-ball arrangement of hair behind the head, and the rest plaited all over the head into

Bird's-eye view of Harrar.

tiny little tresses left in their natural curly state at the ends behind. The end curls of these tresses were en-circled in a sort of gauze net, which covered nearly all the top of the head except a small section directly above the forehead. These Galla women were pic-turesque enough in their red, yellow and blue ornaments ; with their earrings and blue bead necklaces.

From the last pass, where I began to descend into the Harrar valley, a fine bird's-eye view was to be obtained. Directly before me to the east were chain after chain of mountains. To the south-east I could see again the high, flat-topped Mount Gundura, and above a streak of green vegetation rose a white dome on the slope of a central elevation with a white square building at the side. Other white dots were near it and two towers. As I descended, I left behind and soon out of sight to the south and south-west the Bara Muldatto range, and towards sunset I approached the small, walled outer city, higher than the larger Harrar, and with a pic-turesque castellated gate. This smaller enclosure is used now as a grain store. Remains of the formerly-existing English fortress can be seen near the small suburb of conical-roofed Galla huts outside the town.

As one approached the larger city, only a few yards further down the hill, it reminded one strongly of Arab towns. The figures of men in their white clothing, draped over the shoulder, a fashion common also to the north coast of Africa, rather served to accentuate this illusion.

The city gate was not impressive, and just large enough for a horse and rider to get through. As one stepped through the gate in the city wall, one looked down upon the numberless flat roofs of houses built of stone and mud. There was no regularity about the streets, and as one meandered round endless corners, always keeping to the left in Arab fashion, through narrow lanes, one finally emerged into the market square. There stood Ras-Makonnen's palace to the west, and on the north side of the square the Custom House sheds, with quantities of ivory, coffee and foreign goods waiting to pay duty.

Next to Ras-Makonnen's palace were the cavalry barracks, closely guarded by soldiers. I happened to peep in at the gate, when the sentry shouted to me that I was a *ferenghi* and could not enter. There was nothing to be seen except a few partitions of brushwood dividing the stalls for the horses, and a few stacks of spears and rifles in a more or less dilapidated condition. That was all.

The gates of the city were closed at sunset and opened at sunrise, and I was fortunate to enter the town only a few minutes before the gate was barred. The first person I met in Harrar was Mr. John Gerolimato, a Greek, who fulfils the duties of British vice-consul in Harrar. He is a man of superior education, extremely well informed and most enterprising as a merchant. He was held in much esteem in Harrar. He had considerable influence over the Ras, who put absolute trust in him ; and in one or two walks which I had with the vice-consul he seemed, indeed, to be everybody's adviser in the place.

As we were going along the streets, a swarm of soldiers came towards us, and two men, evidently chiefs, moved out of the centre of this rabble of armed men and came to greet Mr. Gerolimato in a hearty fashion. They were Fitawrari Gabri, Governor of

Ogaden, and Atto Karokorat. Further up the road another man in his black toga came along, followed by more soldiers armed with Gras rifles. This was Abdalla Taha, the Governor of Jig Jiga.

As we prowled here and there in the narrow streets of the city, we came upon more chiefs in their black or brown cloaks, and invariably surrounded by strong escorts. Here and there we met Greeks and Armenians, ever distinguishable by their unshaven faces and ill-fitting clothes and hats. In the principal market-place, with its humble but picturesque gateways of Makonnen's palace and of the police station, were hundreds of black faces, some with heads shaved clean, others with short frizzly hair. The men were generally draped in ample white garments, whereas the women struck brilliant notes of colour in that already lively scene, dressed as they were in their red or blue gowns, much draped over the head not unlike the Indian fashion.

Under low sheds constructed of a piece of cloth supported on three or four sticks were Galla traders, selling narrow white, striped, or blue cloth, beads, ornaments and ribbon. They seemed to carry on a brisk business.

Children unable to walk were slung low upon the back by the women, and nearly every man one saw in the square possessed a long stick resting upon his left shoulder, to which he attached packages of food, or other purchased articles.

Near the square was the bazaar, a narrow lane so crowded with people that it was difficult to force one's way through. The merchants were mostly Indians, and Greeks under British protection. They sold almost exclusively cotton goods from Manchester or from

America, American cottons having lately gained considerably over British manufactures.

In a smaller square we came upon the butchers' market, with its many wooden tables strewn with more or less appetizing meat. This place seemed to be the *rendez-vous* of all the women of Harrar, who came in the afternoon to talk scandal while making their purchases.

When you have seen these two markets, the Coptic church and the Mosque—all of no artistic importance —there is nothing else to see in Harrar. The tortuous streets, with the mud-plastered walls of the houses, are all more or less alike. The heat of the sun has baked the mud of the walls to such an extent that it has become as hard as stone.

No one is allowed in the streets without a lantern after nine o'clock in the evening, and even with a lantern one always runs a risk of being arrested. Little harm would come to a European, who with some slight *backshish* would soon be released ; but natives, and even Greeks or Indians, would be involved in considerable trouble if found out during the night, and they would be heavily fined and the former possibly even beaten.

When I was in Harrar the Bank of Abyssinia, newly formed, was about to start a branch in this important city, and Ras-Makonnen, who had been elected one of the directors, had given one of his palaces outside the town to be used as the Bank building. No doubt, the Bank will have some uphill work in the beginning, as banking in European style was quite unknown in Abyssinia, and people preferred to hoard their money rather than trust it to any commercial concern. Of course, lending money is a very popular custom in Harrar, as in all Oriental countries, but an interest of

A street in Harrar.

at least one thousand per cent. is expected for the convenience, and it remains to be seen whether the three per cent. or four per cent. interest, which the Bank will pay on money deposited on current accounts, will be sufficient to attract the capitalists of Harrar.   Mr. H. M. Goldie, who had just arrived to take charge of the Bank, was studying the best ways of establishing suitable relations with the people, and no doubt with his vast experience of banking matters in Egypt he will be able to do what is possible in the interests of the Bank in Ras-Makonnen's country.

From the beautiful house, at an elevation of 6,150 feet above the sea, which had been given to the Bank by Makonnen, one obtained a delightful view of the town, with St. Michael's Church in the foreground upon the hillside. The city itself was some 250 feet lower, or 5,850 feet in its most central part.

The approximate population of Harrar is from forty-five thousand to fifty thousand people. Among these we find about a thousand people under British protection, mostly a shifting population of Somalis, Arabs, Berbers, and about one hundred and fifty Hindus.

The export trade of Harrar consists principally of hides and coffee, which find their way to Aden *via* Djibuti. The caravan route to Zeila in British Somaliland, which was formerly much used, has now been almost entirely abandoned.

One very curious point about this city is that a special language, the *Harrari*, absolutely different from the Galla spoken in the surrounding country, has been adopted by the town people.

We find a great mixture of types in Harrar, of Galla, Somali (Issa and Haberual), Danakil, Arabs,

Abyssinians, Ogaden Somali and specimens of minor tribes.

Although vanquished by the Amharas, the Harraris have never been morally affected by the Abyssinian conquest, and they consider themselves quite as independent as they were before. They look upon the Government as a protection rather than as a subjection. A certain rancour is still preserved in their hearts against the Abyssinians, and I think that had they a suitable opportunity they would soon shake off the Abyssinian yoke.

They are not of the Coptic religion, but are Mussulman, with firm religious notions on the subject. Even between the Ras and the Mahommedans there is an intermediate chief, with whom the Ras has to settle all differences with those practising the religion of Islam.

Early in the morning, accompanied by Mr. Gerolimato, I proceeded to the palace, where Ras-Makonnen was expecting me. We did not enter by the main palace gate, surmounted by elongated crouching lions, but we went through a back entrance, first through a court, the walls of which were decorated with Gras rifles, spears and circular shields ; then from a second court we mounted the staircase of a modest building. On the first floor, at the door of a whitewashed room of the simplest description, Ras-Makonnen greeted us with effusion. He beckoned us to sit down, and he seated himself between two large red cushions upon a low divan. He looked quite worn and ill, and he had the pathetic look upon his face of a man whose end is near. He seemed absorbed in deep thought, almost as if he were in a trance. He breathed heavily, and it was an effort for him to speak, but he struggled through it

Ras Makonnen and his son.
(This photograph, taken by Author, was the last shortly before the Ras' death.)

bravely. With long pauses between, he spoke in a faint voice.

" How are your King and the Queen, and the Prince and Princess of Wales and their children ? The English King was very good to me. We must drink his health in Abyssinian wine. . . . I am very glad to see you in my country, and I want you to accept one of my favourite horses as a remembrance of your visit to me. It is a good ambling horse, and you will find it easy to ride on your journey to the capital. . . . . Yes, England and Abyssinia are good friends, and my wish is that our friendship may continue for ever."

The Ras seemed quite exhausted. There was a long pause, during which I examined our surroundings. The only decorations in the rooms consisted of a few rugs upon the floor, one solitary Japanese fan nailed to the wall and a cheap glass globe lamp.

We sipped hydromel from tall unwashed tumblers, and when the Ras lifted his head again, I told him how much we in England admired his great courage in battle, as well as the sensible way in which he administered the country.

The Ras bowed modestly—for, indeed, this great fighter was in his manner as humble, gentle and modest as a maiden. He was intensely unaffected and soft-spoken, and upon his lips an occasional sad smile lighted temporarily his *sympathique* countenance. It was enough to see the Ras to be struck at first glance by the intelligence of his face and by the extreme kindness and firmness of his character.

" I want you to meet my son," said the Ras, and he despatched a servant to fetch his boy, Deziazmatch (General) Tafari, a little fellow of twelve, with large,

soft pensive eyes and a sad girlish face of refined lines.
He spoke excellent French, and, like his father, was
most charmingly simple in manner.

Ras-Makonnen insisted on rising, as he wished to
show me the interior of his palace. He took us to his
bedroom—in European style—occupying the highest
and loftiest room in the building. Behind a curtain
dividing the room in two was a solid brass bed, of ample
dimensions, with silk curtains of somewhat ill-matched
colours and a silk counterpane. Coloured glass panes
of bilious yellow, green and red tints in the windows,
let in as unpleasant a light to the interior of the room
as one could wish to have when the powerful rays of
the sun penetrated through.

I could not help being amused at the great fear of
the sun the Ras and his son had, when I took them out
on a balcony in order to photograph them.

After many compliments and good wishes for a happy
journey, I took my leave of the Ras, and returned with
Gerolimato to the place where I had put up.

" I think the Ras will not live long," I remarked to
the consul.

" He is sinking every day," was the reply. " He is
going out like a light that has once been brilliant,
but is now fading away. He will be a great loss to this
country."

Neither Gerolimato nor I believed, however, that the
end would come so soon. A few weeks later this the
greatest of all Abyssinian chiefs was dead.

On returning home, I found the beautiful horse Ras-
Makonnen had sent me, and having given a suitable
present to the " Master of the Stable," who delivered it
to me, I took possession of it.

The main square, Harrar.

Again here, as at Dire-Dawa, by far the best store was that kept by the Indian Mahommed-Ali, where a well-selected assortment of articles was to be found, both for European travellers in the country and for natives. While I was in the store, Ganiasmatch Kolouci, who was the late Acting-Governor of Harrar when Ras-Makonnen travelled to Europe, entered the shop, and we had a pleasant conversation together.

I much admired the patience of the Hindu merchants with the Abyssinians. It is, indeed, a good thing that time is worth nothing in Menelik's empire. With the ex-Governor I was shown over the premises of the largest commercial firm in Harrar. Had one desired, one could have purchased anything there from a glass candelabra at fifty pounds sterling, to a military pack-saddle or a cake of soap from the best-advertised English manufacturers. Knives of all kinds and all makers were, they told me, much in demand in Abyssinia, and they certainly seemed to have a great choice of them in their show-cases.

These people have certainly studied the local wants, and their civility in dealing with customers, whether European or native, as well as their comparative honesty, go a long way towards making them successful where European traders become bankrupt.

I visited many of the other Indian shops in the bazaar. The smaller merchants go in principally for native custom, which gives quicker returns. Gras ammunition, grey American and Manchester cottons, are the chief imports from America and Europe. Glass and china ware are much in demand among the richer Abyssinians and Galla. Bric-à-brac articles for decoration, as well as perfumery of the most aggressive kind,

generally come from Austria, Germany and France,
and find a ready market in all the principal cities of
Abyssinia.

I returned to Dire-Dawa by the same route I had
followed on my way out. A mishap, which might have
been serious, happened as we were about half-way on
our journey. My Somali servant, who was carrying a
perfected camera which had been specially constructed
for me, was thrown by his horse, and unfortunately
fell on the top of this most valuable and valued
possession, causing a deal of damage. Fortunately,
carpentering is one of the things I can do best in the
world, and several hours' hard work saw the camera fit
for work again.

I only remained two days in Dire-Dawa in order
to complete all arrangements for my journey, such as
the purchase of pack animals, mules and camels, the
engagement of servants, and the final shopping, in
order to get cooking implements or other things which
I had forgotten at the last moment. The consul, Mr.
Michel A. Michaïlidis, was extremely obliging, and
helped me a good deal to get men and animals quickly.
He also obtained for me an Abyssinian passport, and
assisted me towards obtaining an escort of Abyssinian
soldiers—not a protection, but an additional danger as
one proceeds on a journey across Abyssinia, but without
which no foreigner is allowed to travel in Menelik's
country—and in the more difficult job still of obtaining
a cook.

This is the sort of conversation we generally had with
the candidates for this highly-important post.

" What do you intend to do ? "

" I am a cook."

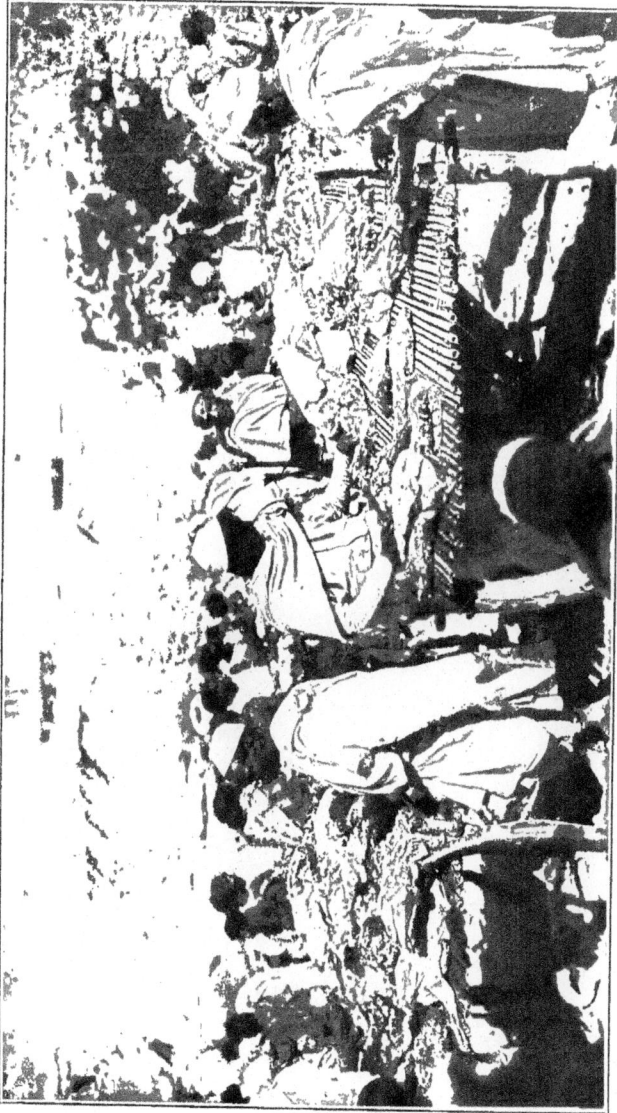

The meat market, Harrar.

" What can you cook ? "

" Oh," said one, with delightful frankness, " I can do nothing. What can you expect from an Abyssinian cook ! "

" What wages do you expect for doing nothing ? "

" Not less than thirty dollars a month, clothes, shoes and blankets."

I suggested that thirty lashes of the *courbash* a minute would be a more appropriate pay for his services, so another cook was examined while the preceding one left grumbling.

Of course, one got the usual procession of " boys " with French and British certificates, praising up the phenomenal qualities of the various servants discharged, but travellers should always be careful in employing these certificated domestics, as certificates are passed round, when one " boy " has obtained employment, to his friends. One certificate does, indeed, for many people. For instance, one certificate I examined, brought to me by a young " boy," some seventeen or eighteen years of age, read that " The bearer of the present certificate, my faithful servant So-and-So, although over fifty years of age," etc., etc.

Personally, I merely go by my first impression, and I find that I have seldom been mistaken in my estimation of the character of the men I employ. Naturally, for journeys like those I undertake, one cannot always get the best people to go, as folks comfortably off will not leave their homes nor risk their lives for any consideration whatever ; so that I have to depend mostly upon finding what suitable material I can from the scum, as it were, of whatever place I happen to be in when I am forming a new caravan. Of course, with men of this kind, no trust can be placed in them, but to trust in other people of any country has never been one of my chief characteristics.

Before leaving Dire-Dawa, a road tax of two *thalers* for each camel travelling upon the Assabot Road (which I intended to follow) had to be paid to Abu Bakir, of the great family of Abu Bakir Basha, the actual chief of the Danakil.

Blankets, shoes and canvas water-bottles had to be purchased for the men, and, according to custom, ten rounds of ammunition were handed to each Abyssinian soldier. It will be seen later how this ammunition was misused, and from that time I took good care never to let any of my men have cartridges in their possession, although I occasionally handed one or two cartridges to men who would be sent after game for the expedition.

CHAPTER IV.

I LEFT Dire-Dawa at 9.30 a.m. on January 18th, my caravan of mules and camels in charge of Somalis and Abyssinians having gone ahead earlier in the morning.

We went along a good trail. There were plenty of cacti and other fat-leaved plants, but with the exception of a few trees here and there the vegetation was not luxuriant.

We perceived a high range to the south-east, the mountains near Harrar, and a high table-land stood to the north-west. Between these two ranges we marched at a steady pace for some eight hours, crossing several beds of dried streams. A few Danakil we met, and a great many Gurgura with their spears, looking after sheep and camels. These Gurgura possess a skin of a deep chocolate colour, and can be divided into two distinct types : one with hair that is woolly, or twisted into tiny curls ; the other, not so common, with smooth hair, which is always left long and reaches almost to the shoulders. These people are akin to the Danakil, and some types I saw possessed Jewish characteristics in a marked degree ; particularly the hooked nose, broad at the base, and the large and prominent lips, the lower drooping considerably. Some grew a slight beard upon the cheeks and chin. They all had eyes the iris of which was of a deep brown, but that portion of the eye-ball which with us is white was with them of a dark yellowish tone, which gave a peculiar expression to their countenances. The women went about with breasts exposed and adorned themselves with numerous beads round the neck. The men wore a loin-cloth down to the knees. They invariably carried a leather amulet with green beads round the neck, and a pendent string hanging down from the back of it.

It was glorious after the gloom of London to travel in the pure, clear air of these highlands under a cloud-less sky in the sun which, far from deserving the accusations of treachery which people shower upon it, seemed to give one fresh life and vigour. One is always told that a sun helmet should be worn if sunstroke is to be avoided, and some people go so far as to protect the whole spinal cord with a thick pad against the rays of the sun, but, personally, I think these precautions do one more harm than good. That is to say, if, when you start on a journey, you are in good health and your blood is in good condition. There are precautions which are based on sound sense and which are really precautions, and there are notions which are forced, occasionally with much success, into people's brains under the name of precautions, but which, indeed, are just the reverse. The helmets, the spinal pads, the cholera belts, etc., seem to me to belong more to the latter class than to the former. For instance, the helmet, which protects you, if anything too much, from the sun, renders the back of the head extremely sensitive and has been known to procure its wearer an immediate sunstroke when accidentally blown off by the wind. Whereas men like myself, who accustom themselves to the hot rays of the sun by wearing a mere straw hat or a cap, can have their head-gears blown off fifty times a day and be none the worse. Any average man in good health can get accustomed to the tropical sun in two or three days at the most by observing a little caution for the first few hours in going out during the great heat of the day in equatorial countries. In preference to the hat, the pads, and so on, precaution against the sun should be taken, not by exterior protection, but by a sensible diet and by keeping one's digestive organs in good working order. Intoxicants, for instance, are fatal in tropical countries, and many a sunstroke, many a nasty skin eruption, many a severe attack of fever might be traced with more reason to the disintegrating effects of whisky, brandy or absinthe upon one's blood than to the treachery of the sun's rays. The two combined, of course, are deadly. I have always noticed in my travelling experience that people who drank in moderation, or not at all, could stand tropical climates with no difficulty, where those indulging freely in alcohol generally died. The sun, believe me, is the friend, not the enemy, of healthy, sober men.

We halted for a night at Ursu, where two wells of fairly good water, somewhat muddy, but quite drinkable, were found. There were several caravans with flocks of black-headed sheep, which had made their camp in the neighbourhood, and the men were busy filling skins with water.

Perhaps it does not always do to see what one drinks; for instance, at the wells where the water was taken for my camp were men standing with their feet in the water in the pool about four feet deep, and the water was scooped into the bucket generally with the hand. When they had finished filling the buckets they generally ended by washing the face and head in the well, and it was better not to investigate how many faces had been cleansed before we got there.

An ingenious arrangement was made to allow the animals to drink without further contaminating the water of the pool. A hollow had been made in the ground with a circle of stones around it. When animals were brought up, a skin was spread over this hollow and filled with water, which this improvised water-tight basin perfectly contained.

The Abyssinian soldiers of my escort began to give me trouble from the first day. I had selected the Bilen road across the desert as it was the shortest and flattest for my animals, although the natives of that portion of the trail had been particularly nasty of late. We unfortunately met some caravan men, who told us that two Abyssinians and an Arab had been killed and mutilated by the Danakil in the Bilen desert. My Somali were quite willing to come along, but the Abyssinian soldiers were so frightened and worried me to such an extent that, in order to save delay and annoyance, I eventually agreed to proceed by the Assabot trail. It was quite amusing to notice the contempt which my Somali had for the Abyssinians. One of my camel-men particularly, who was quite a character, did not spare the Abyssinian warriors some humour of his own, not always the essence of refinement.

Several picturesque Somali came into my camp armed with spears and one or two with excellent Gras rifles. Just before the sun had gone down, I took out my camera in order to photograph the group, but they all stood up and refused to be taken, as they said they

Danakil chief and attendants.

knew all about the harm white people did with these instruments, and many of their friends had already been killed by them.

As night came on, more people from the other caravans came to my camp, and while under my tent, by the light of my lantern, I could see outside a row of human eyes, upon which the light was reflected, moving up and down, following the movements of my hand while I was eating. The colour of their skin was quite indistinguishable in the blackness of the night, which it well matched. They were respectful and peaceful.

We left Ursu the next morning at 3.30, going along a flat highland, then over slight undulations, travelling first southward; then, leaving behind the high, flat-topped plateau to the east of us, which we had so far skirted, we went due west at elevations never more than 3,400 feet in the first four hours' marching. We passed a few deserted huts here and there, a square structure somewhat more solidly built on the saddle of a hill, a few goats and some cattle and a green patch or two of cultivation. A lot of vultures (the *amora* of the Somalis) were circling overhead with their weird, piercing shrieks; as we drew nearer hundreds of them were pecking away at the carcase of a dead cow.

We had by now reached the charming little Herrer river, with its clear water, quite a refreshing sight after the long march over arid, semi-barren country. We arrived in camp at noon, the last four hours of our march having been in a south-westerly direction over undulating country. We were now 3,610 feet above sea level. There were here hot-water springs, to which the people called the Hawuya, who live here, attribute medicinal qualities, especially for curing sores and skin eruptions. In fact, when I went to the springs, some sixty feet higher than my camp, I tasted some of the water, which seemed slightly sulphurous.

The Hawuya, like the Gurgura, speak Somali, and some also understand the Galla language.

During my dinner in the evening, there was a fine concert of hyenas prowling around my camp, and while I was enjoying "stewed pears and rice" for dessert there was a great excitement in camp, animals stampeding in all directions and men shouting. When peace was restored we discovered that one of my camels had a large slice of his left hind leg bitten off by a panther. This left the camel minus a big semi-circle in his anatomy, but except that the animal walked lame, he was apparently not much the worse for it, and we were able to proceed the next morning, wending our way between various camps of Hawuya. The natives were squatting down round big fires, and possessed large numbers of donkeys.

Over open, undulating country we came, after one and a half hours' march, to the beautiful, clear Gotha stream ; then up and down over wavy ground with absolutely nothing to interest one on the way, skirting a fairly high range to our west and south-west, we arrived at the camp of Ella Balla (altitude 3,950 feet). There was a big well, some thirty feet deep and thirty-five feet in diameter, and around it quite an interesting scene. Some dozens of Danakil—since Herrer we were in the Danakil country—were busy watering a large herd of cattle. Two troughs were provided on the upper edge of the well, while three sets of men had taken positions at intervals up the incline of the interior of the well, the last man below standing in water up to his waist. Small buckets were quickly filled and thrown up with great celerity and skill ; they were emptied in rotation and returned down, not one ever being missed.

The Danakil are a morose, ill-natured and suspicious people, with evil manners and cruel faces. I nearly got into trouble with them in endeavouring to take a photograph of the scene at the well. When I pulled out my camera, they all made for their spears, which were bundled against the trunk of a tree, and with suggestive signs and angry words gave me plainly to understand that I must go or they would hurl their weapons. I snapped them all the same ; but we had quite a row with these fellows, and they insisted that we must not stop even to look at them near the well. My Abyssinian soldiers were so scared that they made things a great deal worse ; they behaved like silly children and took refuge behind me. I refused to go away from the well until it suited me, as it is fatal in any country to show weakness, but it was all I could do to prevent the Abyssinians running away. The Somalis behaved well and were quite cool and collected. When all the Danakil had gradually left off using violent and threatening language against us, I pitched my camp some fifty yards from the well up on a high position.

These Danakil are well known for their treachery, and they are said to have a particular craving for killing white people and mutilating them in the most horrible fashion. It was near this spot that the French newspaper correspondent, Monsieur Dubois-Dessaulle, was murdered and mutilated, as has been described in Chapter II.; and, as I have said, an Arab—whom the Danakil also look upon as white men—and two

Abyssinians met with a similar fate only a few days before I went through.

It is considered dangerous to go away even a few yards from one's camp while in their country, for these Danakil lie in wait with their spears ; they see you get away from your caravan, and when you are within reach they fling a spear at you with such force that it sometimes goes right through the body. If spectators from their own tribe are present to witness the killing of a man the body is left intact, but if there is no one to see the performance certain organs are cut out and tied in the centre of the shield in order to be produced to the tribe to show that a man and not a woman has been killed.

Certain tribes, wilder than others, remove also the heart of the victim and give it to their horses to eat. One can generally recognize Danakil who have killed one or more victims by the number of feathers they place in their hair—one for each man—or else by the number of bracelets and amulets.

We met a good many of these fellows, and I tried on many occasions to make friends with them, but they were always extremely suspicious, especially when one treated them politely. In the middle of a conversation they would suddenly jump up and dart away, and no coaxing would induce them to turn round in their flight and return to continue the conversation. Their saluta-tion was quite original and well showed the diffident nature of these people even among themselves. One could not persuade them to be grasped by the hand. On meeting even members of their own tribe they would strike each other's palm with outstretched fingers quickly and rapidly, in order to prevent any possibility of having the hand seized. They say that the French correspondent, M. Dubois-Dessaulle, met his fate by wanting to teach his murderer how to shake hands properly in European fashion. The Danakil, having had his hand seized by the Frenchman in a hearty fashion, became alarmed and thrust his spear through him. This, at least, was the excuse given by the Danakil chief, when Menelik sent soldiers in order to capture the murderer, as Mr. MacMillan, the leader of the expedition, would stand no nonsense and insisted on having the murderer punished.

Another early start was made from Ella Balla. About sunrise we saw any amount of wild game : gazelles, jackals, and a magnificent panther, creeping gracefully along the ground like a huge cat and only a few yards from me. Jackals, of which there were thousands about at night, were amusing and often somewhat trying little animals. They sneaked silently into one's camp and stole whatever small articles they could find, especially if made of leather or canvas.

At Ella Balla, for instance, they actually came into my tent and carried away my shoes. It was only after a search which lasted nearly an hour that my men were able to recover them some good distance from camp.

Another night, further up country, they stole a belt and revolver belonging to one of my Abyssinian soldiers and dragged it some hundreds of yards from where we had halted.

Besides these jackals, or *caboro,* as the Abyssinians call them, and the *medafiher,* or gazelles, lions are plentiful in that country, and one has to keep big fires at night in order to keep them at large.

The Danakil, too, have to be kept at a respectful distance, as they are unscrupulous thieves and will steal anything they can lay their hands upon.

At about 11.30 a.m. we arrived at Magu (3,450 feet), an unimportant place, with fair drinking water. The Danakil we met were troublesome. They were being hunted by Menelik's soldiers in order to obtain the surrender of the murderers of the Arab and the Abyssinians. Near Magu were some Danakil huts about five feet in height, domed and covered with matting. These huts, generally in groups of three or four, were inside a kraal of thorns, in which the oxen were kept at night. The gate of the kraal was made with tree branches to prevent wild animals coming in.

On January 17th, at 4 a.m., we were off again over undulating country, skirting the big mountain range on our left. By eight o'clock we had arrived at Delladu, sometimes also called Kalladu, where a large well and two smaller dry ones were to be found. From this point we were again out of the Danakil country and found Hawuya people, who possessed a lot of cattle with gigantic straight horns.

I continued up and down steep inclines, and then along an interminable hot plain. We mistook our way, as we made for an old well, which we found dry, so that we only arrived at Mulluh at 1.30 in the afternoon. A well was found there dug in the rock and some sixteen feet deep. A similar method to that seen in the Danakil country was employed here for watering cattle by throwing up buckets of water. My instruments registered the elevation of Mulluh at 4,000 feet.

Kamil Pasha, chief of the Danakil, came to my camp to pay his respects, and presented me with a

Danakil and Gurgura filling skin-bags with water at a well.

goat, which necessitated a return visit to his tent with a suitable present of money. He was extremely civil, and I took this opportunity of snapshotting him and his men. In the photograph, which is reproduced in one of the illustrations, it will be seen how some of his lieutenants were covering their faces in order not to be photographed.

The next morning, three hours' marching over undulating country and across beds of streams now devoid of water, took us to Maisso (altitude 4,300 feet), called so because of a small plant found there in quantities and named *mais* (not to be confounded with *maïs*—the French for Indian corn).

We left again in the afternoon, and marched at a good pace over undulating country quite picturesque in some parts, with the rugged Assabot mountains on our right. Herds of antelopes gracefully ran before us and were soon out of sight. Among plenty of trees, but with no water, we eventually descended at Laga Arba into a sort of cañon, rising again on the other side, where I made my camp, obtaining a beautiful view of the extensive plateau we had crossed and left behind, and of a curious isolated mountain standing upon it.

We were now at an elevation of 4,600 feet, and it was quite cold at night.

Whether it was the cold air which brought out more forcibly the racial dislike, or whether for other reasons, there was a violent quarrel in the evening between my Somali and the Abyssinians. Both swore that they would kill the others before the morning came. I separated them, and placed the Abyssinians on one side of the camp and the Somali some way off on the other side.

The soldiers built up big fires to keep jackals and other animals away, while the horses and the mules were tethered close to my tent. The camels squatted in a circle near the Somali.

It was the habit of the Somali camel-men when we made an early start to sing to their hearts' content— more so than to the content of the ears of whoever had to listen to them—but that morning the Somali were sulky and grumpy and did not sing nor speak. The Abyssinians were morose and unpleasant. I found the best thing on such occasions was to take no notice of either of them and pretend they did not exist at all.

From Laga Arba we descended considerably on our march, and at one time we got a magnificent view of the Bilen desert, of a bright yellow colour. More gazelles, more jackals.

The camp at Laga Arba, so cold at night, was extremely hot in the daytime. The horses and mules stampeded again for some reason or other, and gave us no end of trouble to recapture them. This incident brought peace afresh among my men, who all joined in the chase of the animals.

Near Laga Arba were a few Ito inhabitants, with their flocks of sheep, goats and some cattle. A sheep is worth about one thaler, or two shillings, in that country. These Ito speak the Galla language, and they are quiet, gentle people, quite unlike their neighbours, the Danakil. They belong to a different race altogether and have a language of their own, whereas other people we have met, like the Hawuya, the Issa, the Gurgura, the Haberual or Hawaraoer, the Ghedebursi and the Dahrot, speak Somali.

Beyond the beautiful Gadjenna mountains to the

south-west over the Hawash river, we had a lovely sunset, resembling an *aurora borealis*, with huge red and blue streaks radiating from the centre—the sun—and shooting skyward half-way across the heavenly circle. The glorious effect lasted a long time.

Camp Argaga (altitude 3,550 feet), where we stopped next, had no particular fascination, and nothing happened except jackals coming into camp again during the night and stealing another revolver case and two soldiers' hats.

Shortly after three o'clock in the morning we moved out of Argaga, and some two hours later came across the telephone line on the high caravan road from Harrar *viâ* Tchertcher, leading to Adis-Ababa.

We travelled mostly over flat desert country, with some short grass upon it here and there. The Katchenua mountains before us were a typical instance of Abyssinian scenery—curious isolated mountains rising abruptly above flat country.

A small shed for caravans had been built by Menelik on a hill by the wayside, but we did not stop there. We went along and crossed the small Katchenua stream, then continued for another hour and a half's march to the Hawash, meeting on the high road many caravans of coffee and hides. The men in charge of these caravans suffered from sore eyes, caused by the dust which is raised in clouds by the animals walking in front of them. Nearly all these caravans were in charge of Galla. The hides were carried mostly on camels. We came across several caravans of mules also, but these were chiefly laden with coffee.

After a steady march of seven and a half hours from Argaga we arrived at the new bridge on the Hawash

river, a somewhat shaky construction, spanning the
stream some forty feet across. This bridge has been
given into the charge of the Carayu, a tribe of Galla.

It was from this bridge, where the high volcanic walls
were closer together, that I obtained the first and last
really beautiful view in the way of scenery since I
had landed in Abyssinia. We suddenly came upon the
deep cañon in which the Hawash river runs, a huge
vertical crack in the bluish volcanic rock, in one portion
with quite vertical walls on both sides of the stream
for some hundreds of yards. In other sections it is
broader and with slanting banks.

The Hawash river was the largest I had met since
leaving the coast. During the rainy season it carries
a considerable volume of water. I made my camp
on the west side of the stream, but there was no shade
of any kind to be obtained and the heat refracted by the
volcanic rock was terrific.

Hawash river, showing volcanic fissure.

CHAPTER V.

At the Hawash bridge, where the river ran in the volcanic fissure from south-south-east to north-north-west, the vertical sides were, especially in the lower portion, baked quite black, as if they had been subjected to intense heat ; in some places, too, even high upon the wall, one could see where the flames had licked the rock. Directly north of the bridge was an oval " cuvette," which appeared to have been a crater, with huge black, round boulders on the east side. The altitude of the river by the water at this point was 2,700 feet, the wall-like rocks by its side along the stream varying from fifty to one hundred feet high above it. The elevation of the place where I made the camp was 2,800 feet.

South-south-east of the bridge, and only a short distance from it, the stream flowed northward for a long distance in an almost straight line between two high slopes resembling natural gigantic railway embankments, some two hundred feet higher than the level of the stream.

The strata of the parallel embankments, which correspond exactly on both sides of the stream, would seem to show that the earth had opened, leaving this enormous fissure, which, owing to the erosion of water and wind, and possibly to other minor causes, has gradually assumed a slope in the upper and softer strata.

My camel-men, having met many of their tribesmen here on the river, again became troublesome, and were dissatisfied with everything in general.

The purchase price of camels in this region was from fifteen to twenty-five thalers. For the hire of camels from Dire-Dawa to Adis-Ababa, a journey from twelve to thirteen days, Englishmen were made to pay as much as thirty dollars for the hire of each camel.

Several Carayu women came to barter milk and butter with my men. It was a relief to find people who would not take money. These Carayu were flat-headed, with curly hair, left hanging down in twists over the neck, as far as the shoulders. They wore peculiar semicircular earrings, three or four inches in diameter, with a broad metal bar in the lower part. Around this bar were coil ornamentations. The semicircle of the ring was heavy with silver or copper wire wound round it ; in fact, the weight was such that a leather strap had to be attached to it to go over the ear in order to support it, so that the lobe should not become torn. Only one earring was worn, generally on the left ear. When an additional earring was worn on the right ear it was invariably of a different shape, such as an elongated ring of bone or metal, or else a lozenge. Old women wore a strap over the forehead. Broad bangles were worn upon the wrists. Necklaces of small white and red beads were fashionable when I passed through the country. Beads of other colours were on no account accepted in payment for goods supplied.

With nearly all these tribes, except in young women, the breasts were abnormally pendent. The arms were well formed and beautifully rounded, but the hands were coarse.

The women had on leather skirts, extraordinarily dirty and shiny at the knees, and the better dressed draped over the shoulders a cloth shawl. Brass anklets adorned the lower limbs and drew attention to the well-formed and dainty ankles which the Carayu women possess.

Slung upon the back these ladies carried gourds of rancid milk and butter. Some of these gourds were handsomely decorated with white shells, others were covered with a protective, finely-made basket-work, with pendants of bits of discarded sardine tins.

Upon examination, the principal thing which struck the observer in their otherwise well-proportioned heads was the flatness of the upper portion of the skull. The nose was small, broad in its upper portion, but not so much at the base, where it had rather clearly-defined, well-curved nostrils. The eyes were wide apart, the lips fairly ample and the chin receding. In profile, the outline of the lower jaw formed an almost straight line from the chin to the ear instead of the more common angular form of most African tribes.

Carayu men possessed skulls more elongated backwards than the women. They twisted the hair of the head in a similar way to their female companions. Some were proud of a slight moustache and beard, but they did not wear many ornaments, except round the neck a string, generally of leather, and perhaps an occasional brass or copper bracelet round the wrist or a larger ring above the elbow.

We had amusing scenes with these people, bartering empty sardine and corned beef tins for buckets of milk and pots of butter. Only, as we generally threw away empty tins, we soon came to an end of our currency.

I wished to buy a bag of grain, but the woman who owned it would on no account accept silver money for it, nor any article which she saw about my camp. My Somali servant had a bright idea—the only one he had during the entire journey across Africa. He went to one of the boxes of provisions, and tore off a highly-coloured label from a corned-beef box. Having licked it copiously, he stuck it in the middle of his forehead. Inquisitive like all women, the Carayu asked him what he did it for. The Somali said that he had been seized with a violent headache. The coloured paper was a quick and certain cure. The Carayu at once offered the bag of grain if the Somali would part with the magic paper. Her wish was satisfied without delay, and the woman departed quite happy.

In this camp animals and men suffered considerably from the terrific heat. During the day we were simply roasted by the refraction from the volcanic rock. It actually burnt so that we could not touch it with our hands.

We left early in the afternoon and rose on the top of the plateau to 3,000 feet, some three hundred feet above the river at the bottom of the volcanic fissure. The moment we reached this elevation we got a pleasant breeze and began to breathe again. We were now travelling upon an extensive flat high-land, with hardly any vegetation except a little grass and a few shrubs.

To the south-east was the Katchenua mountain; to the south in the distance the Arusi Mount, and to the west the Fantalli mountains. The Bulgo and the Ansobar mountains stood beyond. The entire country over which we were travelling was of volcanic formation, and was strewn everywhere with eruptive boulders.

Adem bartering with Carayu women.   Silver dollars useless

On nearing the Fantalli mountains, which we crossed by a low pass, we passed over stretches of volcanic, cellular, spongy rock, which seemed to have been subjected to high temperatures. North of the Fantalli mountains, in the immense plain stretching before us, and only about one hour and a half's journey from my last camp, were to be found hot springs, the Filoamelka, the steaming water of which, the natives say, has curative powers.

Before getting to the Fantalli camp we came upon two trails, one proceeding by the hot springs, which is the better of the two and quite level for camels ; the other, more picturesque, which I followed, going over the Fantalli Pass.

A Frenchman had started a plantation of tobacco, cotton, coffee and vegetables a short way beyond the hot springs.

We halted at 6.30 p.m., and as there was no wood we were unable to make fires and do our cooking, so my coffee, which I always like hot, was brewed over a candle. There were many hyenas howling round our camp with their funereal cries. We had seen a lot of large antelopes during the day. Since leaving the Hawash we had descended to 2,900 feet, and the march in the hot afternoon sun was trying for my animals. There was near the Hawash river little vegetation except a few shrubs bent and baked by the heat of the sun, but in the Fantalli region there was absolutely no wood.

On January 22nd we again made an early start shortly after three a.m., and although the moon would not be up till an hour or so later, we were able to see our way quite clearly by the brilliant light of the stars. The trail was rocky in many places—quite bad, especially for camels, as there were high steps to go over upon the rock. The heat was stifling all through the night, and we only got a slight breeze when we reached another pass, 3,250 feet high. On descending, we again encountered the camel trail *via* the hot springs.

We reached the Tadetchimalka river, which we followed, making a temporary halt at eight o'clock. On a height above our camping-ground was a freshly-built village of circular straw huts with conical roofs, the quarters of a guard of Abyssinian soldiers.

This point was well known among natives. They said there were many robbers of camels here. In fact, as I was lying on my camp-bed after breakfast, waiting for the hot hours of the day to go by, one of my camel-men came to me in great excitement, spear and shield in hand. One of the camels had been stolen—the best of the whole lot, of course—and he would go and kill the thief. I heartily consented to that, upon which he leapt in the air brandishing his spear, and ran to and fro in trace of the missing animal.

Nearly all camel-men I have employed in my journeys in Asia and Africa seem to have ill-balanced brains. Whether it is the heat of the sun upon the desert, the company of camels, or perhaps the unnatural life they lead, constantly marching at night and sleeping during the day, or other causes, I could not say, but the fact remains that I have never yet seen a camel-man who was absolutely in his right mind.

The fellow who had approached me in such a warlike temper was a curious type. Tall and slender to a degree, with a dreamy face like a poet ; a great lover of music, if music there was at all in the songs which he gave in a rasping falsetto voice when he was awake and every-

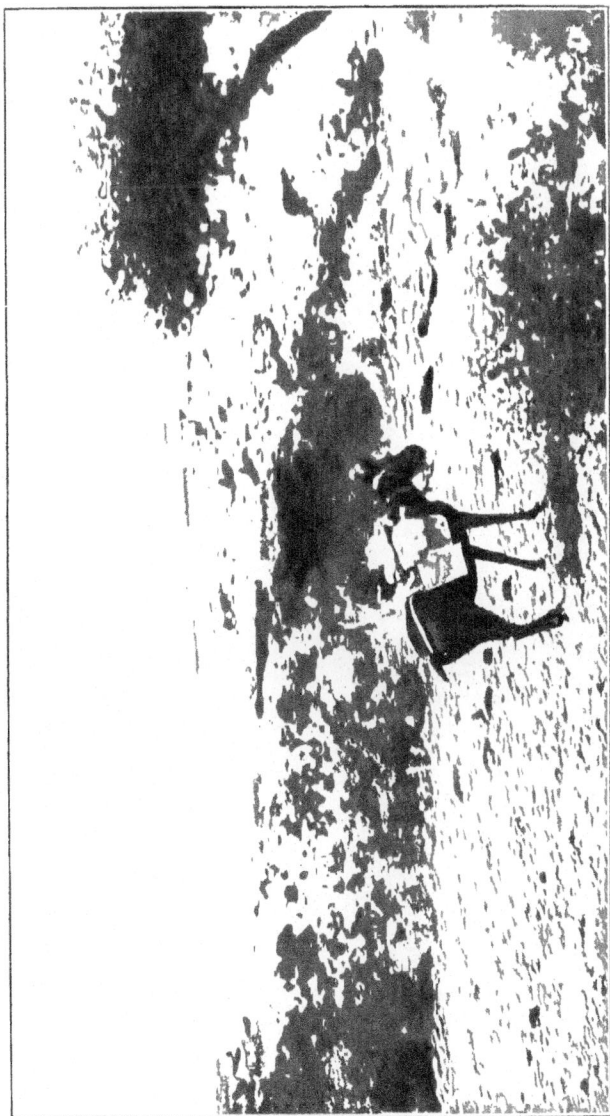

View of escarpment along the Hawash river (Abyssinia).

body else trying to sleep ; loving to a degree to the animals of which he had charge ; moody and disobedient as only an African can be. One moment he would cry bitter tears, and the next he would laugh to his heart's content. Sulky and unpleasant for hours he made himself, if I spoke to my other men and took no notice of him. His delight had no bounds one day, when, tired of incessant begging, I presented him with a pair of trousers. The first thing he did with them was to cut them so that they should reach five or six inches above the knee, the remaining cloth being exchanged there and then for three pots of butter. His only baggage was a wooden pillow, which he always carried under his arm. When in a fit of temper he took great delight in throwing things about, and he was constantly bent on quarrelling, until I applied a cure for this bad habit.

While the camel-man went about accusing everybody of stealing the camel, and threatening to run his spear through them, two haggard, worn Danakil dragged themselves to my camp and saluted me by slightly touching the palm of my hand. Extreme suffering was depicted on their faces, and upon inquiry I learned that they had been three days without food.

"If that is so," I inquired, "what is it that you are chewing now ? You have something in your mouth."

In fact, to allay his hunger one man had for the last two days been chewing a piece of hard wood. I had some food given them, which they at once ravenously devoured. Their gratitude was such that they grasped my hands and feet and kissed them repeatedly. I also gave them provisions to last them for some days until they could get back to their own tribe.

Tadetchimalka was the first place where we found real Abyssinians, as none but savage tribes had been met until now except officials or soldiers, as at Dire-Dawa or on the railway. Many picturesque people passed the camp in their white clothes and long curved swords, and numerous caravans of donkeys, mules and camels. We had only met one large caravan from Dire-Dawa as far as the point where we joined the Tchertcher Road, but now that the principal roads to Adis-Ababa had converged to this common meeting-point the landscape before us was brightly animated. One could see that civilization was making progress in the country by the number of animals laden with corrugated iron roofing bound for Menelik's palace.

To the north of my camp the Wassil mountains extended westwards behind the Barrakhet mountains, which were somewhat lower, and both chains were rather barren.

On leaving this camp we rose between mountains to 3,820 feet, and we got a glimpse to the south of the high Bohsat mountains in the distance. On quite a good road made by Emperor Menelik, in order to take the traction engines purchased from the English firm of Fowler and Co. to Adis-Ababa, we still rose further to 4,250 feet, where, owing to the night coming on, I had to halt by the small *meziid*, or " praying ground," on the hillock which marks the grave of a Mahommedan. The view from that point described an immense arc of a circle from south to north. To the south-west was the Galla country ; beyond the Arusi region were mountains in several consecutive ranges ; then below us the Carayu country, with its bright yellow desert and its peculiar isolated hills rising island-like sheer from the flat country. One to the south-south-east, more peculiar than the others, had the appearance of a large crater in a conical mountain.

Nearer us, lighted by the last rays of a dying sun, were the Fantalli mountains, with a table-land in two superposed terraces spreading a considerable distance to the west of Fantalli. To the north-east was now the Wassil. The Barrakhet mountains stood out prominently and appeared of a curious yellow colour in hundreds of little rounded humps. With the golden rays of the sun shining upon them each mount projected a deep blue shadow over the hollow between it and its neighbour, and the effect produced was curious and most picturesque.

Down below on the winding road the stillness of the evening was disturbed by the weird song of camel-men, interrupted by an occasional " hop," the favourite cry of caravan men to urge the animals up an incline. All was barren around us, except a slope on which a crop of barley had been grown, and was now being cut and collected into high-domed stacks.

As the sun set, the distant mountains became more indistinct and inky in colour ; those in the foreground taking dark, powerful tones of a deep bluish brown. Then gradually night set in with a strong wind howling, and men and animals shivered with cold. We made a later start in the morning at sunrise. It was impossible to get the Abyssinian soldiers out of their blankets, as they said they were frozen and ill.

On January 23rd, we travelled over a high plateau, on which cotton and *dura* (sorghum) were grown. Small villages of Mussulmans and Christians were to be found. Near Tchoba is an Abyssinian Custom House, where traders are sometimes given, I am told, considerable trouble unless they are willing to bribe the officials and soldiers in charge. They gave me no bother whatever, and, indeed, on hearing that I was a British subject, they were extremely civil. I was only detained a few minutes on my march to allow time for my servant to go up to the Custom House, perched at a height of some two hundred feet above the trail, a wall being built all along and across the slope, in order to prevent caravans passing through except by the road.

To the west of us we now had the Magaghes mountains called Magassi on Marchand's map.

The general elevation of the Tchoba plateau is 4,700 feet, the highest point we crossed over that day being 5,080 feet, and later in the day occurred a second pass 5,020 feet high, where two stone walls marked the tomb of a chief, Aba Jambar, killed at Fantalli by the Carayu. As one goes along the high Tchoba plateau, one still continues to obtain a fine view to the south-east, the south and south-west. Lake Bata Hara, or Mata Hara, to the south-east of us, with a lot of little isolated hills near it, was now becoming disclosed; then to the south the mountainous mass of Bosseta, with a series of parallel terraces spreading north-north-east, and with a high terrace to the north-west.

We kept at an elevation varying from 4,900 feet to 5,000 feet, descending to the west by a gentle incline to 4,850 feet, then rising again on a higher plateau in a gradual slope to 5,275 feet. Portions of this plateau were cultivated with *dura*. We went on rising until we reached another plateau (5,610 feet), on which, after travelling a long distance, we encamped near the former

Guagura woman.

Galla woman selling butter.

lakelet of Menabella. The lake which formerly existed at this place was now quite dry, and we had difficulty in getting any water at all.

My first glimpse of real Abyssinians in their own country was certainly not an enticing one. The women with shaved heads, or else with their hair in dirty little curls, were as ugly as it is possible for women to be. A lot of them came into my camp endeavouring to sell eggs, barley and *dura*, but we had great difficulty in buying anything, as they would not accept money, whether Abyssinian or foreign, and only Gras cartridges were accepted in payment for their goods. I had some of these cartridges, but even then most annoying discussions took place to discover whether the cartridges were good or not. Even the slightest scratch on the paper surrounding the lead bullet, where it is inserted into the brass envelope, was enough to cause the rejection of the good cartridges as bad ones. So, after hours of bargaining, we were able to obtain nothing at all from the natives. My Somali attendant was more fortunate, and after two hours of steady talk, purchased seven eggs for one cartridge—the only bad cartridge, it may be observed, that we possessed.

We moved the camp away to a place where the Abyssinians said we should find good water. After marching some time we got away from the trail, and I was led to a very secluded spot, a fact which rendered me suspicious. Having gone a considerable distance from the road, my Somalis rebelling all the time against going in that direction, as they said there was no water at all, at one moment when the Abyssinian soldiers were ahead, the mad camel-man came to me and made a sign that this was only done because the

Abyssinian soldiers wanted to play us false. I had suspected as much from the beginning.

Having reached a distant spot away from everything and everybody, the Abyssinians professed they had made a mistake, and that no water was to be found. They said they were tired and worn, and could not go on any longer and we must stop. I had watched them carefully and had seen them confabulating in an excited manner. I saw that this was one of those occasions when tact would be required.

We encamped, and, contrary to my usual habit, I had my tent pitched at once. Under it, unseen by my men, I unpacked a heavy 44-calibre revolver, which I happened to have in one of my trunks to give away as a present to some chief, and loaded the six chambers. I also loaded my Winchester repeater with eight cartridges and my Männlicher with a five-cartridge clip. I had a presentiment that something might happen soon, and, in fact, I was not far wrong. So I laid all these loaded weapons upon my bed. The Somali servant came in presently considerably upset, to warn me that the Abyssinian soldiers had taken me to this desolate spot in order to impose terms upon me. He said that he and the camel-men would stand by me, so I asked him to remain in the tent, and handed over to him one of the loaded rifles. A few minutes had elapsed when the Abyssinian soldiers, rifles in hand, came to the entrance of the tent and in a most arrogant manner demanded a sum of money. Before they had time to point their rifles at me, they found themselves covered by my revolver and the rifle I had handed to my Somali. This answer rather surprised them. I told them that they must put down their rifles or I might shoot them, so down went the rifles upon the ground, and the men were made to stand back at a distance. Their rifles were collected and conveyed by my Somali into the tent. Then only we began to talk, the Abyssinians being extremely excited, partly owing, I think, to a considerable amount of liquor they had imbibed that morning at a drinking place upon the road.

They got nothing, of course, and were considerably scared when I told them that I would now proceed to smash their rifles. I gave orders to that effect. This brought them back to reason, as a rifle in Abyssinia is expensive, and it is the most valuable possession that the average Abyssinian man has. They entreated me to pardon them and not carry out my threat. Upon obtaining a promise from them of future good behaviour, I ordered them to go to sleep and the next morning on leaving camp I would hand them back their property. They were to go out of sight, and not come near me till the moment of departure next day, and to receive nothing to eat for twenty-four hours.

They left camp deeply humiliated, much to the amusement of the Somali, who took great delight in making cutting remarks at their expense. As they walked away unarmed in the humblest of fashions, the mad camel-man, spear and shield in hand, followed them for some distance, every now and then signalling to me that he would protect me with his spear. Men —even Africans—can be so brave when there is no danger !

Early the next morning the Abyssinians returned to camp and were submissive. They said they were very hungry, and I answered that I was glad to hear it. When the camels, mules and horses were ready, their rifles, minus the blocks, were handed back to them.

As we continued along the road I was amazed at the numbers of blind people we met. We passed the Nimjar village, and we at last arrived at the escarpment to the west of us at an elevation of 5,620 feet above sea level at the foot.

This escarpment is quite impressive, as it rises abruptly and almost vertically from a comparatively level ground extending in a long straight line from west-south-west to east-north-east. It makes a magnificent natural barrier for the Shoa country. One portion of this high escarpment displays at the top a stratum of shiny rock forming a broad band all along.

In the plain down below, *dura* and corn were cultivated, and there were a few huts with conical roofs. The people kept a number of cattle. We met thousands of them going through a ravine towards the stream, as we approached the camp of Godoburkha, *godo* meaning " at the bottom," and *burkha* " source," or " source at the foot of the plateau." The camp, which took, of course, its name from the stream, was directly at the foot of the gully leading up to Baltchi, at the summit of the escarpment, a place which was reached by a steep and rugged trail most painful for camels.

Picturesque mounted men, with sheep-skins on their backs, rode after the cattle, while many caravans were waiting, giving their camels a rest before ascending the steep incline.

The Godoburkha stream came from the north by the great gully of Baltchi, and flowed along the escarpment.

The high escarpment at Baltchi (Abyssinia).

CHAPTER VI.

My camel-men were anxious to wait here one day to rest the animals before going up, but I would not hear of it, and late in the afternoon we started on our way to the Shoan plateau. Panting and stumbling all the time, the camels struggled up, encouraged by the yells of the camel-men. Every few yards they stopped, looking most disconsolate and helpless. The camel is certainly not built to climb mountains.

We followed on the left side the great valley in which the Godoburkha stream flows, and after a good deal of trouble, for the loads of the camels kept sliding down, we reached Baltchi village on the edge of the plateau, 6,610 feet above sea level, or nearly one thousand feet above the Godoburkha camping ground.

Baltchi is a typical Abyssinian village, the houses cylindrical in shape, with walls of matting over a wooden frame and a conical thatched roof. There is only one aperture in these dwellings : the door, but no windows. A stone wall is to be found on the south side of the village, and from the edge of the plateau one obtains, of course, a beautiful view over the cultivated fields in the valley below to the east. To the west, the only thing that strikes the eye is the trail to Adis-Ababa, with its ups and downs over undulating country.

No sooner had we arrived than an old woman came

into my camp with two large bags of barley, a load of firewood, two gourds, one of fresh, the other of curdled milk, and one large jar of native wine, the whole of which she presented to me.

"I have no husband," said she; "no father. No one to whom to give all this. I only have this little child. So I give all to you."

"Pray, not the child," I hastily replied. "But I will take the wine, the milk and the barley."

On my rewarding the lady with brand-new silver dollars, her eyes gleamed with joy, and she expressed her gratitude by throwing herself down to kiss my feet and then my hands. The latter she kissed first upon the knuckles, then under the palm. Her little child was, after much shaking, made to imitate the good woman's example. The end of it all was that the infant was further persuaded to throw his arms round my neck, and he kissed me on both cheeks with quite unusual fervour. The child had a dirty face. The old lady returned to camp many times to express again her gratitude—she said—but I took great care to keep mother and baby at a distance.

There was a "grande douane"—to use my Somali's expression—at Baltchi. The Abyssinian officials in charge of this "douane" came clothed in long brown cloaks to see me and were quite civil. They did not wish to inspect my baggage.

"Oh, no, indeed! They would not do such a thing to a traveller"—but they had only come to count my numerous loads so that they might advise the next post to let me go through without trouble.

Counting was easier said than done for them, as none of the three who called at my camp seemed able to sum beyond ten. After trying repeatedly they eventually gave it up, and said it would be all right. They consumed a whole tin of biscuits and a tin of jam while on their visit, and they were further presented with sundry pencils and paper, as they possessed neither in their office, with and on which to write the official pass.

Many women came to the camp in the evening to sell things. One has to go to Abyssinia fully to understand how plain some women can be—all with shaved heads and body dressed up in a long, loose robe, coarse to a degree and disgustingly unwashed.

Bargaining in Abyssinia takes time and gives endless trouble. The people are extremely suspicious and are always under the impression that they are being swindled. Well, they often are. It would be unfair to blame poor, ignorant people—mere barbarians after all—for not mastering the difference between Greek and Armenian traders and people of a different calling—who are for them all white people, therefore all scoundrels.

That day was mostly used by the Somali in giving trouble in camp. I think they rather felt the effects of being at a greater elevation, and with their nervous temperament they became depressed and morose. The mad camel-man in particular groaned and moaned the whole evening, declaring me responsible for his death and that of the camels, which had not occurred yet, but which, he said, would unavoidably take place before the morning.

During the night the cold seemed indeed intense after the heat we had experienced down below. On no account could I induce the men to get out of their

blankets until the sun was high upon the horizon at
nine o'clock the following day.

We left soon after, crossing two small streams during
our march, and going over two passes, one 7,150 feet
high, the other 7,550 feet. There were cultivated
patches of wheat and barley, but most of the country
was barren and treeless. Over numerous undulations
we rose still higher to 7,650 feet, and further on, when
we had reached an elevation of 7,720 feet, we found
ourselves on a flat plateau, and we began to discern
in the distance to the west the mountains near Adis-
Ababa.

We marched steadily over what the Americans would
appropriately call " rolling country." Volcanic rock
showed through, here and there, strewn with black,
quadrangular pebbles also of volcanic origin. Passing
through barren country, but with fair grazing in spots,
we arrived at 4.30 p.m. at Tcheffedunza (7,700 feet),
where I pitched my tent under a solitary cluster of trees.
There was a charming little stream of clear water. To
the south-south-west we could now see the Tchukhala
mountain, or Mount Zougouala, as Marchand calls it,
on the top of which was an Abyssinian church and
monastery.

One does not find many places of archæological interest
in this portion of Abyssinia. Probably one of the most
interesting in the Galla country is the underground
monastery of Goba, of which my friend, Monsieur Franz
de Zeltner, who visited it while taking part in the
" Bourg de Bozas " expedition, has given an interesting
description.

He tells us that in the valley of the Mitcha stream
what the natives call a church, but what is in reality a

monastery, is to be found in the shape of a grotto dug in a cliff some sixty feet high. This excavation is only an annexe to an upper building, to reach which it is necessary to haul oneself through a narrow and almost vertical gallery some nine or ten feet long, in which rough steps have been cut. By this primitive stair-case one enters a suite of five or six chambers.

The first, twenty-one feet long, twelve feet wide, and nine feet high, is lighted by a sort of garret window overlooking the valley. Besides the entrance above described, there are two other small holes permitting a descent into the adjoining chamber. A natural pillar of rock supports the ceiling, and near one of the corners, opposite the entrance, is found a rectangular trench covered with wood, which the Abyssinians say is a tomb.

By a gap six feet high one gets into the second chamber. Evident signs can be seen upon the rock that a door or a gate was placed at this entrance. In the middle is a grave similar to the one in the first chamber, and in one of the angles a niche has been made in the wall. In front of the window the ground has been raised about three feet, forming a platform in which two holes have been bored, one leading out of, the other into, the fourth chamber. In the wall opposite the window a tunnel, fifteen feet long and only one and a half feet high, leads to a long passage, on the side of which is a small semicircular recess.

The third chamber, which is probably the most interesting of all, has a strong, square pillar in the centre, hollow in its interior, and a window on each face. A circular seat has been carved in the rock in-side this pillar, so that eight people can be accommodated inside this stone tube, the interior diameter of which is about four and a half feet. This arrangement, says M. de Zeltner, is common in the convents of the Thebaïd, where it has the name of *Cathedra*. The chamber itself has no windows, as it is far inside the rock.

In the fourth chamber, lighted by a large window, is a square trench and a seat carved in the rock. Facing the window is a low door ornamented by a rudimentary moulding, the only attempt at ornamentation noticeable in the entire monastery.

A passage, thirteen and a half feet long and one and a half feet high, leads to the fifth chamber, where two niches and a seat have been dug into the rock. M. de Zeltner says that this monument is still in perfect condition, and has in no way been damaged by atmospherical changes nor by the destructive hand of man.

A small layer of sand covered the floors and some fragments of bone and stone were found, but unfortunately M. de Zeltner was unable to dig in the trenches for fear of offending the Abyssinians in charge of the place.

The grotto next to the monastery is a natural cavity of no interest whatever. An isolated rock, with a hemispherical excavation in the centre, is said by the natives to have been used by the monks as a mortar. A tunnel of considerable length is said to exist at the end of this grotto, but the aperture is blocked by stones.

In the Mitcha valley, near the grotto, are also several small cells cut into the cliff at various heights, and in which live Abyssinian priests in charge of the subterranean church as well as of an inevitable miraculous spring, such as one finds near most places of sanctity in any country.

According to M. de Zeltner this must have been a Christian monastery, identical with those of the Thebaïd. The Galla maintain that it was a Christian monastery, and upon Mount Fasila, dominating the Mitcha valley, they show the tomb—a simple circle of stone—of King Atie-Fasil, who, they profess, was a Christian. The identity of this king has never been properly established, and whether he was a Christian Galla king or not is uncertain.

Several of the tribes in Abyssinia have been known to dig grottoes in the soft sandstone of cliffs, making habitations for themselves, and it is possible that in this locality, so suitable for excavations of the kind, the example had been imitated by the monks who made this monastery. Its Egyptian appearance, so far away from the valley of the Nile, has not quite clearly been explained yet, unless the theory brought back by Raffray is correct, that the Negus Lalibela in the twelfth century imported an Egyptian who constructed some monolithic churches, which were copied afterwards all over the country. M. de Zeltner, who has studied the question more than any one else, seems to be strongly inclined to adopt this opinion.

On January 26th we went up another higher step of the plateau, now 8,050 feet. By Mount Herrer, which rises high above the table-land on our left (the south), we ascended still higher to 8,150 feet. Except for a short dry grass everything was burnt up. Mount Herrer throws out many spurs in the shape of hill ranges. They radiate especially towards the north, and we had to get over them on our march. The highest on our trail was 8,150 feet. From the last of these, towards noon, I obtained my first view of Adis-Ababa to the north-east of the Manangesha mountain (not to be confounded with Mount Magaghes).

We then descended abruptly, almost precipitously, from 8,050 feet into the basin and gorge of the Akaki, or Aghaghi, a river flowing from north to south at a level of 7,610 feet, and on the other side we quickly rose again to 8,480 feet upon another flat plateau. It was, in fact, the continuation of the one we had so far followed, divided merely by the deep cut in which the river flowed. This further portion of the plateau was quite level, with black, volcanic, gravelly soil.

We had now an interesting horizon line cut up by mountains all round. The Tchukala mountain to the north was most prominent of all. My men told me that a lake was to be found on the top of this mountain, on the shore of which were an Abyssinian church and monastery. Many hermits and monks were said to live in grottoes and caves in the mountain side. Monks from this locality were frequently called before the Emperor to predict his future. They wore a burnous of hide and a skin cap.

In the Godjam and Tigre countries—one north-west, the other due north of Adis-Ababa—were many monks and hermits.

The road from Adis-Ababa to Mombassa passed at the foot of the Tchukala.

The Dalatti mountains stood in the foreground. Then between the Dalatti and the Furi mountain in the far distance emerged, in a faint blue, the Soddo Range, inhabited on the north-east side by Galla, and on the south-west by Guraghi. The Yekka Mehel and Yekka

Emperor Menelik's palace, Adis-Abeba.

Abbo were two low mounts to the north of the Abyssinian capital.

As one got nearer the city one saw prominent on a height various white buildings and factory chimneys which, I was assured, made part of the Imperial Palace. Here and there upon hills one saw groups of scattered houses.

Adis-Ababa cannot be called a city in the proper sense of the word. There are thousands of white tents about, but few permanent houses, and it really impresses one more as a big encampment than a town. On the spurs of the hills to the right as one approaches the place, one sees the modest buildings of the British Legation, then a grander one where the Russian Minister lives.

Up a steep road I made my way to the hotel in the centre of the town. The accommodation consisted of one solitary room, from which the landlord, a Frenchman, and his wife turned out every time a traveller arrived. They were polite and the cooking was unmistakably good.

Of late years Menelik has been bent on making good roads in the capital, and bridges over the many streams which intersect the town, and which are impassable during the rainy season. I noticed, on going up the main road past the palace, that nobody walked on the road itself, but all crowded into the gutter at the side. Not knowing the laws of the country, I rode in the middle of the road upon my horse, much to the amazement of the passing crowd, many of whom made remarks which I did not understand. It seems that when the roads are made and well-metalled according to European ways, nobody is permitted to tread on them, so that they may be kept in good condition for the time when the rainy season arrives.

Since the arrival of two traction engines in the capital, Menelik, followed by many Abyssinian grandees, spends most of his time walking behind these engines while they are at work crushing stones upon the road. Sometimes Menelik himself gets on the platform of the engine and takes the keenest interest in its working, including the stoking. Thousands of soldiers and a great portion of the population form a procession behind the Imperial chauffeur.

Strangely enough, when, owing to its weight, the engine sinks into the new road, prepared in sections by men under various chiefs, Menelik, with true wisdom, does not blame the foreign-made engine, but takes the workmen to task and punishes them severely for not making the metalling of the road sufficiently hard to bear the pressure.

Menelik certainly gets a deal of amusement out of the traction engines. He uses them for all sorts of purposes besides road-making. I have seen the Emperor sawing wood with a circular saw driven by one of these engines upon the racecourse where a stand was being erected. When he did not actually work, hours were spent by the Emperor watching the saw at work, and he did not restrain his admiration at the evenness of the divided planks.

The day after my arrival I received a letter from Sir John Harrington, our Minister in Abyssinia, asking me to stay at the Legation during the time I should be in Adis-Ababa. After a day or two I left the single-roomed " Hotel Terrers " for the more comfortable quarters at the Legation.

A sad and curious incident happened the moment I arrived. The Russian Minister sent over a letter to Sir John, asking him to lunch, and an hour or so later a Cossack came over to the Legation bringing a message that the Minister had suddenly died of apoplexy, news which caused a great gloom in the European community, as well as among the Abyssinians.

Menelik, preceded and followed by thousands of warriors, hastened in great state to the Russian Legation. The rabble of soldiers in their white robes—a most impressive and formidable rabble—ran before him in no order whatever, carrying the rifles in any fashion to suit personal convenience. Then a swarm of horsemen in brown burnouses came up the hillside by the British Agency, quite a picturesque sight. Here and there upon the white clothes of the soldiers were touches of red, which added brilliancy to the striking scene.

The crowd approached with the characteristic whizz of Abyssinian mobs, quite loud as it drew near, all talking and dragging their feet upon the ground. The chiefs, mounted upon their horses, were noticeable above the sea of heads—most of them with their hair tightly bandaged in a white *shash*, others sporting cheap grey or black felt hats. All the infantrymen, thousands of them, carried Gras rifles, but the chiefs only had revolver-belts. It was not easy to recognize the Emperor among the horsemen unless his face were familiar to one, as he was garbed like other people, and like some of the other chiefs, he wore a cheap, large-brimmed felt hat, grey with a green lining under the brim. It was only after one had identified the Imperial figure in a black silk burnous that one had time to cast a glance at the magnificent mule he rode with its gorgeous harness and gold decorations.

On coming out of the Legation, where he was shown the body of the Russian Minister lying in state, Menelik seemed greatly upset.

I had selected a fine point of vantage upon a wall from which to photograph the Emperor as he came out, and I was amused at the way in which the African potentate actually drew up his mule for a moment in order to be snapshotted. With him was Mr. Ilg, his *Conseiller d'État*.

On January 30th, the funeral of the Minister took place, and Sir John Harrington and I, with an Indian escort, duly attended it.

The body was lying in state with wreaths of flowers from members of the community deposited upon the coffin, and numerous candles burning everywhere around. Cossacks in tunics of the crudest red and blue formed a line at the head, the corporal reading and chanting prayers in a hoarse voice.

Outside the house a choir of Abyssinian priests chanted plaintively, waving to and fro censers of silver and brass. A youthful priest who wore a gilt mitre over a silk kerchief upon his head, was the centre figure of this picturesque group. Above him was held a gay sunshade of Parisian pink satinette and silver lace. Another priest was sheltered under a sunshade in sections of green, yellow, red and white. Others were protected from the rays of the sun by pallid green, others by multi-coloured sunshades.

The more important figure had donned a long cloak of deep red and green brocade, with a shoulder cape of lighter-coloured tints, and a white turban wound round

The single-roomed hotel at Adis-Abeba. The sleeping quarters were in the central pagoda-like structure.

his head ; while several of the younger priests were
garbed in similar robes but of black silk. Many of
them carried crosses of silver or brass upon long
staves.

Menelik and the *Abuna* had sent these men over as a
compliment, and I think they rather felt a slight at not
being admitted inside the house.

When the prayers were finished in the lying-in-state
room, we all marched after the huge coffin up the hillside to a favourite spot in the Legation garden, where
the Minister, in his lifetime, used to spend many hours
of the day. After more prayers and firing of rifles the
body was laid to rest.

CHAPTER VII.

ABYSSINIA, not unlike other countries placed in similar conditions, like Persia or Afghanistan, owes its present independence mainly to the jealousy of the envious powers surrounding her. Nevertheless, Abyssinia seems to have now reached a stage when serious development is expected of her or division of her land among her grasping European friends must follow. With the French and the English on the Somali coast, the Italians in the Danakil country and Anglo-Egyptians in the Sudan pressing her on every side, it is not possible for Abyssinia to remain much longer in her present semi-barbarous condition.

While Menelik lives, his power is so great that it carries everything before it. His word is law and is everywhere obeyed in a manner quite amazing to Europeans. Menelik is a kind of god to the Abyssinians themselves, and if not exactly worshipped by subjected non-Abyssinian chiefs in the country, like the Galla and others, is regarded with wholesome fear by them.

The Abyssinians owe, I think, their constant victories in colonial wars rather to their fame than to their present fighting qualities or their skill and courage in warfare. The conquered and neighbouring tribes are in positive terror of the Abyssinians and of Menelik himself, more than of the Abyssinians in general, I think.

Abyssinian soldiers waiting for the Empress Taitu.

At the death of Menelik, and with the knowledge which the natives are beginning to acquire from foreigners visiting the country, perhaps matters will change. The tribes will know their own strength and the actual weakness of the Abyssinians. Perhaps then it will not be so easy to hold the country together.

One cannot help admiring Emperor Menelik personally. He possesses an abnormal amount of sound sense. He is as just and fair to his countrymen as is possible to an emperor ; he is generous enough with what he possesses, and tries at all times to do all that is right and proper. He is shrewd and has a more calculating brain than many a foreign emissary has given him credit for. His simplicity and natural charm of manner are quite delightful. Perhaps were Menelik a younger man, and were he persuaded to take a journey to Europe, a great many sensible reforms—and possibly some not quite so sensible—might follow.

As matters are now, Menelik does all in his power to improve his country up to the limit of his knowledge, but his knowledge would perhaps still further benefit by making a careful examination and selection of European ways of administrative government.

His country has now only reached a stage of semi-civilization, at which it cannot possibly remain. The empire might still hold its own were it established on a sound basis for natives and foreigners alike, with a proper government and administration, and, above all, with some stability of laws.

Abyssinian administration to-day, quite of a patriarchal kind, is good in a way, and when properly applied is, on the whole, just. The principle is that you must give an eye for an eye, one tooth for one tooth, and so on. The injured person has frequently the delightful privilege of himself enforcing the punishment upon the offender. For instance, an assassin is handed over to the parents of a murdered man, who can do with him what they please. There is charm in that undoubtedly, but abuses must be frequent.

Justice may not always be law, and we all know that law is not always justice, but with civilization coming in, with intercourse getting more frequent between natives and Europeans of all nations, some sort of a code of written laws must be made, as the present state of affairs leaves the litigants entirely at the mercy of the temporary fancies of the official called upon as an umpire in the various quarrels.

Menelik well knows this, but he thinks it wise to leave the country under present conditions—personally, I think they suit the natives better than a regular code —which do away with the ruinous lawyers and pleaders and lengthy and expensive trials that only bring discontent and ruin to a great proportion of the population.

All the more serious cases to be tried go before Menelik, and although he endeavours to be just, perhaps a touch of indigestion or a fit of bad temper, or a natural sympathy or antipathy for one litigant or the other undoubtedly influences his decision. Innocent men meet their death where criminals, if clever enough, are set at liberty.

Six men were shot one day in Adis-Ababa while I was there, and an interesting incident happened showing Menelik's good nature. One of the men who had been sentenced to death was discovered by some passersby some hours later to be still alive. He was taken to the Russian Hospital, and Menelik, on being asked, said that God had protected that man and he would now be pardoned.

Everything in Adis-Ababa is referred to the Emperor. It is quite amazing what an amount of mental work Menelik must go through daily. While attending to most important political affairs matters of the most trivial character are brought to him for assent.

This is practically what happens every minute of the day at the palace : Menelik with his head bandaged in a white *shash*, as it is called, a sort of silk kerchief, and with a cheap French felt hat with a large brim, far back upon his skull, is pondering with some Foreign Minister over some political problem of great importance to his country, let us say, the projected railway between the sea and Adis-Ababa. The Emperor is deeply absorbed in thought.

Enters a servant, who whispers in the Emperor's ear, regardless of the presence of the foreign representative of a great European country :

" Your Majesty, the carpenter wants some more nails to mend the verandah."

" Here are the keys. Give him twenty nails," says the Emperor. " If he needs more, come again to tell me."

The Emperor is again in deep thought. Intruder number two comes up and whispers that a mule has escaped from the palace.

The Emperor jumps down from his throne—a high packing-case covered with Oriental carpets—slips quickly into the shoes which he had discarded, and hastens to his telescope, scanning the country all round with it, in order to see whether the missing animal can be detected upon the hills near Adis-Ababa.

No signs being apparent of the Emperor's wish to

resume the conversation about the railway—the escaped mule being much more important to him than all the railways in the world—the Foreign Minister vainly attempts to drive the Emperor again to his throne. Attention is called to the interrupted discussion. The Emperor on his side endeavours to induce the Minister to come and look for the mule.

The subject of the railway is again tactfully approached, and the conversation, thinks the Minister, is proceeding satisfactorily, when a fresh disturber rushes in to inform His Majesty that the machinery in the mint adjoining the palace has stopped ; so down goes the Emperor to see what has gone wrong, and cannot be removed from the workshop until the machinery is set going again. He then calls for pieces of lump silver and gold, and with his own hands amuses himself in striking fresh coins, which he then places in his pocket.

By this time the Foreign Minister is getting anxious about the railway, and would like to argue some of the points of interest which might concern both his country and Abyssinia ; but Menelik will convey his illustrious visitor instead to examine a patent rifle or pistol which has just been sent to him as a present, or else will press him to listen to such sweet songs as " Honey, my honey," on a talking machine, which has been sent over to him. This over, the Emperor will enter into a lucid and graphic description of how he succeeded in hauling up a beam which should support the roof of a new church he is building here or there in the neighbourhood of Adis-Ababa.

Anything, in fact, distracts him when he is made to talk about affairs of State.

While I was in Adis-Ababa the question of the railway greatly interested the Ministers of the leading European countries. It was not therefore surprising to me to find that the various representatives were getting old and worn-looking. Nothing could be more trying, I should think, than talking politics with the Abyssinian Emperor.

Menelik, as a man, is certainly one of the most charming, thoughtful men I have ever met, a fact one appreciates a great deal when one remembers that his people —I am speaking of the Amharas or pure Abyssinians— are possibly as mean, ungrateful and abject as it is possible for men to be. There is with them no real paternal, maternal, fraternal, marital, or any other kind of love, and all is suspicion and treachery among them.

There is no "Thank you" in Abyssinia for anything, no matter how big a service has been rendered. In fact, I do not think the expression " Thank you " exists in the Abyssinian language. If it does, it is never used.

There is no finality about the word of an Abyssinian, nor about his deeds, nor anything he may undertake. *Eshi*, which many people take to be " very well," or " very good," but which really means " something like," or " possibly," is their invariable answer to anything you tell them. It only means conditional assent, the right to alter their minds being always reserved to themselves.

For absolute and unscrupulous lying, I never found people who could beat the Abyssinians. They will swerve from one statement to another diametrically opposed without flinching, and for barefaced impudence it is impossible to go further than these people. One moment they will swear one thing by all that is most sacred to them, and the next moment, for no reason whatever, they will swear exactly the reverse. It is, indeed, most difficult to know where you are with them. The more one knows them, the more contempt one has for them.

Great devastators of the country, it is in their nature to destroy everything. Improvident, living at the expense of the people whom they raid, robbers by nature, these people have succeeded in gaining a reputation for bravery largely undeserved, and obtained only by the fact that they possessed quantities of excellent imported firearms, where others merely fought with spears and arrows.

They themselves maintain that in their war with Italy they only gained a victory because God knew the Italian cause to be a false one, and wished to punish the invaders for trying to seize a country over which they had no right. The Abyssinians fully recognize that it was not the fighting qualities of their people that gained so great a victory over the white soldiers. They say that had the Italians wished they could any day and at any moment have easily beaten the Abyssinians. This, of course, emphasizes the shocking mismanagement, the inexperience of the Italians in colonial warfare, and their absolute lack of topographical knowledge of the country they were traversing. We will not further refer to the political ambition of Cabinet Ministers who were cabling to General Barattieri that he must win a battle on a certain day in order to carry an election at home, which no doubt procured or hastened the Italians so terrible a disaster.

All this, mind you, Abyssinians know well, for despicable as they may be, one must recognize in them

The Custom House and Market in Adis Ababa.

a certain natural reasoning power which can gauge matters accurately on certain occasions.

Many of the better Abyssinians have told me that this war with Italy has been a ruin not only to Italy, but to the Abyssinians themselves, who will some day surely pay for the conceit they have now acquired. Barring some of the people in power, it is difficult to make the public at large differentiate between nations of Europe. For them beating one white nation means beating the whole world of white people.

So, especially in Adis-Ababa, one has to stand a good deal of insult and rudeness from the public. I do not think that I have gone once alone through the market-place without overhearing remarks I did not particularly like. Of course, when going about with an escort, as one generally does, the people are more guarded, and one does not hear these things. It is only when alone that the natives are more or less offensive.

For instance, when they see a European go by, they generally hasten to stop up the mouth and nose, in order, they say, not to be suffocated by the fetid, corpse-like stench of white people.

To be just and fair, white people do certainly exude an odour, quite strong, which may be offensive to the natives of Africa, just the same as the effluvium of the people of Africa—much more powerful than ours—is disagreeable to us. It is also beyond doubt that the smell of white people does remind one forcibly of the neighbourhood of corpses. This I have noticed myself after having been abroad for long periods in the open air in countries far away from Europe. Upon my return to civilized towns one of the things that strikes me most potently is the unpleasant, rancid odour of most people.

I think this comes a great deal of stifling the body in musty clothes, by living in stuffy rooms, and from the terrible condition of people's digestions—as well as of their blood—in big European centres.

In America, where the people live even more unnaturally than we do in England, this peculiar odour is much accentuated to anybody whose respiratory organs and sense of smell are in excellent condition. There are unfortunately few Europeans, indeed, and fewer Americans, who can claim such a privilege, owing to the catarrh complaints which are so general in people leading a civilized existence.

The people of the country smell strongly, but less bad than the people of the towns, whereas the people of dry countries are less offensive than those of wet countries. It takes some little time before one gets accustomed to the peculiar natural odour of the people about, and it is only then that one does not notice it any more.

CHAPTER VIII.

I HAD several audiences with Emperor Menelik. He was always extremely kind.

Abyssinia is a land where time is not money. One has to wait days and weeks for everything one wants. It is always at the last moment that everything happens, and then always with a great rush. Being quite ready to abandon Adis-Ababa, my entire caravan of mules had been for some time under orders to start at any moment. I was delayed no less than fifteen days in order to wait for the Emperor's return to the capital. I was to do a sketch of him to be elaborated into a larger picture which Sir John Harrington wished to present to His Majesty King Edward.

Every minute the Emperor was expected back. I was told that he was busy building another church upon some mountain—he is always building churches—and that he was now occupied watching the construction of the roof. At last, when I was one day pleasantly disporting myself calling on various friends, a mounted horseman was despatched all over the town to tell me that the Emperor had returned and wished to see me at 4 p.m.

The messenger found me some two miles from the Legation at 3 p.m. Up and down various hills I galloped back to the Legation and got into my best frockcoat.

Sir John Harrington was waiting somewhat impatiently. We got upon horses and raced to the palace, where we were first ushered into a sort of open-air reception hall. Then, without waiting any time, we were shown into the presence of the Emperor, who sat himself cross-legged between two red pillows upon a couch in the doorway of the highest building in the palace grounds. A pair of shoes had been discarded on the floor.

In a black silk coat, a white band round his forehead and his favourite grey felt hat, His Majesty smiled good-naturedly and extended his right hand—not particularly clean—in the most jovial of manners. It seemed the handshake of an honest man.

Menelik certainly had the best-natured face, not the handsomest, of any Abyssinian I had seen. There was something leonine about his countenance, although his eyes, very prominent and bloodshot, had more the suavity of bovines. He was badly pock-marked. He possessed a capricious turned-up nose, narrow at the nostrils, and prominent lips, the lower rather too drooping to suggest strong will. His Imperial Majesty's skin was as black as coal and rough ; but although the face was altogether rugged, it was absolutely devoid of vulgarity. Intelligence and sharpness of wits showed clearly in his expression.

I was interested in his conversation with Sir John, and the good-natured, friendly chaff between the two, especially when I suggested complimentary remarks upon the Abyssinian climate, which brought a grateful smile from Menelik and threats of murder from His Britannic Majesty's Envoy Extraordinary.

Sir John maintained that the climate of Adis-Ababa was homicidal, and to prove this he said that all the

H.M. Emperor Menelik.

doors of the Legation had become so warped owing
to the alternate heat and cold, dry and damp, that it
was impossible to close them.   Upon which Menelik,
with really humorous sarcasm and with an explosion
of laughter, very wittily answered that the climate
would not affect good wood, but would certainly affect
bad wood.   Also, he exclaimed, doors were of absolutely no use in Abyssinia, where everybody was honest.
It did not matter at all if they could not be closed.   They
might, of course, be of the greatest use in countries where
such good people as the Europeans lived.

We had a most charming and amusing conversation
with a deal of repartee on all sides, and it was delightful
to see on what excellent terms of real, sound friendship our Minister was with the Emperor.

In a more serious moment, Menelik was asking our
representative's advice on some important matters, and
it was a pleasure to hear the Emperor say words to this
effect to Sir John :

" I like to ask your advice, because I know you always
tell me the truth, and you have always given me good
counsel for myself and for my country.   I can trust you
in every way."

Menelik was extremely jovial and polite to me, undoubtedly because of Sir John's introduction, and also,
I think, perhaps, because I assured the Emperor that I
wished nothing from him.   I wanted no concessions, no
decorations ; nor did I come to buy or sell anything.
It must have been rather a relief for Menelik, as the
majority of foreigners who visit him worry him considerably, trying to obtain something or other.

It was arranged that the next morning I should go
and call again, and he would give me a sitting for the

portrait. He would then put on his regal robes for me
and a huge gold, jewelled crown, a sort of gigantic
mitre.

"Oh, I do so hate putting it on," said the Emperor
jokingly. "It is so heavy and it hurts my head. I
much prefer my felt hat."

"Can you paint my portrait in fifteen minutes,"
said Menelik to me, "and can I wear my crown and cloak
only for one minute, as the cloak is hot and the crown
is heavy ? And can I talk to Sir John while you are
painting me ? "

When the crown and cloak were produced, I was really
sorry for the Emperor, and there and then agreed to
his terms. Then I was sorry for myself, as, indeed, it
meant painting under difficulty. I would try, anyhow,
and see what I could do. The Emperor promised to
let us know the next morning at what time he would sit.

Having been kept up till 4 a.m. in a deeply interesting
conversation with Sir John at the Legation—Sir John's
reputation for keeping people up all night with interesting conversation being well known among friends who
have visited him—I was roused from a heavy slumber
at seven o'clock in the morning, and was informed that
Menelik would sit for his likeness at 7.30 sharp.

Well, if there is a time of the day, any day, that I
never can do anything, it is just at 7.30 a.m. I am
generally too sleepy to be awake and too awake to be
asleep, or, in other words, in that unhappy intermediate
state when thinking—much more drawing—is quite out
of the question. I did not bless Menelik. A lightning
shave ; an extra lightning cold douche ; no time to dry
myself ; a jump into some sort of clothes ; up on the
horse ready at the door and a race to the palace, about

one mile off, and then, in a soaking perspiration, I was immediately dragged before the Emperor.

We had kept the Emperor waiting half an hour, but Menelik was gracious in his manner, and again expounded what a nuisance it was to have to dress up in his official robe.

When it came to the crown, Menelik exclaimed, child-like, " Feel the weight of it," and he handed the regal emblem first to Sir John and then to me, all the time laughing heartily. " The last time I wore it, it gave me a terrible headache for several days. That is what comes of being an Emperor ! " he soliloquized.

In fact, when the crown was placed upon his head, Menelik made an excruciating grimace, as if it caused him intense pain.

" Mind you, only for one minute by the watch," he ejaculated as he was half smothered under the heavy golden jewellery.

I took two lightning sketches of him and then hastened to take several photographic negatives, in order to have a record of the detail, as so many and complicated were the jewels upon his headgear and so uncommonly elaborate the ornamentations upon his yellow robe—not to speak of the European decorations of all sorts cover-ing his entire chest—that it would have been quite im-possible for any man to draw all that detail, which has to be reproduced with accuracy in a picture, in so short a time.

Harrington, who is more of a racing man than a painter, was actually timing me, watch in hand, and I was so hustled—there is nothing more fatal when you are drawing than being hustled—that when I came to take the photographs, I took several on the same plate. Having discovered my mistake, I took others, but Menelik's head was shaking so violently with the effort of supporting the imperial emblem that they, too, were not successful. The photographs were taken inside a room where a long exposure was necessary.

I took a number of other negatives without the crown, and these were slightly better.

Within the fifteen minutes, the Emperor was through his sitting, and he seemed so delighted with the gold-point sketches I did of him that he proposed to sit again for me whenever I wished. The sketch-book was passed round to some of the Abyssinian officials who were present, and was duly returned to me after many exclamations of admiration and covered with finger marks.

Sir John Harrington approached Menelik that same morning on so serious a matter as forming a reasonable and stable system of government and establishing a Council of State. He had for the purpose drawn up a lucid circular, copies of which he had distributed among the leading chiefs of Menelik's court. Menelik pondered deeply.

" Oh, look, look ! " said the Emperor, jumping to his feet, his eyes fixed upon a distant mountain where thousands of white tents had been pitched.

Anything is ever more important to him than serious matters of State.

" Do you see," he continued. " Here they come, thousands of my soldiers. I expect 7,980 people to lunch with me to-day."

He strolled upon the wide verandah, and could not repress his excitement on seeing the huge mass of white figures quickly descending the road leading to the

Menelik watching 7,980 guests arrive for lunch.

palace. He gazed upon them with his telescope with exclamations of delight, as he recognized one chief or the other in the crowd. He asked us to remain with him to see his guests arrive.

He also most kindly invited me to lunch with him. He said it might be an impressive sight. Meanwhile, as it would take some time for the guests to come, he inquired whether I should care to go over the palace grounds. He possessed some magnificent lions in a cage and a lot of rat-catching blackbirds, and other animals which were loose in the palace gardens.

I inspected the old circular Court of Justice with a tower and clock (a final court), in the door of which Menelik sits to judge cases, while the great Ras sit in the windows at the side. A little further, another building was in course of construction entirely of masonry, also circular in shape, with green doors for the Ras to take their places and a red door for the Emperor. In front was a space for the public.

Between the old and the new court was the façade of the great reception hall, a building of great size, showing in its decoration strong Indian characteristics. It was constructed by Indian workmen. The older audience hall was a typical Abyssinian building.

After that I went to see the arrival at the palace of the thousands of soldiers who were to be the Emperor's guests. There were guards at the gate with sticks in hand in order to keep out people who had not been invited. These attendants were said to possess wonderful skill in recognizing people who endeavoured to obtain admission to the palace and have a free meal at Menelik's expense, and upon these deceivers they used their sticks freely—so freely that the sticks had frequently to be renewed. Bunches of them were near by where a fresh supply could instantly be obtained.

A picturesque group of chiefs—early arrivals—squatted under the shade of trees. They were wrapped up in white cloaks, none of them over-clean ; in fact, most were absolutely ragged and dirty. The court was in mourning, and mourning in Abyssinia is observed by putting on unclean and shabby clothes.

At about ten o'clock a messenger came saying that Menelik wished me to go to lunch, and I was ushered in the politest of fashions into the great hall. It was not unlike a huge railway station in course of construction, with a double row of cantilever supports for the roof lavishly coated with blue and vermilion enamel-paint of the crudest tints. The interior of the hall was more notable for the ornamentations it did not possess than for those which were there and which were certainly not an attraction to the eye.

A large portion at one end of the hall was screened off by a cotton curtain, through which one could distinguish the burning lights of two candelabra. These lights, burning in the daytime, were placed there in order to follow an ancient custom, when Abyssinian houses had no windows and artificial lights were required. So upon European candelabra of dubious artistic beauty cheap European candles were set alight.

As the curtain was raised for me to enter the Emperor's enclosure, Menelik, who sat most nobly under a baldaquin of red cloth, on a raised throne of Oriental carpets and gold embroidered cloth, bowed graciously, and begged me to come and sit at a small table which he had placed by his side in the place of honour. A gilded chair was at once brought for me to sit upon.

Round me, seated upon the floor, were many important chiefs, such as Ras-Tassama, the powerful prince of Western Abyssinia, Dejazmatch Lelesaged, Dejazmatch Damise, Dejazmatch Balow, son of the chief of Guja, and Dejazmatch Wabe, all chiefs who had come in that day under the supreme command of Ras-Tassama. Behind me, when I turned round, I perceived the head priests of the Church, the high judges and many of the leading men of Adis-Ababa.

Two or three prominent foreigners were also present that day, but they were made to sit at low native tables, upon which was served Abyssinian bread and some native dishes.

Menelik seemed much concerned about the special lunch in European fashion, which he told me he had had particularly prepared for me. Various officials were despatched at intervals to find out how the cook was getting on with it.

"Here it comes," exclaimed the Emperor, whose face beamed all over, and with extended hands he made a sign to the attendant to lay the dishes upon my table.

Behold, the lunch had indeed arrived! I was much overcome by noticing who were the people waiting upon me. One of them was one of the three men who, in warfare, impersonates the Emperor, parading about in similar clothes under a red umbrella, in order to deceive the enemy and to be shot at instead of his regal double. The other men were also high officials, such as the chief of the Emperor's Forestry Department. All waited upon me with the utmost care and thoughtfulness. Half a dozen eggs were laid upon my plate to begin with. Then Abyssinian cake, so hot with pepper and spices that it gave me a violent cough when I tried a mouthful.

" Do not eat that if you don't like it," said Menelik, quite perplexed when my cough would not stop and nearly choked me.

Two large cutlets were next deposited on my table and three huge pieces of steak in the best English style, but not size. By their side (by way of comparison, I suppose) were three more pieces of steak in Abyssinian style, with a great many incisions upon them, so that the heat might penetrate inside in the course of cooking. A dish with a mountain of rice also towered before me.

Menelik was all the while turning round in the kindest way possible pressing me to eat some of this and some of that, saying that it was all cooked for me. I ate what I could to please him, but the Emperor insisted I must eat more. All my excuses that my appetite was now fully satisfied, that I was in delicate health and could not partake of more food, that my poor skin— never too elastic—had already reached its highest state of tension . . . . all was of no avail, and Menelik signalled to the Forestry man and to his " warfare double " to pile upon my plate more chunks of meat and hillocks of rice.

I was getting quite alarmed. Menelik said I must eat more. If I did not eat, it must be because I did not care for his food and he would punish his cook. So, in order to prove to him that this was not the case, and with a failing heart, I again endeavoured to demolish a second and third mountain of food upon my plate.

"The Emperor thinks you do not like Abyssinian bread," said the Forestry man, laying before me half a

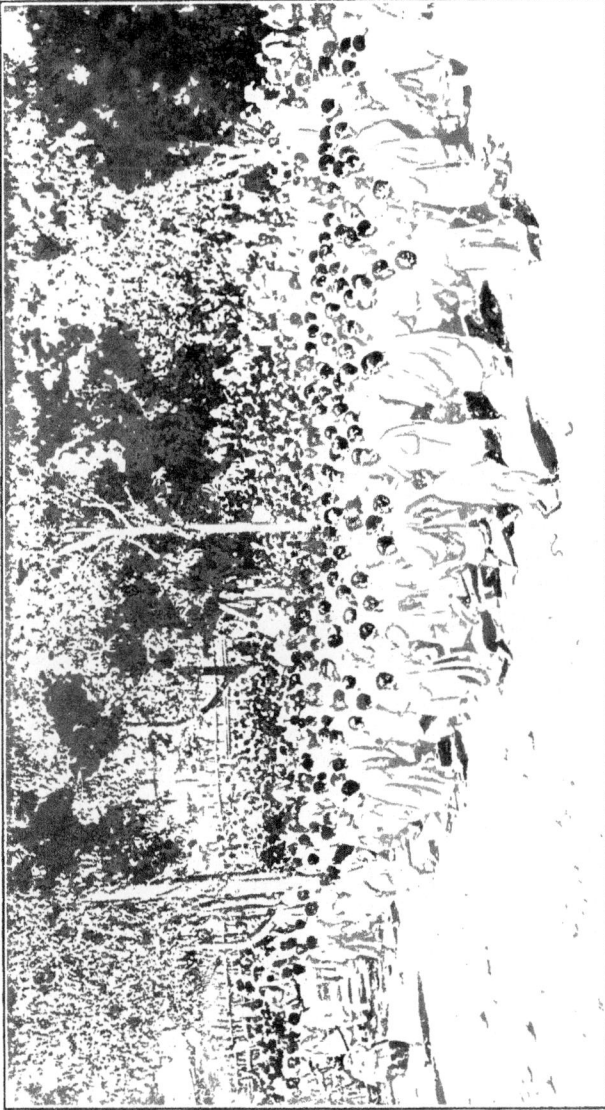

Guests on their way to Emperor Menelik's lunch party.

dozen huge, pancake-like half-baked native breads each about three feet in diameter.

"Oh, yes; yes I do," I mechanically remarked, shoving into my mouth a large piece of the heavy paste. The breads took so much room—in fact, the whole table —as they were spread flat, that all the plates, forks and knives had now to rest upon them.

Were this not enough, Menelik, who was certainly the quintessence of thoughtfulness as a host, immediately ordered loaves of European bread to be brought up.

In the way of drinks, not only was every spare inch of space over the breads—the table could not be perceived any longer—occupied by bottles, but bottles with all kinds of labels were standing upon the floor all round me. Abyssinian *tetch*, a kind of hydromel, native beer, claret, burgundy, white Rhine wine and champagne of an unidentifiable brand, but of a highly-explosive character, all were produced, and out of each I— practically a teetotaller—had to drink and tell the Emperor what I thought of it. Well, I thought a great deal more than I could say. That was one of those occasions when even an honest man had to tell big stories—that is to say, if he possessed a palate. Poor Menelik is terribly taken in in matters of foreign wines by merchants who supply him with all kinds of filthy rubbish in bottles with high-sounding labels. It somewhat pleased Menelik that I preferred the *tetch*—the native drink, by far the least poisonous of the various liquids which he at much expense placed before me.

The Emperor took his own lunch at the same time, and before him were laid various Abyssinian dishes, similar to those eaten by his leading guests seated within the curtained enclosure.

The Abyssinians were squatting upon the floor. Each had a circular basket before him containing several huge breads, like those which had been served to me, and some sauce. A small bottle of *tetch* was given to each man and constantly renewed when empty.

At last, when the Emperor had finished eating, the curtain was drawn. Before me was one of the most impressive sights I have ever witnessed. The huge gates at the further end of the hall were thrown open and a flood of sunlight was projected upon a stream of white figures entering the building in a dignified and orderly manner, each going to their respective seats along low tables close together occupying the entire hall. Each table was covered with five or six layers of flat breads, the top layer being sprinkled copiously with red sauce from large buckets which servants conveyed to and fro. Tabasco is mildly hot as compared with this red sauce.

At a top table near the platform on which was the throne were seated the older sub-chiefs and officers. At the further tables were the soldiers. At the four tables on the left sat the officers' servants and followers.

No one paid obeisance to the Emperor on entering, as all seemed to look upon this feast as a right. In fact, a similar feast was given by Menelik every Sunday to some or other of his people.

All the men entered and sat themselves down, proceeding at once to make a hearty meal. Hundreds of huge pieces of raw meat were passed round by attendants, and each guest cut a chunk with his knife and ate it, tearing at the raw meat with his teeth. Tall, enamelled iron tumblers of *letch* were given to the soldiers.

One of the typical sights of this banquet was a huge mountain of bread upon a central table, the mountain being eight feet high, fourteen feet long, and four feet wide, some 448 cubic feet of bread. This was besides counting the thick layers already laid upon the tables, which were fast being demolished as each relay of guests came in. Large as the hall was, it was not sufficient to hold the guests at one time, and they came in by instalments, each set of guests being expected to consume one layer of bread.

As soon as one lot had been fed and departed, the crumbled top breads were hastily removed, the under layer quickly besprinkled with the red sauce, the carpets and rugs shaken so that the dust from the people's feet went to settle down upon the food that was to be eaten by the next lot.

And so the hours went by. Swarms of figures kept pouring in with their black faces and white cloaks, giving quite a Biblical appearance to the scene. They sat with their stolid faces round their chief, who, in his turn, was the very representation of one of the ancient patriarchs one imagines from reading the Bible. To him these people paid their oxen and cows, their grain, milk and butter, and as he knew no better way to get rid of his wealth, so he gave back to his people plenty to eat and to drink, to show the fatherly interest which he took in his subjects.

I studied Menelik carefully. He really seemed to delight in having his people around him, and in watching them feed heartily and enjoying themselves.

I asked the Emperor how many oxen and sheep had been killed that day, and he told me that over one hundred and twenty oxen had been despatched and several hundred sheep. Each one of these feasts costs Menelik several hundred pounds sterling.

On the raised platform on which we were, many interesting scenes took place. Officers with bare heads, others with white turbans, streamed in to converse with Menelik. After talking for a few moments they sat themselves at the table at the foot of the platform. The higher officers remained in jovial conversation with the Emperor, paying him compliments and relating anecdotes which seemed to delight their Imperial host.

Each time the Emperor wanted to pick his teeth, blow his nose, or rearrange the white *shash* around his head, a screen was made by the attendants around him, raising with outstretched arms their shawls round the throne, thus obscuring the Emperor from the sight of the people. It was considered *infra dig.* to let the Emperor be seen by the public in such earthly pursuits.

By this time the afternoon had come. Menelik was incessantly urging me to eat and drink more. I had long ago reached a bursting point, and I cannot tell the suffering I went through in order to please the Emperor. Every time I caught Menelik's eye more food and drink were pressed upon me, and a constant stream of delicacies kept pouring in for me to try.

To work off the effects of over-eating, I had several interesting discussions with the head priests and the *Abuna's* secretary, with the Emperor's double, and the leading lawyer of Adis-Ababa, all men of great intelligence and quick wit. They were indeed remarkable at repartee. They never seemed at fault to find an answer. We had a thoroughly good time.

It was not till 4.30 p.m. that coffee was passed to a

Menelik's mule and escort.

few of the principal guests, and the Emperor got up to leave. As I stood by his throne, he bade me a hearty good-bye, and while I thanked him for his charming hospitality he apologetically explained how sorry he was my lunch had been delayed half an hour—I wished it would have been delayed a good many hours—as he had ordered special European dishes which had taken more time than he expected. He was so charmingly simple and frank about everything that really one could not help liking him, notwithstanding the intense agony he had procured me.

A curious scene occurred when I came out of the Grand Hall. Menelik's mule stood beautifully decked with silver and gold ornaments upon the head and saddle and round a huge collar. Near by lazily rested in the easiest of postures hundreds of soldiers upon the ground. When I produced a camera to take a photograph, they all sprang to their feet and begged me to wait. They buckled their belts, arranged their clothes and stood at attention with rifles pointing in all directions. This was because they feared if Menelik were shown the photograph of his soldiers in all sorts of reclining positions, instead of being upon their feet and on guard, he would certainly punish them severely.

CHAPTER IX.

ONE talks a good deal about the civilizing influence of Christianity, and there are many people in Europe who imagine that when a native becomes a Christian he must be a fine fellow in every way. In my own experience, I know that from a sanitary point of view, at least, if one wishes to see natives who are really filthily dirty, one has only to turn to Christianized masses of natives. This does not mean that I have not once or twice seen Christianized individuals who may have been clean, but these were quite the exception. To Japan, China, India, Persia, the Philippine Islands, and to Abyssinia—all countries where non-Christian natives indulge a good deal in ablutions—the above remarks may apply.

Abyssinians proper belong, as you know, to the Copt religion. What do we find? Whereas the Mussulman Galla, their conquered countrymen, wash considerably, the Christian Abyssinians themselves only bathe once a year at the feast of the Epiphany. They stay, on that occasion, nearly the whole night near a stream, and at dawn they sing, fire guns in the air, and then fling a cross into the water. They all jump in after it.

Even the Emperor and Empress indulge in this immersion on the Epiphany morning, but this, the only bath Abyssinians take in twelve months (thirteen months according to their calendar) is in no way intended to clean themselves, but is merely a religious performance. When in the water they wear, in fact, the *shame*, or shawl, over the shoulders, and the *surri*, or trousers, over their legs.

It is quite enough to look at any well-to-do Abyssinian, male or female, to perceive that even face and hands are quite innocent of soap. Of the body we will not speak —the seldom-changed clothes discharging a fetid odour which leaves no doubt whatever on the subject.

The only other bath an Abyssinian takes in his life-time is forty days after birth in the case of a male and eighty days in the case of a female, when during the ceremony of baptism they are plunged into the water.

The Abyssinians do not give their dead much chance of coming back to life again. When people die they are interred the same day. If death occurs at night, the burial takes place early in the morning. The relatives of the deceased rub the sides of their own foreheads with a woollen burnous until the temples are quite sore, and they attach pieces of cotton wool in sign of mourning.

Women on such occasions cut the hair short, clumsily, with scissors, in order to diminish what little attraction they may possess, and also to show their sorrow for the death in the family.

Before dying a confessor, not always necessarily but usually a priest, is called in. This is a man who goes by the name of *nefsabat*, and who is well posted in the secrets of the confessed.

Every Abyssinian must confess before death, or his body will not be admitted into the Church graveyard. If he dies unconfessed, he must be buried outside the

Church grounds. Many of these confessors are mere blackmailers, who take advantage of the opportunities offered to impose upon the afflicted family. At the death-bed they have been known to make mercenary bargains by threats with the dying man. When the confessor comes out of the dying man's room, it is usually found that the man who has expired has bequeathed his mules, his property, even the bedclothes and the very clothes he is wearing at death, to the confessor. Hence disputes between the relatives of deceased and these " soul-pacifying " individuals are common. Perhaps it is a sensible precaution for these people to have the body buried as soon as life seems extinct.

Although the Abyssinians consider themselves highly civilized, superstitions are rampant among them, even among the highest people. Curious methods are used, for instance, in order to discover the perpetrators of thefts or other crimes. A man called a *lebassai*—the title of a profession descending from father to son—is employed by chiefs and even by the Emperor. This fellow proceeds to the spot where the theft has taken place, and with him go two slave boys, not older than eight or ten years. These boys must know nothing about sexual intercourse, nor must they have ever used intoxicants. The *lebassai* gives one boy a specific medicine of his own, after which the lad, bound in a white sash, is made to prostrate himself face downwards, when a glass of milk is produced, into which a white powder is mixed. Then the boy is made to rise; he is by then in a dazed condition, whether from the stuff he has swallowed or in a hypnotic trance. They say that the boy will then unconsciously reproduce all the movements of the thief or other criminal during the crime,

Menelik's High Court of Justice (Adis Abata).

and proceed directly to the spot where the offender has found shelter.

Notwithstanding the faith of the people in the accuracy of the *lebassai's* medium, all Abyssinian bystanders make a hasty stampede at his approach. There have been mistakes made even by the *lebassai*, although I am told that many a real offender has been traced in this way.

The way it is done I think is this. The *lebassai* is a highly-observant man, who spends his entire time in his detective work, and who acts generally on information previously received. For a consideration he will surely spare the culprit and accuse an innocent man. Wealthy people who refuse to be blackmailed are often selected by the *lebassai* as culprits, and folks maintain that the *lebassai's* profession is one of the most remunerative in Abyssinia. His recognized fee alone amounts to five silver thalers.

Many other superstitions prevail among the Abyssinians. For instance, if an overladen mule gets a sore back, they say it is caused, not by an ill-fitting saddle, but by a great vulture—the *gibri*—which, on soaring above, has projected its shadow upon the animal's back.

They are great believers in the evil eye, which they call *metf* (eye), or *aen* (the Arabic term for eye). In magic they also place absolute faith.

On St. John's Day none of them go out early in the morning, as they believe that by doing so they might fall victims to the incantations and exorcisms of hidden enemies who have the power on that day to inflict punishment. The only way to counterbalance this evil influence, they believe, is by obtaining a grey lamb, a jet-black sheep, or a white or black fowl, as the magician may direct, or, if the whole animal would cost too much, a piece of meat from any of these animals. These offerings, placed on the road with some incense and a special stone, are held sufficient to break the spell.

Abyssinians of certain classes do not leave their sons alone on that day, nor do they eat in public. If possible, they remain inside the house the whole day, as they fear that if bad luck should come on St. John's Day it will go on for the whole year.

Abyssinians are great believers in spirits of the mountains and ghosts. They cannot be persuaded to pass by a church or a graveyard (near the church) in the hours of the night for fear of these spirits. Nor will they travel alone at night, as they fear the spirits of dead people.

Medicine as a science is not much advanced in Abyssinia, but the people possess a few remedies of their own which do no great harm, if they do not do much good.

They use cupping for stopping headaches. Also, they always wear round the neck a black ribbon, to which a small silver lamb is attached. When suffering from headache they place this little lamb upon the forehead with the string tied round the head.

For fever they make several incisions upon the scalp or in the back of the neck. This bleeding process, which I have seen applied on several occasions, gives good results.

Molten butter is swallowed when a good purge is needed, and for tapeworm, from which they nearly all suffer owing to the habit of eating raw meat, they drink a decoction of powdered *cossu*, which has been soaked in water for at least four or five hours. They drink this early in the afternoon, and will see no one until the medicine has acted, for fear the " evil eye " should stop its effects.

Many diseases are put down to the "evil eye"; and great chiefs, for instance, will not let their children be seen by strangers, even going so far as to change or misstate the baptismal names of their young, for fear of spells being cast upon them if their real origin were known.

The Emperor and Empress themselves largely indulge in superstition.

For fifteen days before New Year's Day a number of Abyssinian priests are fed only upon roasted beans and water, and are not allowed to go out at all. On the first day of the year they are conveyed into Menelik's presence, when they predict the events of the forthcoming year, and advise him what to do. They say that Menelik is greatly guided by their counsel. The many churches which he builds are due to these yearly consultations, and it is said that such predictions are responsible for his having yielded up to the priests his palace of Adis-Alem, which had been constructed at enormous expense in a spot formerly a forest. The priests have turned it into a church.

The priests I met in Abyssinia were most unattractive. Depravity was plainly depicted upon their features; their unctuous manner never rang true, and they had the conceit of men who obtain high positions by false pretences. In short, I never had much liking for them, but I would not care to state that all were bad. Perhaps the *Abuna*—the chief of the Coptic Church of Abyssinia, who is ordained by the Coptic Patriarch of Alexandria in Egypt, and possibly some of the high priests under him—ought not to be classed among the common herd, but one and all, I believe, show much tendency towards intrigue. Their indirect influence in politics is considerable.

The *Abuna*, like the Emperor and Empress, has the right to have a red seat—a kind of throne—as well as a red sunshade over his head. There are thousands of priests all over the country, and in Adis-Ababa alone, I was told, there were no less than six thousand of these religious expounders.

The *Abuna* can impose Church taxes at will, and the Emperor has no word in the matter, the taxes being duly paid by devotees.

One Sunday I went to hear the service in the Church of St. Michael, situated opposite the Imperial Palace. The building was simplicity itself inside, with no idols nor pictures. The church was formed by two concentric walls with spacious windows and doors in each. Within the central circle sat the Empress in a screened enclosure of gauze, while the *Abuna* officiated in the space between the inner and outer wall, attended by a gaudily-dressed staff of priests.

The Emperor seldom goes to this the swell church of Adis-Ababa, but attends service inside the palace grounds in a smaller church called the Hedan Emrath.

The Abyssinian Church is national and independent, as everyone knows. The *Abuna* is the resident chief of the church. With only such variations as are suitable to the locality and the people, much the same doctrines as those of the Coptic Church are taught, except that several additional rites are observed, such as circumcision of both sexes, adult baptism and certain love orgies. The Mosaic laws regarding food are also observed.

During the service the porch and wooden lintels, as well as the walls and supports of the church, were kissed with great fervour by devotees, and this kissing formed a good portion of the service. The Abyssinians talk a good deal about "kissing the church," and on passing the holy places they always stop to kiss the wall or the ground near it. They also throw stones as they pass or heap them up in a cairn, or else deposit offerings of strips of cloth or rope as they go by a church.

In some Abyssinian churches bells are made of two long pieces of slate suspended from two poles.

A good deal of chanting went on during the ceremony and shaking of the *sistrae*—the *tenatzil*, as it is called by the Abyssinians.

In front of St. Michael's Church, for instance, which is upon a well-beaten road, a humble telephone pole standing near the church had been decorated with strips of cotton, and its base was quite greasy with the constant kissing of passers-by.

Whether because of the evil consciences they possess, whether from fear of the revenge of the gods or the reprisals of evil spirits, I am not certain, but the Abyssinians are decidedly charitable. This virtue, as with us, does not always come from a good heart. Oh, no ; perhaps penitence is more responsible for it. The poorest people will give away sums vastly out of proportion to their wealth when anything is weighing upon their minds.

I noticed in the Abyssinians I employed that after they had committed some misdeed they were always charitable, and gave away nearly all they possessed. This surely was because they had great fear of God, whom they believed to be their protector until angered.

Of course, in a country where people are charitable, there are bound to be a lot of beggars. Lepers and appalling cases of elephantiasis swarm in Adis-Ababa. Sores of the most purulent character are displayed to the public with the utmost gusto, while clouds of flies feed peacefully upon these and then come and settle on your face as you go by. To all these fellows—dozens of them near the churches particularly—the Abyssinians give freely.

The Abyssinians have many official holidays, but perhaps the most important falls on September 14th (Coptic calendar)—the day of the Virgin, which is celebrated with horse-races, games and rejoicings of all kinds. During that day crimes and accidents go unpunished. On the eve of the 14th everybody must go with a gun on his shoulder to the church, and when the cross is taken out they all follow it, the Emperor included. They then form a circle round it, the Emperor depositing upon the ground a wooden stick, all the others imitating his example, until a high heap has been accumulated, which is then set on fire. Many of these sticks have yellow flowers attached to them—the *ababa* (a generic name for flowers, but used specifically on these occasions).

The following morning (the 14th) they all return to the spot and make a cross upon the forehead with the ashes from the burnt wood.

At Easter the people fast, and also on Good Friday, the last food being taken on Thursday, and the next not until Saturday at about 10 a.m. They then proceed *en masse* to the church with their sisters and sweethearts, the head of each encircled by a wreath.

A strange custom is practised on New Year's Day.

People go about with flowers in their handkerchiefs, which (the flowers) they present to their friends on meeting them, wishing the *un Kututash* at the same time. If one happens to touch the flower while the words are pronounced, one is compelled by custom to offer a present to the giver—something like our Philippine trick.

Christmas, of course, does not exist, the Epiphany being the most important holiday after September 14th.

In a country where hypocrisy and sanctimonious bigotism are rampant, we necessarily find saints in great force. St. George is the most revered of all, but for every month there is a special saint, and once a year a great holiday is dedicated to each. In a way these saints are useful, as they serve to let people fix dates exactly, which they would otherwise have difficulty in doing, owing to the lack of printed calendars.

The Abyssinian year has thirteen months, twelve of thirty days each, and a thirteenth—the *Kogumeh*, which comes after the end of August—of only five days.

CHAPTER X.

MARRIAGES in Abyssinia are sometimes performed according to the rites of the Coptic Church, and in that case, when a legal separation between man and wife is demanded, the property, such as houses, land, cattle and furniture, is divided into two equal shares. So, as Abyssinians are seldom honest, even among themselves, the wife never knows exactly what the husband possesses, nor is he aware of the wealth of his bride, the facts being concealed in case domestic quarrels should arise.

A more frequent form of marriage consists in swearing by Menelik's name, the price to the husband of Menelik's oath, the *samagna*, as they call it, being at the most some one hundred and twenty thalers. This form of marriage is the one generally preferred by the better people, but the poorer classes do not always go through any official ceremony at all, and marry or divorce somewhat promiscuously—as fancy takes them.

No faithfulness exists in marital relations among Abyssinians. Owing to shocking diseases of the blood, women are not prolific. The percentage of infant mortality is also high, so that the population is neither increasing nor improving. When a mixture of blood occurs, as with Galla, Somali, or with black tribes, a slight general improvement in the physique, as well as in the mental capacities, is noticeable in the half-breeds. Also, these mixed unions are generally more prolific than those among pure Abyssinians—a race to my mind quite exhausted physically.

Roughly speaking—as accurate statistics do not exist—I do not suppose that there are more than a couple of millions of *fairly* pure descent, and very few indeed *absolutely pure* Abyssinian individuals.

The Emperor himself, and many of the leading Ras, show evident signs of mixed descent, and it is the mixture often of negroid races which has given them the strength to rise above the average individuals and rule them.

It is curious in this case to note that the crossing of two weak races can produce satisfactory results.

The purest of all Abyssinians are to be found in the Tigre, Godjam, Gonda and Meus, as well as a few at Ankober—the best by far of all these being the people of Tigre and Meus. The latter never intermarry with other races, and until the death of King Johannes, the Tigrins, too, deemed it quite a dishonour to marry even a Shoan. Nowadays marriages between members of the two races are quite frequent.

Owing to the singular state of affairs in Abyssinian marital relations—the men and their wives indulging in promiscuous love—it is sometimes difficult to trace the exact parentage of children. Whether legitimate or not, all are taken into the family while cordiality lasts in the home, and when separation comes, as it often does, the girls are taken charge of by the mother and the boys by the man, whether their father or not.

The Tigrins are perhaps the noblest-minded and most generous of all Abyssinians, but the others are incredibly *mesquin,* dishonest and dishonourable, among themselves more even than with strangers. There is no family affection—which is absolutely non-existent with Abyssinians—and the people are suspicious of one another and treacherous. There is no word of honour with them, nor the faintest notion of the meaning of truth. An under-thought is always present in their minds, whatever dealings they may have with anyone. Their cruelty to human beings and animals is disgusting.

The better class might be excepted, but the men at large seem to have no ambition in life except carrying a gun upon their shoulders. It is generally a good gun, but owing to his diseased vision and unsteady hand, the average Abyssinian cannot hit a haystack at twenty yards. The rest of his time is spent searching for vermin (they all swarm with lice), of which there are legions in his clothes. There is a happy existence for you !

Abyssinians do not care for trade, they detest agriculture, they are too proud and impatient to be good shepherds, and they are in too great terror of the water to be good boatmen or sailors. They are first-rate people for destroying everything, for pillaging, burning and rendering barren and miserable the richest of countries. Even upon the now barren and arid Shoan plateau, in the neighbourhood of Adis-Ababa, over which we have travelled, there were formerly beautiful forests now absolutely destroyed. The agriculture of Abyssinia is now practically in the hands of the Galla.

The Goraki, who are Mahommedans, with inclinations towards tree-worship, and who inhabit between Tulidumtu and Burani Arusi, are a superior race as far as regards mental capacity. They have the entire native trade in their hands, especially in Adis-Ababa, where the market is solely run by them, and even in the Imperial palace everything is managed by these people. Fitaurari Apti Gorghis and Dajatch Baltcha, for instance, two of Menelik's most intelligent chiefs in the palace, are Goraki. The telegraph and telephone operators upon the Dire Dawa—Adis-Ababa—Gori line are nearly all Goraki.

These Goraki possess a language of their own. They never intermarry with other tribes, except when their women have been raided and necessity compels them. Few—very few of them—have ever accepted the Christian religion. They bear certain Egyptian characteristics in their general appearance, and they are the whitest and best built men and women I saw in Abyssinia. The Goraki women, with their large, well-cut, softly-magnetic eyes, are much admired by the better class of Abyssinians. The wives of most of the great chiefs are, in fact, Goraki.

The Goraki are fairly numerous, and they are clannish. The Goraki, like the Jews, are great at helping, even supporting, one another. Anything that is done at all in Abyssinia is done by Goraki. The arts and crafts—whatever there are of them—are in their hands. The Goraki are the masons, the carpenters, the traders, the goldsmiths and blacksmiths. They manufacture the saddles and harness. They tan the leather and dye it of a dark red tint. The Abyssinians also try to tan and dye, but they do it badly.

I was told that close upon ten thousand Goraki workmen and traders are to be found in Adis-Ababa alone.

It is astonishing how inartistic the people of Abyssinia are. Only seldom one sees attempts at painting or sculpture, and these attempts are ridiculously weak. Occasionally one notices a crude representation

of Menelik and the Empress Taitù under their red umbrellas, but that is about all.   In the Tigre and Godjam,
jewellery, especially in silver, is manufactured, but is of
no artistic beauty.   The only ornaments which I saw,
and which were quite interesting ethnologically, came
from South-Western Abyssinia, from the Kaffa country,
and from the kingdoms of Kulu and Kunta.

There was a forehead ornament sticking out horizontally, and suggesting an enlarged conventionalized
representation of virility, worn by the Kaffa men, especially in battle.   It is a simple design in brass, and usually
rests upon a ring of ivory fastened to a cloth band which
goes tight round the head.   A brass chain is attached to
it with conical pendants hanging in front of the ears.

The women, too, wore a series of such conical em-
blematical ornaments of silver––only smaller—in a row
upon the forehead, with a superposed chain of beads and
lozenge-shaped additions.

A man who had performed a brave deed in the Kaffa
country was entitled to wear an almost circular ornament
of rats' teeth attached to a skin.   Long coil bracelets,
such as those presented by the Emperor to his subjects
who have killed many enemies in war, are also found in
the Kaffa region.

Ivory trumpets of great size, which produce a hoarse,
loud sound, and ivory flasks for civet-scent are wonderfully well turned, although the methods of turning are
extremely rudimentary.

Baron Mylius, who had travelled extensively in the
Kaffa, Kulu and Kunta districts, showed me a curious
collection of belts for women and ivory bracelets with
certain marks, small perforations, recording the number
of lovers the wearer of the belt had possessed.   If the

records were correct, some of these Kaffa ladies seemed to have had a lively life.

Kulu spears, with elongated heads and brass rings attached to them, were interesting. The shields—about three feet in diameter, much larger than those of most other tribes—were made of cowhide.

Among musical instruments there were conical drums with a triangular six-stringed frame attached to them, and the *kaficho*, or trumpet, of antelope horn, eight feet long, into which was inserted a bullock horn, with a perforation about six inches from the bottom. Where the horns met the trumpet was decorated with a horse's tail.

Among the attempts at representing living objects the conventionalized wooden dove seen on the huts of Kulu Chiefs, and upon the poles of their tents while on a journey, was one of the few to be noticed in the country.

The Abyssinians proper are given to constant orgies and are inveterate drunkards. It is amazing what quantities of *tetch* they can drink. They have one redeeming quality ; they do not smoke.

There is a legend telling how at one time the Abyssinians had become so fond of tobacco that even priests chewed in church. Whereupon good King Johannes made a law that whosoever was seen smoking or chewing tobacco should have his lower jaw amputated.

This is, of course, a pretty legend, but there is a better reason for this, the Abyssinian's only virtue. They are indeed ready to take up almost any vice which gives them pleasure, and if they do not smoke, it is simply because of the unpleasant, even disastrous, effects which smoking has upon the human heart at the high elevation of this plateau. So that the abstinence from tobacco is more a necessity than a good quality among these people. In my experience I have always noticed that people living at high altitudes, even in Asia, seldom indulge in tobacco—the Tibetans, for instance.

As we are about trying to discover good qualities among the Abyssinians, we must give them unbounded credit for another excellent virtue they really do possess. I mean their absolute contempt for degrading and disgusting unnatural vices between individuals of the same sex. They are in no way degenerate in that direction—if, perhaps, some of the priests are excepted.

The ignorance of these repulsive priests is unlimited. Few of them can read, fewer still can write. They teach in schools—what, I do not know ; perhaps prayers.

The school hours in the towns are from seven till 8.30 in the evening and from three to five in the morning, as the children are needed during the day to go and fetch wood and water for the family and help their mothers in the duties at home.

People in Europe have a most erroneous idea that all countries in Africa must be highly picturesque, but, indeed, there is no continent in the world where anything is more difficult to find than is picturesqueness among the people, scenery or buildings in the zone of Africa I traversed. There is no attractive colour to speak of in the landscape, the light being too brilliantly diffused in the middle of the day, and the contrasts too hard and violent in the morning and evening. As for the people—take Abyssinia, for instance—they are ungraceful and ugly, and wrapped in clumsy clothing, usually white or brown, and always too clean to be pictorial and too dirty to be captivatingly clean.

The men's heads are bandaged up most inartistically in the white *shash*, the tails long behind only in the case of the Emperor, but quite short with other folks. Above this is worn a felt hat of the ugliest description. These hats come mostly from Italy.

Both men and women must undo this *shash* in sign of respect before the Emperor and Empress, and it is on such occasions that one can smell to the full the rancid odour of Indian oil and molten butter mixed with pinks, cinnamon and myrtle leaves which the ladies use for smearing the head. This mixture gives the hair a greenish colour.

One cannot accuse Abyssinian women of being extravagant in dress. The *sipsipo*, or national costume, consists in a mere sacque with extraordinarily long sleeves pulled up at the elbow. The sleeves of the richer women are as much as three yards long, and have to be gathered together up the arm by slaves, and then buttoned up tight at the wrist. Of similarly ample dimensions are the women's trousers, the *modante*, also three yards long, also pleated up and buttoned at the ankle.

The chief luxury and ambition of Abyssinian women is to possess, or rather to display, sunshades of any brilliant colour, except *red*, which is forbidden, being the colour reserved for the Emperor, Empress, and *Abuna* only. The sunshade is held over the head regardless of atmospheric phenomena by a slave, seldom by the lady herself.

In countries away from European traders the natives make tiny cane umbrellas, undoubtedly of Mussulman origin. They are common, as we shall see, among the Islamic Galla.

CHAPTER XI.

Politically Abyssinia has but a relative interest.

For the last few years we have heard a great deal about neutralization or the internationalization of the Djibuti-and-Adis-Ababa railway, and, I think, many people confuse the neutrality of Abyssinia with the neutrality of the railway. It does not take a clever man to see that were the railway entirely in the hands of one foreign Government, the interests, the commerce or ambition of other countries might suffer. Menelik himself, from what I could understand, was not partial to a scheme which might endanger his country considerably. The construction of the railway to Adis-Ababa had to be suspended owing partly to fear of a revolution in the country, the masses of the Abyssinian population being much discontented—in fact, quite opposed to the continuation of the railway as far as the capital. Were the railway completed they felt they would soon have their country swarming with foreigners, with whose methods they can in no way compete, and perhaps the country would eventually be altogether absorbed by one or more foreign nations.

Menelik himself is fond of reforms, but not so his people, who are bigoted and conservative. Anything European brings bad luck upon the country, they believe.

I understand that lately an agreement has been arrived at between Great Britain, France and Italy regarding the completion of the railway, and naturally, both from a political and commercial point of view, this completion will be a great stride towards the rapid development of Abyssinia. All the nations interested in her resources will benefit in a greater or lesser degree. Commercially, France, I think, is bound in the end to come out first, because Djibuti, on French territory, is undoubtedly the key to Abyssinia, being the nearest, cheapest and most suitable natural outlet for Abyssinian exports, as well as being the best inlet for imports. It possesses all the practical advantages that can be desired. The Italians, of course, would like to see trade go towards Massowah, but that route is longer, more difficult, and through endless, barren, ungrateful country.

A concession has been given by Menelik for the construction of a British railway from British Somaliland to the Soudan. No route has been specified. Should such a railway be established, the competition between the French and British line might possibly be considerable, as the British line might be made to traverse the richest portions of Southern and South-Western Abyssinia, perhaps crossing the rich Aroussi country (which sooner or later must have a railway), and going into Kaffa, one of the wealthiest districts of the Ethiopian Empire. A junction could eventually be effected with the Mombassa railway along the valley of the Omo river by way of Lake Rudolph, and the line could continue northwards by way of the Didessa valley and the Blue Nile to Khartoum. All this would, of course, come into the giant scheme of the Cape-to-Cairo Railway.

But in my opinion, for commercial purposes, goods will always find their way in and out of Abyssinia towards the east coast, as the freight charges *via* river and rail to Khartoum can never compete with those *via* French Somaliland, or even were the second railway constructed, *via* British Somaliland. The distance would be much greater ; and the difficulties of travel, the many necessary transhipments, are all against the longer lines of railway and water travel combined. This might not apply to goods either for local trade or for direct export to the Sudan and Egypt, which would travel direct to the north-west, but the direct trade with those countries is at present small, what exists being mostly a transit trade.

Possibly a line might also be constructed from Adis-Ababa westwards to the Didessa and Blue Nile, with a branch to Gori and the Baro river, but this line, I think, would rather further help to bring goods from the west towards Djibuti which might otherwise be compelled to travel by the British line to the Nile or British Somaliland.

Be that as it may, Abyssinia is in great need of railways, and whatever effect the various lines may have on the interests of foreign nations, they will certainly be of financial advantage to Abyssinia herself. The country, especially the west and south-west, urgently requires new and more convenient ways of communication than those now in existence.

There are few regions in Africa which are richer than the western and south-western portions of Abyssinia— generally known as the Galla country. Its picturesque mountain masses are well wooded and the valleys are regular gardens. The climate is ideal, water for irrigation plentiful, and the soil so fertile that it will produce anything with the minimum of labour. Two crops a year can be grown without cultivation. All that is necessary is to sow the seeds anyhow ; the land does the rest.

Cotton grows well in the low lands and might be made a remunerative industry. Experiments in the cultivation of cotton have been made by Mr. Gerolimato near Errer. His plantation gave satisfactory results. The climate of the Abyssinian plateau seems suited for the production of this valuable textile. At Errer the plants reached a height of four and a half feet, and on each stem were counted as many as sixty-two blossoms. A higher price was obtained for it than the price fetched by Egyptian cotton of the best quality, the thread being longer and more resistant.

The first year, when the land was but imperfectly cultivated, fifteen *kantar* per *fedang* were obtained. The kind which seemed most adapted to the locality was the " *metafifi*," which is fibrous and silky.

A hectare of land (about two and a half acres) produced about thirty-five *kantars* of raw cotton, whereas in Egypt not more than twenty *kantars* are generally obtained on a similar area. A *kantar* is three hundred pounds. When boiled, a *kantar* of Abyssinian cotton gave about one hundred pounds of clean cotton.

Unfortunately, when things were progressing well, a swarm of locusts arrived and razed the plants to the ground. Other regions of Abyssinia would, I think, be equally, and even better, suited than Errer for cotton plantations.

Higher, on the hill slopes in Western Abyssinia,

Indian corn, dura, barley, wheat, beans, lentils, potatoes, onions, giant cabbages, tobacco, and coffee of excellent quality are most plentiful. The coffee grows wild, and only a small portion of the berries is collected, the rest being wasted, left rotting upon the ground for want of carriage to foreign markets.

The western country is more thickly populated than Eastern Abyssinia, and the inhabitants, the Galla, are peaceful, docile people, easily amenable to reason. They would be good auxiliaries to any one exploiting the resources of the country, whereas the Abyssinians proper, of whom there are but few in that portion of the country, are so independent, lazy, uncontrollable and unreliable, that they are of no practical use in steady commercial enterprises.

The western, the Galla provinces, are the exclusive property of the Emperor, who farms them out to great Abyssinian feudatory chiefs, always reserving to himself the right of deposing them and replacing them at will if they incur his displeasure.

It is in South-West and Western Abyssinia, too, that whatever mineral wealth exists in the Empire is to be found. Gold has been discovered in various districts, mainly washings in river beds. I am told that forty to fifty thousand ounces a year are collected with the primitive methods at hand. Iron ore, of course, is plentiful all over the country, and the natives themselves smelt it. Traces of copper have been discovered, but whether in sufficient quantities to be workable is problematic. Lignite has been found in several places, especially in Tegulit and at Bulga (east of Adis-Ababa), not far from Baltchi.

Then there are beautiful pasture lands to the east,

as well as to the south-west and west, where cattle and sheep, mules and horses, could be bred in abundance and profitably, if there were easier ways of transport to distant markets where the demand is great. As it is, good animals are kept in small numbers, and oxen, mules, and horses find a ready sale in neighbouring countries. This is only the case because the animals themselves supply their own inexpensive transport for comparatively short distances ; while grain, for instance, which could be produced in immense quantities, can only be disposed of locally. The Adda country, for example, is a rich grain country.

Small trading caravans visit the smaller markets in Western Abyssinia, where cotton goods, arms, silk, hats, ammunition and glass ware are exchanged for oxen, sheep, horses and mules. These animals are then conveyed to bigger centres. Abyssinian mules are excellent as transport animals for mountainous countries, and the horses are also quite good.

In North and North-East Abyssinia we have a different state of affairs. The complete destruction of forests has left the land barren and has had a deplorable effect upon the climatic conditions of that region, making the rains irregular and causing disastrous storms with violent winds and hail.

The Abyssinian inhabitants, such as the Amharas, the Gondari and the Tigrins, who sparsely populate the country, are humble proprietors of small fields where barley, *bagoussa* and *tief* are grown in meagre quantities, just enough to suffice the wants of the family. No export trade worth considering exists.

On the other hand, this region would be a good market for imports, as the climate, being severe, the natives require articles of clothing, and their contact with civilized people has already created in them several new wants.

Hats, for instance, find a ready sale in those regions, as well as coarse black woollen materials, with which the natives make their burnouses ; also red stuff for ornamental jackets. Parasols are most popular among Abyssinian ladies, white, black or brilliantly coloured (except red), and come mostly from India, Germany and Italy. There is a slight sale for cotton velvets, made up into cloaks by the chiefs to be worn on solemn occasions. These velvets, like the woollen cloth, are imported chiefly from France, Germany, England and Belgium, whereas the cotton materials, which are most in demand in white, red, yellow, green, and blue tints, come almost altogether from Manchester and America, passing through many intermediaries before they reach the final buyer.

There is an ever-increasing demand in Eastern Abyssinia and Somaliland for good camp equipments and supplies, such as sensible cooking utensils, camp beds, blankets, tents, water-flasks, etc., but above all for tinned provisions of good quality, which find a ready sale among Europeans residing or travelling in the country, as well as among the wealthier Abyssinians. Sardines, for instance, are much relished by the natives, and tons of them—of the very poorest kind—are sold.

It is to be regretted that most of the foreign merchants import merely condemned provisions, which they purchase at little cost and sell at immense profits, or else damaged tins from wrecked ships, or from the stores of extinct expeditions. Some of these tins are quite deadly ;

nor would it do to speculate on the age of tinned provisions one buys in Eastern Abyssinian centres.

There is one great thing in Abyssinia—goods travel in
absolute safety, when not accompanied by a military
escort. Caravans can travel from one end of the country
to the other, provided the necessary passes are carried,
without fear of being robbed.

CHAPTER XII.

In Adis-Ababa I had the pleasure of meeting the Europeans connected with the development of the country, and prominent among them stood the stalwart Monsieur Ilg, Councillor of State to His Majesty the Emperor.

This gentleman, a Swiss, has been in Abyssinia for many years, and has played an important part in Abyssinian politics, in a way, I think, beneficial to the Abyssinians, as well as possibly to himself. One does not generally go to live in countries like Abyssinia merely for one's health. The Abyssinians should decidedly be grateful to him for his work during the Italian war, when he displayed much energy and faithfulness to the Negus. Possibly his work may have clashed at different times with British, or Italian, or French interests, for which he received unbounded abuse in Europe according to which country happened to be affected, but I think that M. Ilg always endeavoured to do what he honestly believed best for Abyssinia.

For those who abuse the climate of the Abyssinian plateau and its evil effects upon foreigners, there could be no better answer than to show them M. Ilg and his family. Both parents and their charming children were the very picture of health and vigour, although the children had lived there all their life and the parents longer than any of the foreign officials I met in the Abyssinian capital.

It is a pity that M. Ilg does not write his memoirs, as he has seen Abyssinia during its transition ; he knows the country, the people and their language more intimately than any other European, and he has gained the affection of the people to such an extent that the natives regard him practically as one of themselves.

M. Lagarde, the French Minister, I also met, a highly intelligent man. When I called, I found him in a semi-nautical, semi-official costume, indiarubber top-boots such as mariners wear in stormy seas, long, white, accordion-like trousers, tucked with difficulty into them ; a black frockcoat, with rosettes, and in his hand a white helmet. He was most affable. This man has done good work for his country, and there was a time previous to Sir John Harrington's appointment to Abyssinia when he was practically a second emperor in the country. In the town he was in those days saluted with such respect as is in general only commanded by the Emperor. His influence then had no bounds at the Abyssinian court.

Things have changed a great deal during the past few years. The Abyssinians, like most Easterns, are capricious people. One day they cry you up to the sky, and the next a rapid descent may befall you. Instability of success is always to be expected in one's relations with Eastern nations.

When the interests of England in Adis-Ababa were in severe conflict with those of France, M. Lagarde certainly made a great fight against Sir John Harrington. He did not leave a stone unturned to regain his former power, but for some reason or other the Emperor placed more confidence in Sir John Harrington than in the French envoy, and of late has been acting chiefly upon the advice of the British Minister.

I understand that M. Léon Lagarde, who has now returned to France, is not to go back to Abyssinia.

Perhaps there is no more admired Frenchman in Abyssinia than Colonel Marchand, of Fashoda fame. He could do for France in that country what few other men could do, the prestige he gained there during his journey being enormous.

Major F. Ciccodicola, the Italian Minister, was absent when I was in Adis-Ababa, but I frequently met Don Livio Gaetani, the first secretary, a versatile and able young diplomatist, whose name is well known in connection with the siege of the Pekin Legation, as well as with a recent interesting expedition made by him in South-Western Abyssinia. We might doubt the wisdom of sending a military officer as Minister to Adis-Ababa, however able he may be, after a disastrous war ; and, in fact, the Italian envoy found himself from the beginning a good deal handicapped in diplomatic negotiations with the Emperor. Nor do I personally believe that the extravagant presents constantly given by Italy to Menelik help much in restoring the prestige lost during the war. It might of course be said that a military officer was selected because Sir John Harrington, the British Envoy, is also a colonel in the army, but matters stand somewhat differently as regards Abyssinia in our case and in that of Italy.

Expense was certainly not spared by the Italians in order to impress the Abyssinians, and formidable fortress-like towers of solid stone were built as a gateway for the Italian Legation, which stands near the market square. They seemed rather out of keeping with the modesty of the buildings in the enclosure. The Abyssinians were somewhat amused at seeing these fortifications put up on one side of the enclosure, whereas a galvanized wire—not even barbed—was deemed sufficient to keep people out on every other side.

The Russian Legation buildings were outwardly the most imposing, but perhaps when the new buildings of our Legation are finished they will surpass in beauty those of our Slav neighbours.

So far, the low native conical roofs and cylindrical walls of the British Legation appear outwardly more like a florid growth of mushrooms than the residence of His Britannic Majesty's envoy extraordinary; but the buildings inside are extremely comfortable and well furnished.

From the summit of the hill on which the Legation stands one commands a fine view of Adis-Ababa—a lot of huts in patches, like so many villages scattered upon various hill summits, and the Kabana stream, one of several intersecting Adis-Ababa. It was in this stream that, returning from a party, a secretary of the Russian Legation was carried away by the current and drowned, so that getting about the Abyssinian capital is not always quite so easy as it sounds.

Further one saw quite prominent in the landscape the house of Dejaz Matjubado (commander of the right wing), a two-storeyed house, with hundreds of soldiers' tents pitched around it.

On the summit of the hill was a stone fort, and I was told that upon many of the hill-tops commanding Adis-Ababa similar forts were to be found.

Down below stood the spacious foundations for the

new British Legation, and, in fact, the stables of solid masonry were nearly completed when I left. The living quarters for the humans connected with the Legation will be constructed later on higher up on the hill.

Sir John Harrington needs no words from my pen. His work is too well known for me even to refer to it. Perhaps, however, it is not so generally known as it should be, that this man, with his remarkable personal influence, has been able to save British prestige in Abyssinia at a moment when every atom of power had been lost in that country, and that region was about to slip out of our hands altogether.

To-day, thanks to the immense respect which our Minister commands in Abyssinia, we have but little to fear in political competition with other nations. Anyone who has travelled in Abyssinia can bear witness to the absolute reverence which he commands from every side. His good, honest advice to the Abyssinians is much appreciated by Menelik, and undoubtedly the few beneficial reforms that have so far been carried out in that country have been due to a great extent to the sensible suggestions made by the British Minister to the Emperor.

Much attention was aroused by the establishment of the Bank of Abyssinia, quite an event in Abyssinian development, as the natives had so far been accustomed to hoard their treasure. When it came to depositing their silver and gold, they preferred to do so in a deep hole in the ground rather than in financial concerns. Perhaps they were not altogether to be blamed, but all this may gradually change.

The National Bank of Egypt having obtained a concession from His Majesty the Emperor Menelik for the constitution of the Bank of Abyssinia, a company was formed with a capital of half a million pounds sterling. Shares were offered to the public on November 7th, 1905, and the result of the issue was satisfactory, the required amount being subscribed many times over, chiefly in Italy, Paris and London. The object of the Bank was to transact commercial, financial, or industrial, as well as banking, operations in Abyssinia.

By the concession given by Menelik the Bank obtained the following privileges for fifty years :

That no other bank should be established in Menelik's Empire ; that the Bank of Abyssinia alone should have the right to issue bank-notes ; that the Government should not by itself issue coinage of any kind, but that the coinage should be made jointly with the Bank of Abyssinia ; that all public funds should be confided to the Bank, and Government payments effected by cheque drawn upon the Bank. The Bank of Abyssinia was to have the preference over the issue of all Government loans, and the authorities were to establish warehouses where merchants could deposit their goods as a guarantee for the Bank's advances. The Government was furthermore to supply gratuitously the necessary sites for the Bank buildings, its agencies and warehouses.

The employees of the Bank of Abyssinia were to enjoy the same tariffs on the railway as Government officials.

As the Emperor had taken the leading part in the establishment of the Bank, it was hoped and expected that the general mass of the people would support it. Also, Ras-Makonnen at Harrar was one of the directors, and it was believed that his influence would help considerably in the success of the Bank. Great difficulty was of course anticipated in starting business in a country like Abyssinia, where the natives have no idea whatever of the work of a bank, and no doubt the shareholders and directors will have to show a great deal of patience for the first few years, before any real headway is made in that country.

Fortunately, according to the concession given, there can be no opposition or competition. Foreigners of all nationalities welcomed the arrival in Abyssinia of some system by which business could be transacted in an easier and safer way than it had been so far.

Perhaps the profits of the Bank will develop chiefly with the growth of the agricultural resources of the country. In order to bring this about, however, it is necessary to establish first a sensible mode of transport. Menelik, and with him all Abyssinians, I think, are quick enough at choosing anything which is likely to be in their own interest.

The Bank has already obtained the entire control of the national funds, and even the Emperor is obliged to pay into the Bank the silver money as well as the gold hoarded in the palace. Eventually, with this wealth to fall back upon, paper money will be issued, repayable on demand in gold or silver.

I was told that an attempt would be made to change the obsolete currency of the country, only the time did not seem ripe for that yet. The people of Ethiopia are still so ignorant that it will take some time before they can be made to change their old system.

One cannot help considering that a country with a silver currency liable to fluctuations of exchange places itself in a precarious situation in view of large purchases from outside countries. The Bank will attempt to put the currency on a gold basis as soon as practicable, a change which should be welcomed in every way, especially by those having commercial relations with, or in, Abyssinia.

The Bank was formally opened by the Emperor on February 15th, 1906, at nine o'clock in the morning. Menelik went over and inspected the various buildings, and paid into the Bank a few thousand thalers, his being the second transaction the Bank had made in Abyssinia, the first business done actually before the Bank was opened being with me in cashing money upon a letter of credit.

The day the Bank was inaugurated, Menelik was surprised to find that the Bank had not brought over a lot of gold and silver into the country. Menelik had at that time little idea in what the work of a bank really consisted.

In order to avoid international complications, the Bank of Abyssinia is not a purely English concern, but is an international affair, with a Board of Directors, in which one noticed names of many nationalities, and with a cosmopolitan staff of employees. The Bank was to have branches at Harrar and Dire-Dawa, and it was proposed later on to establish one in Western Abyssinia at Gori, as this point will some day be of great importance, being on the Khartoum and Adis-Ababa route.

The idea of starting the Bank was due, I think, to Lord Cromer and Sir John Harrington. Mr. D. P. MacGillivray was appointed Governor of the Bank of Abyssinia, as he had gained much previous experience in the Bank of Scotland, and then in the National Bank of Egypt.

Menelik at one time purchased a quantity of German machinery, and established a mint in the Palace grounds, where we have already seen him at work, but had so far been quite unable to produce coins fit for circulation. Efforts would probably be made to put the machinery in order, but as the privilege of the concession does not allow the Government to mint its own coin, it is doubtful whether the machinery will ever be used again on a large scale. The coinage could be struck in a better way at a smaller cost in other countries.

The agricultural resources of Abyssinia may be considerable some day, and, maybe, also the mineral. The latter perhaps will be of secondary importance for a long time to come. The Bank, if it has the strength to keep alive for many years, should be in a way the means of holding the country together, if all goes as expected. Even the natives may eventually be induced to deposit the money they now keep buried in order to prevent robbery or extortion, but no doubt the task of teaching them extra-civilized ways of doing business will by no means be an easy one.

One should not lose sight, however, of the fact that in Abyssinia there is at the present day immense wealth in gold and silver money and in ivory lying idle.

Owing to the peculiar way of administering justice, in a country where no one speaks the truth and blackmailing is usual, where the accused, whether innocent or not, is not judged according to his crime, but is first of all imprisoned and his property confiscated—the *urs*, as the Abyssinians call it—it is no wonder if those who possess wealth keep it carefully buried. Also, the fact that a wife on divorcing her husband can claim half his fortune tends to promote this attitude of suspicion towards all neighbours.

Enormous quantities of ivory, I am told, are buried in Abyssinia, and are gradually getting spoiled. Menelik has a vast amount of this valuable possession stored away. Possibly ivory, with its ever-increasing value, may be used some day as a deposit security in banking concerns of Menelik's Empire.

It is said that Menelik has considerable sums of money buried at Ankober, in the mountains north-east of Adis-Ababa, and also at Mongoresa. In the latter place and upon the mountains of Tadetchimalka, where he has built extensive fortifications, he is declared to have stored munitions of war. There are there two Krupp guns, perhaps the best he possesses, which were formerly, in the time of Emir Abdull-Ali, at Harrar. All the rest of his artillery consists mostly of old Italian mountain guns of small calibre, taken from the Italians during the Erithrean war. They have not been cared for, and they are now practically useless.

CHAPTER XIII.

It did not take long for me to make up a fresh caravan. On a Saturday afternoon, which is the market day for horses and mules, I purchased, with the assistance of my friend, Mr. MacGillivray, some twenty-four or twenty-five animals, which, with others I possessed, were sufficient to carry all my loads. In fact, I actually loaded only two-thirds of the animals at a time, the others going along empty. This enabled me to march quickly, being able to change the loads from the tired mules every three days, each animal taking its turn in having a rest.

With the usual rabble of Abyssinian muleteers, a troublesome lot at best to deal with, I despatched my caravan from Adis-Ababa on February 13th, and on the 16th, with relays of horses which had been placed on the road for me by Sir John Harrington, I started at 8.15 a.m. along the good and only slightly-rising road as far as Adis-Alem, a distance of some thirty miles.

I was to cover three marches in one day in order to catch up my caravan, so I had to put on a good speed. There were thousands of soldiers along the road, carrying wood for some construction in which the Emperor was interested.

Menelik's way of obtaining building materials is

quaint enough.   If he wishes to put up another building, in the Palace, for instance, or a church somewhere, he rides out upon his mule and picks up a stone or a piece of wood, which he carries back upon his shoulders to the Palace, or to the spot where the erection is to be made.   The thousands of soldiers who always follow him   must imitate his example, so that by the evening plenty of building material is already at hand.

The soldiers were most impudent, hooting and making unpleasant remarks on foreigners in general as I went along.   At Manangasha, where I had relays of horses waiting for me, the soldiers were particularly offensive while the saddles of our animals were being changed, and it required patience to avoid an unpleasant row.   As far as the language went, I think they got back quite as much as they gave, possibly more.

All the people we met on the road were armed to their teeth, but I had nothing on me, not even my *courbash*, which had gone ahead with my *sayce* and my own horse.

The country was getting less barren than on the east side of Adis-Ababa.   We crossed one or two dirty streamlets.

At Adis-Alem the Emperor's former palace, which is painted white, stands on the top of the hill, with a number of humbler buildings in native style around it within an enclosure.   There is a good road leading direct to this palace from Adis-Ababa.   Several European buildings are found a short distance before reaching Adis-Alem, inside the extensive barbed wire enclosure.

On our right were the Metcha Mountains, which, at a first glance, had the appearance of being thickly wooded, but as a matter of fact were only sparsely covered with trees. There were many shrubs close together, which, at a distance, looked like a forest.

As we galloped along the road, under the shade of every solitary tree ugly women, usually in couples, sat with sacks of grain for sale to passing travellers and caravans.

In the afternoon, at 3.20 p.m., I reached the Hawash river, where I made my camp somewhat higher than the stream at an elevation of 7,410 feet, having ridden about eighty kilometres in slightly over seven hours, including a short rest for lunch.

I left the Hawash the next morning in a pouring rain, and marched along rolling country with good pasture land all the way. This part of the country is inhabited by the Galla, who possess thousands of cattle.

We met many caravans all along ; one particularly, in charge of a few muleteers, a big caravan of mules laden with sacks full of thalers. This caravan was to travel right across the country as far as the most western point of Menelik's empire. One could not help being impressed by the security in these barbarous countries, a security which, indeed, is not so common in more civilized lands. Comparisons are always odious, but it is to be doubted whether a caravan carrying several thousand pounds sterling in solid silver, not locked up in strong boxes, but in mere bags, the mouths of which were fastened with a string, could travel with equal safety across London and reach its destination, not only in safety, but at all.

We were marching between two ranges, one to the north, the Metcha mountains, which extended a greater length and were higher than the range to the south, the Tulinencha, which consisted more of a series of

Galla.

rounded hills. The Tulutatcha mount was the nearest to us, with a solitary tree upon its summit. As we went along, the Metcha range was only slightly wooded near the summit. Lower down all the wood had been destroyed in order to supply Adis-Alem and Adis-Ababa with wood for fuel and construction. In fact, all this country, both east and west of Adis-Ababa, which, before the time of the Abyssinian occupation, was very thickly wooded, is now getting absolutely barren.

Further on I was travelling practically due west over transverse undulations, with not a tree except in the far distance, and grass burnt yellow by the heat of the sun. We came across many Galla, some with picturesque leopard skins draped over the shoulders.

From the camp at Metcha, where there was a limpid little stream flowing into the Hawash, we rose to 7,850 feet, and obtained before us a view of the extensive plain. Here and there were a few *metcha* trees, from which the place has taken its name, and the resin of which is quite good to eat.

The Kulluka, or Nulluka, stream, flowing northwards into the Gouder and then into the Didessa, was the biggest we had met since leaving Adis-Ababa. At the village Ambo, some little distance down in the valley on our right, were to be found hot springs said by the Galla to be good for rheumatism and other complaints. An Abyssinian church had also been built there.

Beyond, to the north-north-west of us, opened a broad gorge with precipitous sides. Having marched some six hours from the Hawash, we met again the giant cacti, the *kulgual* (called *hadanta* by the Somali), which was so common near Harrar.

More Galla women with shaggy hair sticking up above the head and cut straight at the shoulders were met with. They were not particularly attractive, with their unwashed faces and limbs and skinny pendant breasts with extraordinary extended black nipples. Some were simply dressed in the usual sack-like gowns of dirty white, others were further decorated with broad red beads. Blue bead armlets and necklaces, and also bracelets, were occasionally worn. One thing that struck the observer was the pretty shape of their feet, small and daintily formed, whilst the hands were plump, almost swollen, probably owing to the amount of rough work the women do in the Galla country. We found here again the skirt of tanned leather, or else a mere kind of apron enveloping the body from the waist to the knee.

The Galla are, taking things all round, a great improvement on the Abyssinians, both physically and morally. They have a keen eye for business and arrange their manners accordingly. The men are not devoid of good looks, nor are the women when young, as they possess an untamed appearance about them which is not unattractive. They have most lascivious eyes and lips. Unlike women in countries where weights are carried upon the head, who have a graceful stride, the Galla women walk rather badly, with the upper portion of the body at an angle forward, as they are accustomed to carry big round pots of butter or vessels containing water resting upon the back at the waist, and supported in that position by a rope across the chest bones and over the shoulders.

At a place called Tulidumtu there were two great roads branching one to Gori towards the south-west, the other towards the north-west, both eventually leading to Khartoum. The elevation twenty feet above the stream was 7,180 feet. This being a market place, we stopped a whole day in order to buy provisions for my men and to make other purchases from the many Galla who came round the camp to sell animals and food.

I took advantage of this halt and of the excellent water in the stream to do some photographic work, and spent a good portion of the night developing negatives under my tent, a tiresome and trying labour when upon the road.

On February 19th we again made a start. Loading the mules generally took a long time, and we never got away from camp before seven or eight o'clock in the morning. I did not mind this, as I always prefer to march during the day, no matter how warm it is, than to make night marches, which I abhor.

We rounded the dome-topped hill of Tulidumtu, and we proceeded along grassy, undulating country with many *metcha* trees and numerous Galla huts with patches of cultivation round them. We found our-selves practically surrounded by fairly-wooded moun-tains, the Toké Toké range close to us to the west. Then over fairly well-cultivated country with the Agomza mountains to the right of us, we descended in a very narrow groove of clay mud, extremely slippery, down to a river called Tukur, which, in Abyssinian, means " black." It is called so because the forest is rather thick in this part, and down by the water the over-hanging vegetation somewhat prevents the rays of the sun penetrating.

As we had descended, on the other side of the stream,

we had to rise up to a pass 8,350 feet high, going through
luxuriant vegetation with beautiful ferns. We then
descended one hundred feet into an immense undulating
valley of bright green, then of yellow grass, the first
portion reminding one strongly of a Swiss pasture land.
We went along across this valley as there was no drinking water, and further the grass was too dry for my
animals. We saw a few Galla homes. Then we neared
a stream at about 1 p.m. After that we continued our
journey on a flatter part of the valley, upon which the
grass had been destroyed altogether by fire.

On the right, to the north, near by were verdant
hills, with trees upon them, and Galla villages at the
foot. On the left, to the south, were also verdant hills
a long way off above a great stretch of bright yellow
grass extending for many miles without a single tree.
Behind us to the east we left a high range now hardly
visible beyond a sheet of torrential rain.

Marching was cool that day, the sky being clouded
and occasional refreshing showers coming down upon
us. We were travelling practically due west on a fair
trail, keeping at an elevation of over 8,200 feet all along
the highest point of the northern section of the valley.
The valley can roughly be divided into two longitudinal
sections running from east to west and with double
inclines, one from north to south and one south to north
respectively, converging towards a central depression
dividing the valley in the centre. There were, of course,
also transverse undulations.

Galla men came in the evening with presents of goats
and butter, when we made camp. The butter would
not be bad if it had not a peculiar flavour which comes
of mixing with it something, also from the cow, but

unclean according to European notions. The milk also is spoiled in a similar manner. My men, however, liked both milk and butter. Personally, except in cold countries, I never touch butter, and never at any time drink milk, even when pure, and I most certainly draw the line at Galla mixtures.

I was able to purchase barley for my animals, a lot of chickens, and most delicious breads, three feet in diameter, which the Galla made for me. These breads were baked between two large concave iron dishes placed in inverted order one above the other and sealed all round with cow's dung. We purchased a great many eggs, which were always welcome, being a most sustaining food.

I gave the chief some presents, but he said the Galla were not a grasping people like the Abyssinians, and they wished nothing for the few things they had given me as a present. It was the duty of any Galla to receive white people travelling through the country hospitably. These people spoke highly of the Marchand expedition and how kind that leader was to all the natives when the French marched across Abyssinia in the reverse direction to mine as far as Adis-Ababa.

I was interested in the construction of Galla huts and went to visit some. By the aid of candles—the huts being so dark that it was impossible to see inside even when there was bright sunlight outside—I inspected several of the interiors. I crept in through a low door. In the centre was a fireplace with the usual three stones forming a triangle, upon which were iron plates plastered over in the local fashion while baking bread. Above the fireplace, slightly towards the entrance, hung a grating seven feet long. There was a raised portion where the people slept on a bed of straw, also in front of the fire ; while a few pots, pans and milk jars were kept in the central place, and a few spears stuck along the wall. Upon another raised portion the milk and the grain were kept, as well as all kinds of plates, etc., made of closely-plaited basket-work. A few low stools carved out of a solid block of wood and a few wooden pillows were to be seen on the raised platform on which the people slept.

In some huts, which possessed a bigger door, a portion of the hut was reserved for small donkeys and calves. They made part of the family.

The domed ceiling was constructed of basket-work with bent sticks, and was about twelve feet high at its highest point.

There was little else to notice in Galla habitations except the pipes, made of a gourd in which was inserted an earthenware pipe with a channel four feet long, the gourd resting on a specially-made basket upon the ground. In these pipes the natives smoked tobacco compressed into a greenish-black cake, mixed copiously with dung. Its smell was sickening.

In the enclosure outside the hut cows were kept, and many chickens in crates. Near the front door was a large heap of dung.

The outer wall was made of posts close together, laced up with split cane fastenings. One of these structures took about eight to ten days to build, and in this operation all the friends gave a helping hand. The thatched roof supported on the wall was also made of cane and wood, and was held firm by the posts of the inner enclosure inside the hut. Over the door, a removable cane matting was used for preventing people coming in. The entrance of the hut was reached after going into an enclosure made of rough branches of trees, with a pen near the entrance door. The portion used as a stable had a separate door, kept closed with a mat.

The spears which were found in the interior of their houses possessed long, oval iron heads. The rod was about seven feet long. They were mostly throwing spears.

In olden times Galla messengers carried a double-headed spear, upon showing which they could proceed anywhere unharmed. Galla chiefs wore curious hats decorated with shells, and they made their shields— the *maya Galla*—of bullock hide with a rim turned over all round.

Both in the Galla and Kaffa countries a curious instrument is to be found much in use, the *koda-kaya* (in Galla), or *beshe kullo* (in Kaffa). It is an earthenware arrangement used for the artificial contraction of feminine organs. It consists of a small covered pan, with a handle on one side and four perforations in its upper face, with a fifth to which a cylindrical short tube is attached. In this receptacle a powder called the *besye* is burned, the smoke of which is said to produce the desired effect.

CHAPTER XIV.

FROM Camp Tukuri, which is at a greater elevation than
the plain we had crossed to reach it, one obtained a fine
view looking back the way we had come. The plain
spread roughly from south-east to north-west. To the
south we had what at a distance appeared to be a beautiful forest, but in reality was a mere optical illusion
such as we had had before, and when we got nearer
proved to be a scantily-wooded hill range. To the
south the sky-line was quite low, over wooded hills
rising but a few hundred feet above the level of the
plain. In the north-easterly portion the plain was
burned black for some square miles up to the rounded
hill which we had passed before reaching Tukuri. In
the south-western portion of the plain rose a conical
wooded hill.

Tukuri village was at an elevation of 8,390 feet,
whereas the plain was at an average elevation of 8,100
feet.

The next morning, about an hour after leaving camp,
we went over a pass 8,420 feet high, after crossing which
we were confronted with an unpleasantly slippery
descent. We were ankle deep in slimy, oily mud, at
such a steep angle that men and animals had great
difficulty in keeping erect. We descended into a small
basin thickly wooded with *ghirar* trees. From the

metcha, sometimes also called *mĕrcha,* gum is extracted. We had great trouble with the caravan, men and mules tumbling down all the time, and the loads were reduced to a filthy condition.

There was quite thick forest on all the hills around us, and by ten o'clock we were traversing delightful country, with beautiful ferns, raspberry bushes and occasional date palms. Now and then we came upon huge fig-trees, the fruit of which was not bad to eat. Every now and then, however, as we lustily bit large chunks out of these fine-looking figs, we found our mouths and faces swarming with ants, of which the fruit was full—quite an unpleasant sensation.

Much tempting wild fruit of all kinds could be seen as we went along, but it is dangerous to experiment, as most of the fruit one finds is poisonous. The very pretty, small yellow fruit, no bigger than a plum, called the *ombai,* and a small red berry, the *indoholla,* and which grow plentifully in bushes, are both inedible.

We were here in a region of beautiful vegetation, with the gigantic *sigba* trees and the huge *uarca* trees, the latter having most powerful-looking contorted branches. The undergrowth was quite thick in this region and thorns innumerable. There were all kinds of creepers and mimosas. Among the flowers, most common of all were the violet-centred convolvuli and the jessamines.

At last, towards noon, having descended nearly all the time through thick vegetation, we emerged in a flat, open, grassy plain, one mile wide, and surrounded by wooded hills at an elevation of 6,580 feet. Shortly after, at 6,450 feet, we came to a pool of evil-tasting water filtering through a rock. The Galla say that it is poisonous ; in fact, quite deadly.

We continued our journey on the flattish grassy plain, and early in the afternoon, after going through two undulating valleys full of high grass, unpleasantly hot and stuffy to travel through, we crossed the stream Ualtinak, an important little watercourse.

We camped at three o'clock a little further on at a place called Danno, where a few Galla huts were to be found. The Galla, as usual, were extremely polite Many of them came to my camp applying for medicinal treatment. They have an idea that every white man is a doctor able to cure any complaint. So during the whole afternoon people kept streaming in : some with sore throats ; one, an old man, wanted to have his sight and hearing restored to him ; others suffering from indigestion, headache, and last, but not least, numerous people complaining of toothache. I generally carry a pair of forceps, which are serviceable when I have nothing else to do in camp, as many people come to have their teeth pulled out. I do not know whether I always remove the aching tooth, but I generally go on with my work until the pain I cause them quite obliterates the pain they had before, and they go away quite satisfied.

In Abyssinia, venereal complaints of the most terrible kind are general, but little relief could be given, as it is not possible to cure in a few moments complaints of the blood which have descended upon the people for generations. Some had ghastly-looking sores.

Provisions were certainly not dear at this place, although we had difficulty in finding a suitable currency to pay for what we purchased ; even Gras cartridges, which had so far been useful to us in marketing, were here accepted with difficulty. My servant bought for me a chicken and six eggs, as well as some delicious Galla barley bread, for the large sum of one cartridge, the value of which would be about twopence. Money of any kind was of no use here, and Gras cartridges were useful to few, as the Galla are not a warlike race. They are mere workers of the land, and only indulge in spears for their protection. They seldom possess rifles.

Salt, another useful article of barter, they would only accept in compressed form.

These Galla villages were always interesting, with children running about absolutely naked, or with only a goat skin slung upon the back. The Galla were always civil as one met them on the road, invariably dismounting from their horses as we passed by and doubling themselves up in a profound bow. They raised their right hand to their lips and kissed it when no opportunity offered to do that to my hand.

Here, too, as in the Danakil country, they were not fond of shaking hands with strangers. It would be difficult to eradicate a certain natural suspicion of treachery they entertain. Like the Danakils, they quickly withdrew the hand in an apprehensive manner when greeted in European fashion.

We passed many date-palms upon the road, and pretty flowers of all sorts. The vegetation was perplexingly entangled in the wooded parts. We then came to three open grassy valleys, which we crossed. Danno village was slightly higher than the stream (5,700 feet). Here we saw a gigantic *uarca* tree.

When starting with a new caravan of mules there is plenty of work cut out for oneself and followers during the first few days until the animals get reconciled to their new mode of life. They kick and bite one another ;

they purposely collide, with disastrous results to the loads ; and in passages where only one mule at a time could go through, three or four would make a rush to go in at the same time. Result : all the loads twisted or scattered upon the ground. It required a great deal of patience to re-adjust the loads time after time every day.

In the afternoon, of course, the quadrupeds had to be let loose to graze, and getting them back into camp at night and tethering them by the leg to a picket line was not so easy as it sounds.

Of course, when you require to make up a caravan quickly, you have to purchase what animals you can, and not always what you would like to get. Many of the mules I had got had been accustomed to being ridden, and rebelled somewhat when loads were placed upon their backs. Others had never been used for anything at all, and we had many exciting scenes of buck-jumping and stampeding when we were loading them to make a departure the first mornings. It was, however, amazing how intelligent these animals were, and how methodical in their habits. In three or four days they became well trained, and they would themselves know exactly what to do at the right moment. They would every day take the same position in the caravan's procession, and at night, when they were fetched into camp, they would of their own accord put themselves in a row along the picket line to have their legs fastened for the night. Grass, and when obtainable, barley, was served out to them along this line in the evening. It made a great difference in the next day's marching when I could obtain a lot of barley for them, as the grazing was not sufficient for our long marches.

Particularly interesting was the fondness that all the mules had for my stallion, whom they followed everywhere. All that was necessary to bring the mules back to camp was to lead the horse to be tethered. The mules would follow him and be as gentle as possible. But if the horse took it into his head to get away on a wild gallop when he was to be fetched back, then we had a great deal of trouble before us. All the mules would gallop behind him and get much excited, and they took us sometimes for runs on foot of several miles before we could get them back to camp.

I must say for the Abyssinian muleteers that they always enjoyed running all over the country after the animals, and it gave them plenty to talk about in the evening over the camp fires. Sometimes they would sit up the greater part of the night talking over the incident, repeating the same story over and over again dozens of times, each time accompanied by roars of laughter.

The Abyssinians are inveterate talkers, especially at night. I remember one day mounting one of my mules instead of my horse. The saddle which fitted the horse was somewhat too big for the mule, the girdle being quite loose as I was riding. Going down to a stream, the mule slid down the high, steep, muddy bank of the river, and the impetus was so great when we plunged into the water that the saddle and myself upon it slid on to the animal's head. The Abyssinians rushed after me, and just saved me from having an involuntary bath. It was, of course, comical to see the mule with the saddle and rider upon its head instead of upon its back, but this incident lasted the Abyssinians a whole week, and caused more merriment in my camp than anything that happened during the whole journey, the entire first night particularly being spent roaring over this natural and somewhat trivial event.

What is called in Abyssinia " the small rainy season " had arrived. We had heavy rain all day, the greater part of the night, and early the next morning when we were about to leave.

It was not till eight o'clock that we made a departure on February 21st, and within the next two hours we crossed three streams. We were travelling over undulating, open, grassy land, with occasional Galla huts and some cattle grazing. We came upon another huge *uarca* tree which had fallen, and which was over ten feet in diameter. Then we descended to a stream slightly under six thousand feet. To the west-north-west, at 10.30 a.m., we had a high range before us, the Oua Corma mountains, and to the south-west there was a curious conical peak, with a peculiar columnar appearance, which at a distance resembled a basaltic formation. It showed at its summit rock similar to the one on a smaller scale that we had passed, about half an hour earlier, upon an isolated hill, which we had left to the north.

The country we travelled over was pretty, but of no particular interest. Here and there a Galla passed, carrying a load of honey upon the head. The Galla possess many bee-hives, which they hang high on the top branches of big *uarca* trees.

At eleven o'clock, while rounding the conical hill which I have mentioned above, somewhat peculiar scenery disclosed itself before me to the north-west ; a great flat stretch of country with an isolated domed hill slightly elongated on its northern side being pro-

minent in the landscape. To the west was a high peak,
I think the Tulugergo. We traversed this big plain,
which only had short grass upon it ; there were distant
high blue mountains to the north and north-east—quite
a long range ; while to the south and to the west, except
for the high peak which I have mentioned, were merely
low hills. To the north-west of the plain was a gap with
one gigantic grey rock several hundred feet in height,
and also another hill of a similar formation.

We then came to the Gibby (or Djibbé) river, which
is about thirty yards wide, flows at this point in a
direction from north-west to south-east, and, together
with many tributaries, and under the further names of
Guibie and Omo, flows into the northern part of Lake
Rudolph, through the Guragha, the Ualamo, the Kullo,
the Tsara, the Bacia and the Damoo countries. The
elevation of the river at the point where I crossed
it was 5,210 feet. We had here an amusing
incident.

I met several Kaffa women on the road, travelling
in the same direction as we were. I had endeavoured
to photograph them ; but they had shown great fright,
and refused to be taken. When we got to the stream,
I crossed first upon my horse, and having got my camera
ready, waited for the women to wade over across the
water, carrying their loads upon their backs, when they
would be quite helpless. It was taking a mean advantage, I confess. When they got quite near, where the
current was stronger, I produced my camera and took
the photograph. The poor women were so scared that
they for one moment hesitated whether to go back or
come along. They lost their footing and disappeared
under water. We had to go to their rescue and pull

them out of the stream in a drenched condition and extremely frightened.

We came across nothing interesting as we went along. We rose and descended over many undulations covered with such high grass that we were unable to see more than a yard or so in front of us. It was only in the afternoon that we found ourselves upon a height from which we gazed down upon a valley with a two-humped hillock in the centre of it and a verdant conical hill in its north-western part. To the south-west a high mountain range now disclosed itself in all its glory, heavy bluish-black shadows, like spots of violet ink, being cast upon it by the numberless, heavy, globular clouds in the sky. These mountains were, I think, the Mounts of Gabano, and further south-west Mount Sadero. A strange peak of reddish-brown colour stood up on these mountains, in shape so sharply pointed a cone as to resemble when seen edgewise an immense monolith.

At 2.30 in the afternoon we crossed a small stream, and at three o'clock another stream flowing from north to south. The elevation of the place was 5,480 feet. Then we rose to 5,700 feet over a hill on the side of the valley. Here we came to more *ghirar* trees. Along the trail we found large black beans, good to eat and not unlike cassia in flavour.

There were Galla graves near the trail. They consisted of a circle of stones some two feet high and four in diameter filled in with earth, with a central stone pillar rising about one foot above the grave. At the camp where we stopped at four o'clock in the afternoon there was another of these graves, more elaborate, and oblong in shape. It was five feet long and was entirely covered

Author's caravan fording the Gibby river.

with big stones. Above it a shed with a thatched roof had been erected.

The women in the Galla country do all the work. We met many of them near villages carrying huge loads of grass. One young woman had bleached her hair artificially, and thought herself beautiful. This bleaching habit has come to Western Abyssinia, I think, from the country of the Nuers, at the foot of the Abyssinian plateau further west. In fact, as we went further towards the west this custom was more frequently indulged in by the Galla.

Nono was the name of the camp (5,600 feet) at which we stopped. On this side of the mountains all the rivers flowed towards the south, volcanic rock showing through in many places, especially when washed bare near the streams. The hills on either side of us were particularly denuded of earth and rock, and a vertical columnar formation such as we had already met on our journey prevailed.

We left at 7.30 the next morning, and began to rise almost immediately upon a bad and steep trail. We found a barrier on the trail, where an Abyssinian military post was stationed, and Menelik's pass was demanded in a rude fashion without even a salute. As I am in the habit of treating people as they treat me, I gave orders to my men to go on and take no notice of the Abyssinian soldiers, to whom I did not even reply. The soldiers ran after us. I treated them with absolute contempt, and made them sweat going up the steep hill after my mules. The men in charge of the post were getting perplexed, and refused to let us go on if we did not possess a pass. As they were getting excited and insolent, I gave orders to my men to tell them to keep

behind. The fellows got extremely anxious, and dis-
covering they were dealing the wrong way with us
became more submissive. They entreated me to show
a pass, if I had one, or else we must go back, or they
would be severely punished.

I would hear of nothing, and made them struggle up
to the top of the pass (6,400 feet). Before reaching this
point we passed a Galla village, with its neat little
store-houses of basket-work, cylindrical in shape, four
to five feet in diameter, seven feet high, with conical
thatched roofs. They were raised upon supports one
to two feet high. Then we passed along a higher hill
range, where we got to 6,650 feet. Further we reached
an elevation of 6,700 feet. Towards ten o'clock we
came upon the first stream that day. We still could
see the high mountain range to the south. Rising still
higher upon a grassy hill (6,950 feet) we obtained from
the summit a lovely view of the southern range with most
wonderful cloud effects half-way up the slopes. A fine
valley extended along its foot from east to west. On
the north we had hills close by, with high mountains
beyond.

I stopped to look at the scenery, the Abyssinian
soldiers worrying me all the time to produce the pass.
They were quite sure by now that I did not possess one,
and they entreated me to go back. When I did produce
Menelik's letter with its huge circular seal upon it, the
effect was magical. They could not read a word of it,
but the sight of the Imperial seal was quite enough for
them. They saluted their Emperor's writing in the
humblest of fashions, and they wiped their hands upon
their trousers before touching it. They then raised
the paper to their foreheads and made a grand bow. They

asked me what the letter said, and begged me to halt until they could go back to their huts and bring me bread, meat and presents of whatever they possessed. Their obsequiousness and politeness after they had seen Menelik's letter was amazing. They could not do enough for us.

CHAPTER XV.

THERE were some poetic spots upon the trail, and every now and then we disappeared under groves of jessamines embalming—the jessamines, not we—the air with delicious scent. The flowers were pretty and mostly yellow. Under fig-trees we always stopped to gather and eat what fruit we could. Thorns were in profusion, and tore bits of one's skin and clothes as one went by.

Menelik had established a telephone line as far as Gori. We struck it at this place. It had certainly been well laid, with substantial poles inserted in solid cairns of stones. Many yards on either side of the line had been cleared of vegetation, and a straight cut was there formed in the forest over the succession of hills.

Towards noon that day we arrived at the top of a hill, 6,650 feet high. To the west and north-west we were overlooking a more or less barren, brown, undulating slope, with domed hillocks scattered over it, especially in the north-western part. In the west was the Salle, a high table-land extending in an almost flat line towards the west-north-west, and as we got a first view of it in its entirety we could discern in a bluish haze beyond it in the same direction another high tableland, which also formed an almost straight skyline, interrupted only by a higher peak in its central portion. In the extreme south, as far as our view extended, the range seemed to get higher and the summits more broken up.

Having descended to 5,310 feet, we came to a small stream which, unlike the others we had met, flowed in a northerly, instead of a southerly, direction. After crossing a grassy plain we came upon another river at the lower elevation of 4,950 feet, and yet another, slightly below the level of the plain, in which it has cut a groove (4,920 feet), and also flowing from south to north. This last river was quite broad. All three eventually flowed into the larger stream called the Didessa.

Further we skirted rocky hills, and in some portions we followed all along the immense clearing, over twelve yards wide, for the telephone wire, even beautiful *uarca* trees, which stood in the way, having been sacrificed. *Uarca* trees have most beautifully-shaped branches, the image of vigour and grace with their clean, smooth, white bark.

After a good many ups and downs, and passing through large settlements, we proceeded along fairly level country until 3.45 p.m., when we made camp in a pretty spot where several low domed sheds had been erected by passing Galla. The country was fairly well cultivated near these settlements, and we saw structures on high piles where the Galla, mounting by means of primitive ladders, kept a watch over their crops. The Galla till the ground with a wooden arrangement drawn by oxen, which merely scrapes the surface soil. A yoke is used for the oxen almost identical with that found in most European countries. The Galla need few implements in their agricultural pursuits, the soil being extremely fertile. For chopping wood, an axe with a small triangular blade attached to a heavy stick is employed.

As we went further west, we began to notice the influence of black races upon the Galla type. Keane classifies them as Hamites; the Abyssinians (*viz.*, the Tigrins and the Amhara, who are platyoprosopic, that is, among whom flat faces predominate); and the Nbogos, he counts as belonging to the Himyaritic branch of Semites. The Galla are, of course, much darker than Himyaritic tribes, owing to the geographical position of their country and their nearer contact with negroid races.

We had made our camp near a small stream flowing northwards at an elevation of 4,900 feet. On February 23rd we made an early start, proceeding over undulating country at no greater height than 5,200 feet, marching mostly west-south-west towards an isolated mountain, shaped like a section of a cone with a missing top.

All waters flowed towards the north. We descended to 4,650 feet, and travelled along flat, grassy, open country, meeting with a small stream towards eleven o'clock. Beyond this the country again became undulating and showed a sprinkling of *metcha* and *uarca* trees.

We kept at an elevation of between 4,700 and 4,800 feet, and soon left the broken-cone mountain to the south and the low range of hills beyond it. To the north-west was a high range in the bluish haze of the distance, while a domed and a conical hill stood side by side in the middle foreground, being the spurs of a range of higher hills of similar formation. Having risen again as high as 5,920 feet, we obtained yet another fine view of the surrounding country.

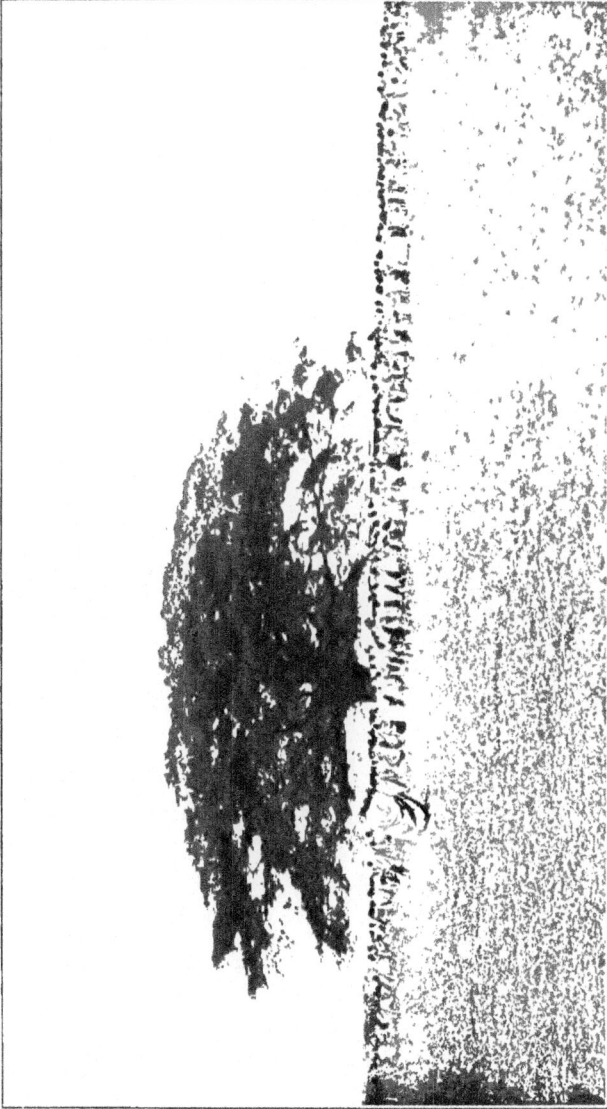

A big *narra* tree at Tchara (Western Abyssinia).

The Custom House of Ras Olde Gorgis we reached before we got to a small stream, which, at this point, flowed south, but further described a curve northwards and discharged itself into the larger Didessa river, a wide and swift stream at which we arrived in the afternoon.

There was a primitive ferry where the Didessa was some fifty yards wide. The depth of the water after the heavy rains was too great to take our loads across upon the mules, so we spent the best part of two hours in conveying the baggage across in a small dug-out, piloted by a Galla, whose knowledge of navigation was slight. He never landed his passengers and goods twice in the same spot. Sometimes he drifted down stream with the strong current for long distances, causing me anxiety. The Galla was indeed rather at the mercy of his canoe than the canoe under control of the Galla.

The Didessa was the first deep and difficult river we had so far met, so the mules were reluctant in entering the water, but eventually we were able to drive them into the stream and we swam them across with no serious mishaps ; they followed the horse led over by us alongside the canoe.

There were plenty of hippopotami in the stream, and during the evening and night we heard many of them roaring and blowing. The river Didessa in this particular portion came from the east, and, making a détour, flowed in a north-westerly direction. We halted by the stream, and for the first time I saw some of my men wash their faces and hands in buckets of clear water from the river.

During the afternoon many Gallas waded across

the river with water up to their lips, shouting all the time and holding their spears in readiness in order to frighten crocodiles away, but I could on no account get my Abyssinians to venture into the stream, and all of them had to be conveyed across in the dug-out. The river was here at an elevation of 5,370 feet.

Many Galla came into my camp, some pitiably ill. Others had leprosy. One of these lepers to whom I gave some carbolic soap to wash his sores with, returned to camp later with some bread which he offered in sign of gratitude.

The chief of the neighbouring village also brought over some gifts of small round breads, so peppery that they made my throat and palate ache for a considerable time after I had tasted them.

Torrential rain came upon us during the night, and in the morning a heavy mist hung over the river banks. Mosquitoes were so numerous that sleep was impossible during the night. We left shortly after seven o'clock the next day, and first went over flat, grassy land, inter-sected by two small streams. Then, towards nine o'clock, at a place where the ground began to be more undulating, we came upon Ras-Tassama's watchmen, perched upon a high, covered shed.

Near this spot was an interesting Galla grave of stones about six inches high, filled in with earth. It had two vertical pillars in the centre, then a square outer wall with two entrances on one side. At each corner upon this wall were upright pillars. Occasionally I noticed four wooden or stone pillars upon these Galla graves.

By 9.30 we had reached a hilly region, 5,300 feet high, with several little villages on our right. We rose

still higher, to 5,450 feet, not far from the village of
Mullu Tunhe, a settlement of some thirty huts on the
hillside on our left. Each hut had a small store-house
near it. There were many natives about, those of
the better class with curious little umbrellas made of
basket-work, which they carried above the head in all
weathers rather as an emblem of dignity than for protection against the rain or sunshine.

In this region honey and tobacco were plentiful, and
we saw numbers of natives carrying loads of these goods
to various markets upon the road.

A new straight trail was gradually being formed
along the telephone line which we followed, being the
shortest. Before us we now had a range with conical
hills. I had great difficulty in identifying the names of
the various villages ; all I could get out of the natives
being that they all belonged to Ras-Tassama.

We gradually descended some four hundred feet, over
a trail rather rocky in some portions, but as a whole
quite good and well beaten. I think that Ras-Tassama's
army marching to Adis-Ababa did a good deal towards
improving this trail.

Another small stream flowing north was met with,
also a tributary on the western side of the Didessa.

I was astonished to find so few butterflies in that
region. Those which I saw were of no great beauty.
They were mostly the common white ones which are
met with in nearly every country ; also the small black
and white, the bright cadmium yellow, and one very
small with blue lower wings. I saw no large butterflies.

Serious trouble with my mules began here, as we
had made long marches and some of the animals were

getting tired.   One mule particularly was   taken so
ill that it was all we could do to drag it into camp at
a market called Tchara (or Tiara), where we halted near
a most beautiful *uarca* tree of immense proportions.
Under its shade a number of men were selling sheep,
goats and mules.

The branches of this colossal *uarca* tree spread across
a diameter of one hundred and sixty-two feet.   The trunk
was over twenty feet in circumference.   The principal
beauty of this particular tree consisted in the wonderful horizontal length of its powerful branches.

There was a great concourse of people, this being
market day, and great crowds collected at the unusual
sight of a *ferenghi* arriving.

On one side of a large square, perched upon stilts,
was the stand of the chief superintending the market.
In it a grey-bearded old man sat upon his haunches
giving wise judgment on all transactions concluded in the
market-place.   For this, of course, he received a com-
mission in kind : cartridges, chips of cakes of compressed
salt, slices of meat, handfuls of grain, or anything—
always the utmost—that people could afford.   He was
surrounded by a struggling crowd as he sat impassive
deciding all questions.

Adjoining this shed was the vegetable market,
where goods lay spread upon the ground.   Galla spinach
predominated, exhibited by unattractive females with
little or no clothing around them.

In another section of the market locally-grown
cotton made into thread and generally dyed red was
for sale.

Several thousand people from the neighbouring
country—all men being armed with spears—were attend-

Galla of Western Abyssinia, with typical sunshade.

ing this market. They followed me about like a human wave from one section of the market to the other, as I prowled around. I was amazed at the respectful demeanour and dignity of these people, in contrast to the Abyssinian arrogance with which we had so far been treated.

These people were quiet and silent, ready to answer politely any question, and making way wherever I went so as to let me pass by. There was nothing at all of the usual idiotic derision and effrontery—sometimes even insult—so frequent in purely Abyssinian centres.

Knives, locally-made pottery, and bundles of long canes for house-building, were to be purchased in different sections of the market.

A variation in the head-dress of the Galla women was here to be noticed. The hair was tied into a conical tuft upon the top of the skull with a fringe of little tresses radiating from the base of this cone. Others preferred a fluffy arrangement of great size upon the head, not unlike a bird's nest upside down. A few only indulged in the Galla fashion, common further east, of plaits in concentric arcs of a circle along the side of the head with the ear as a centre. A great many ladies of this region dyed their hair of a dirty whitish-brown colour.

The type of these people was gradually but continually changing as we went further west. We could see here flat-faced tribes with broad noses and skins of a dark brown-black.

Eye complaints were general, caused not so much by climatic influences, I think, but mostly due to virulent deterioration of the blood, quite universal in this region.

Comparatively young women were of no beauty from

an anatomical point of view.   They had extraordinarily
pendent breasts, the arms and legs were ill-proportioned,
the joints malformed or deformed, particularly the elbows
and the knees.   The body was misshapen, possibly
because of the hard occupations and severe physical
efforts which the women have to endure in the Galla
country.

There are fashionable colours among African tribes
as there are in Europe, and fashions change continually.
Blue beads and brass bracelets were the fashion at the
time of my visit to Tchara.   Only occasionally one saw
a dash of red in the men's shawls.   The characteristic
basket-work umbrellas were carried both by men and
women.

To and fro upon the road leading to the market went
women carrying large red earthen jars and calabashes
with butter.   Some of the smarter ladies were dressed
in gowns not unlike the garments of the ancient Greeks,
with a red border at the bottom and leaving one arm
exposed.

The men were finer specimens of humanity than the
women.   They possessed square, bony faces and the
anatomical details of limbs and body were somewhat
better proportioned and chiselled.   They lead a natural
and healthy out-of-door life.

All the Galla of this country were Mussulman.   Of
late years the religion of Islam has made, and is making,
considerable headway in Abyssinia among the tribes akin
to the Galla.   Perhaps some day this important Mussulman element in the population of Abyssinia may be a
great factor in upsetting the power of the ruling
Christians.

As I was writing my notes in the afternoon a man

with haggard face and staring eyes and his body reduced to a skeleton by hunger, came into my camp—
evidently a case of insanity. Several wounds, which
were beginning to heal, had been inflicted upon his body,
and when he extended his arms imploring for food a
heavy iron chain hung from his wrists where it had
been soldered. He was a murderer. The state does
not keep its prisoners. When not killed outright they
are let loose about the country, driven away like pariah
dogs by everybody and obliged to lead a miserable
existence. This particular man was a raving lunatic
with criminal characteristics noticeable in the formation
of his skull and hands. The fingers were short and
square-tipped, the thumb repulsively malformed. The
forehead was low and narrow, the eyes close to the nose
and the cheekbones abnormally developed.

He entreated me to take him along with me on the
journey, but I thought a companion of this kind would
be rather undesirable, so I gave him food supplies to last
several days and persuaded him to leave my camp at his
earliest convenience.

This market was 5,120 feet above sea level. Due
north was a high, flattish table-land, the Mounts Oua
Corma.

Watching the people provided some amusement.
Many women carried jars upon the back, at the waist,
in the usual Galla fashion, either by means of a cord
over the shoulders or else by simply joining the hands
at the back and supporting the weight partly with their
arms and partly upon the waist. Then there were lots
of Galla boys prowling about with no clothing whatever
upon them, and heads shaved with the exception of
a tuft of hair upon the top of the skull. The procession

of people leaving the market in the afternoon was quite interesting. The women who had done good business during the day put on a great deal of style as they walked off in great state with their dirty and broken-down cane sunshades—not unlike, sometimes, much-worn chimney sweeps' circular brushes.

The chief of the market came to call upon me, inquiring whether he could be of any assistance. In fact, he helped me to purchase a good deal of grain, butter and other things from the natives.

We experienced a heavy thunderstorm in the evening—in fact, we had had one nearly every night since we started from Adis-Ababa.

CHAPTER XVI.

Up and down over undulating country we descended
to the stream, about one hundred feet lower than the
market-place, and about an hour from Tiara we came
to a larger rivulet flowing north. Further we crossed
the same stream a second time, flowing south. It described a curve, bending subsequently towards the north
again, where we had met it before. From this spot we
began to rise over a hill range, the summit of which
(6,700 feet) we reached by an unpleasantly steep ascent,
and we continued travelling more or less at that elevation, and sometimes slightly higher, when we went over
ridges on the summit of the hill range.

Tiresome as these ascents were for my mules, I was
always glad to get upon these high points of vantage,
as generally lovely views were obtained of the landscape
around. In this case, looking back to the north-east,
we had the very high plateau we had seen before, the
Oua Corma, standing all along the skyline, and south of
it the valley we had traversed. Our old friend, the
broken conical peak we had met on our journey, stood
quite prominent in the landscape.

Owing to one of my mules being seriously ill, I only
made a short march that day, three men being employed
to drag the poor animal up the bad road.

I was furious with my Abyssinians that day for their

infamous cruelty. The head muleteer, who was left to look after the sick animal, pulled out his knife, and before I could stop him cut a good portion of the mule's ear, in order, said he, to make the animal march faster. He was, of course, then and there, severely punished for it.

We eventually reached a village called Addis-Jebbo, where, at the summit of a hill enclosed by a wall, were three round buildings and a square one, the country-seat of Ras-Tassama. Near this palace was a hamlet.

As ill-luck would have it, my men obtained a big pot of liquor from the village. During the afternoon, while I was sleeping in my tent, there was a great commotion in camp. When I came out to see what was the matter, I saw three of my men, knives in hand, engaged in a fight. The Abyssinian soldiers I had with me were making for their rifles, and they all seemed excited. Only my Somali—always impassive on such occasions—stood on one side with his hands behind his back, watching events with a sarcastic smile upon his countenance. He hated the Abyssinians, and I believe he was glad to think that possibly that day we might get rid of some of them.

Before I could determine exactly what the row was about, the fight became general. Blows were exchanged freely all round, as the men evidently took opposite views in the quarrel. Taking from my tent the heaviest rifle by its muzzle, I began to administer thumps with the butt end of the rifle right and left, and mostly in the face, indiscriminately to all the men who were fighting, in order to separate them. The men who brandished the knives got the severest knocks, and with the help of Adem—the Somali—I disarmed them and tied their hands. I conveyed one of the blood-thirsty men a hundred yards from my camp towards the west, where I tied him to a tree ; then I went back and led the second irascible creature three hundred feet to the east, and bound him to another tree. The third cantankerous individual we dragged by the nape of his neck an equal distance to the north and made fast with ropes to a convenient *ghirar*.

Sentence : the whole day without food. They were in a highly-intoxicated condition, and had to be shaken considerably before they could be quieted down. Their clothes had been torn to shreds in the fight, and they were bleeding profusely. Fortunately, none of the wounds were of a severe character. Their eyes, blood-shot, were bulging out of the sockets with anger. One fellow nearly bit a chunk off my hand when I was tying him.

Abyssinians, in a way, possess some sense of humour. The auxiliary combatants became amused at the punishment inflicted on their companions, and after an excited conversation eventually quieted down, promised to behave themselves, and went to sleep. The prisoners, too, after a deal of copious salivation—they spat angrily and shouted when anyone went by—eventually collapsed with heads hanging loose, and snored heavily. Late in the afternoon, when I untied them, they were submissive and penitent.

The Abyssinians are by nature uncommonly quarrel-some, and when drunk they are offensive to each other, and difficult to handle.

There were many complaints of headaches and bruises in my camp among the Abyssinians the next morning, and the Somali took the greatest pleasure in laughing at the aching muleteers and soldiers.

We kept along the crest of the hill range at an average elevation of 6,650 feet all along. There were plenty of wild raspberry bushes. After crossing two tiny streams, we arrived at the market of Bedellé (6,600 feet), upon a nice, flat, green, grassy plain. The usual long sheds were to be seen and the small tower for the chief of the market, also a number of *ghirar* trees giving pleasant shade, and avenues bordered by polished stones, upon which the people sat themselves on market day.

Near this place, close to the west, was a fairly high conical mount, cultivated in its lower portion and wooded at the summit. South-west, as we emerged from the market-place, we beheld, between the slope of the above-described hill and the one on which we travelled, an extensive view of picturesquely-wooded hill ranges beyond.

We met another magnificent *uarca* tree of great size, but the majority of trees in that region were *ghirar*. We were travelling at an elevation varying from 6,300 to 6,400 feet, until we descended to a large stream, the Dabana, a tributary of the Didessa, ten yards wide and some four feet deep, flowing north-west at an elevation of 6,020 feet.

On the west of the Dabana we rose again to 6,400 feet over rolling country, and our camp where we halted in the afternoon was in a green little valley intersected by a small stream, the Dabasso (6,120 feet). The country was mountainous all round, particularly to the south-east and to the south, where we had a long range before us, with Mounts Seccia and Ghescia.

Author's Abyssinian muleteers.

At this place I met the first Shankalla, a name given by the Abyssinians to all barbarous tribes. The ones we saw formed an entire family, with dear little children. The " mamma " was gaily dressed in a tall hat with a flat French brim, the whole made of basket-work. She also wore some beads round her neck, but that was about all. The people had pleasant faces—much pleasanter than those of the Abyssinians or even the Galla.

A heavy dew fell during the night, soaking everything, and in the morning my men felt the cold intensely.

There was a nasty stream to cross on leaving this camp, only about twenty feet wide and flowing north, but with such a muddy bottom that we stuck and gradually sank, making it most difficult for the animals to get across. A bridge had been constructed, once, over that stream, but had tumbled down, and it took us a long time to repair it sufficiently for us to get to the other side. With a few mishaps we at last got all baggage across, and then we swam the mules over.

There were more hills on the other side, and, in fact, hilly country all round ; all the hills fairly densely wooded, with tiny streams flowing between.

The rivulets we now met were not more than five or six feet across, and yet they gave us endless trouble in crossing them. There was always soft mud in which one sank deep, and the more one tried to get on or out, the more one became involved without making any progress. The animals became perplexed and scared. Their legs gave way and the loads tumbled off. It made one's heart sore to see in what a terrible condition the loads were when we rescued them out of these muddy streams.

For one bar of salt, worth about fivepence in Adis-Ababa, I had purchased the previous night a hundred pounds of barley, some grain and a dozen eggs ; so my animals were in excellent marching condition that day. This was an advantage, as the trail was hilly, up and down all the time. The small valleys between were swampy, with beautiful verdure upon them.

We were going slightly north, and from a high point we obtained a charming view of the undulating country, the portion in the foreground being quite clear of trees and of a most beautiful green, only equalled by the meadows of England. During the first part of the march we had been at elevations between 6,450 and 6,350 feet, but towards noon we went over a pass 6,900 feet high, from which point we obtained another lovely panorama looking back towards the east.

We struck the telephone wire again, stretching in a direct line over the undulating plain. To the south-east in the distance were high mountains, the Mounts Seccia and Sadero, and due west a mountain range stood before us, ending abruptly in its north-western portion. To the south, close to us, was a wooded hill, and to the south-west, in the far distance, high mountain ranges one behind the other.

We then proceeded on a rapid descent of one thousand feet by a precipitous trail to the bottom of the valley, where, among wooded hills, a stream (5,900 feet) flowed northwards, spanned by a bridge. No sooner had we descended and passed the headland to the south of us, when we ascended again by a steep trail to 6,300 feet at the village of Tchora Uta, where, owing to the exertion the animals had undergone that day, we made camp early in the afternoon.

There was at this place an interesting village of half a dozen huts within a stockade. When I passed within this barrier, I came to a small circular hut with a bundle of spears at the entrance. In this hut lay the chief, spread out flat and ill with fever, some twelve men sitting around him along the wall of the hut. He struggled to his feet on my arrival, grasped me warmly by the hand, and willingly undertook to show me round the village.

Each man's property was encircled by a fence. The chief's habitation stood in the centre of the stockade, the roof being supported on a double circle of wooden pillars, instead of upon a solitary central pillar, as was the case in other huts I had so far inspected. There was a fire burning in the centre, and part of the hut was partitioned off as a dining-room, with a coarsely-made table and divan. Another portion, the chief told me, was the sleeping quarter and dairy. The roof was neatly made, the well-matched rafters radiating from the centre and braced up with numerous lacings in symmetrical sets of concentric circles.

A separate hut was used as kitchen by the wealthier people. Shankalla, or barbarians, were employed by them as menials, practically slaves. A few pots and vessels, a basket or two, a few gourds—that was all they seemed to possess in the way of furniture, if the interesting weaving looms, quite ingenious in their simplicity, were excepted.

The men in that country, not the women, do the weaving. The weaver while at work sits in a hole dug in the ground. The cloth in process of weaving is held in tension over the men's knees. The cross threads are beaten home with a heavy wooden comb when the shuttle has been passed from one side to the other between the sets of threads ; two vertical sets of heddles, each set attached to a frame, and holding the threads in position, are ingeniously raised and lowered by means of two treadles giving motion alternately to each frame. The threads, in order to save space, are not stretched their full length, as is frequently the case in weaving looms, but are rolled up over the framework of the loom. The woven cloth is seldom more than two feet wide.

There were small store-houses near the huts, where the natives kept grain, principally lupin beans, an important article in their diet.

The Galla gave me an interesting exhibition of spear-throwing. They give the spear rod a gradually-increasing vibration, holding it with the palm of the hand upwards at a point where it can be well balanced. The spear is only thrown when fighting on foot ; when on horseback the spear is never hurled.

Again, in this camp dozens of people came for medicine. Most of them suffered from the worst of venereal complaints in its most violent phases, from itch, eye-sores, abscesses upon the jaw, toothache and fever. A little child was brought to me whose foot had been broken during birth. The fracture was a compound one, and the poor baby seemed to be in agony. The parents were quite distressed. They entreated me to set the foot right and stop the pain at once, but this was easier said than done. I did what I could, trying to get the bones in their right position and bandaging the foot up in improvised splints of cane. I have never heard a baby shriek more than this poor little mite did when the operation was performed.

With an empty glass that had contained French

jam I purchased a handsome fat chicken and some eggs. I think that travellers in regions where money does not pass would do well to take provisions in glasses and bottles, which when empty can always be easily exchanged for foodstuff. The natives, I found, do not always care for empty tins, which generally get distorted and spoilt.

Chief Liban, to whom I had given a strong dose of quinine and a quantity of castor oil, partly owing to the faith that these people have in the powers of white people to cure any illness, partly perhaps to some good the medicine did him, came in the afternoon, to say his fever had disappeared. He brought with him large presents of butter, Galla bread, red sauce of terrific strength, milk, and a bag of lupin beans.

CHAPTER XVII.

WE left camp at 7.30, and half an hour later, by a steep, slippery descent, we arrived at a swift river, the Gabbai, about one hundred and five feet wide, and with strong rapids near the only place where it is possible to ford it. After the heavy rains we had experienced of late the river was unduly swollen.

Chief Liban, with many Gallas, had come to the stream to help us cross it. A high suspension bridge of vines had been constructed, but was available for foot passengers only, as, in order to use it, it was necessary to climb a high tree, from the branches of which a sort of network of vines had been stretched across the water. Two large pillars of basket-work filled with stones held fast the opposite end of the bridge on the other side of the stream. I crossed safely, but we had no end of trouble to get the mules and loads across. When I sent the mules into the water with some natives, some were washed away by the current and carried down the rapids. It was only some hundreds of feet lower down stream that we eventually succeeded in saving animals and loads.

The river, at an elevation of 5,600 feet, was picturesque at this spot, flowing in a north-westerly direction between thick forest of the most luxuriant kind.

After describing great détours this river eventually flowed westwards into the Baro.

On the steep ascent on the opposite side of the stream a gateway and watch-house had been erected. We climbed up to 6,850 feet, leaving behind a high, hilly region thickly wooded, with two headlands in the southern part of the scene before us. When we emerged from the forest upon the high pass we found ourselves in a basin with a number of villages on our left, and the slopes of the surrounding hills extensively cultivated.

To the north-west we obtained an ample panorama of long hill ranges, parallel to one another, while to the north near us was another abrupt headland quite characteristic of Abyssinian scenery.

By eleven o'clock we reached the summit of the range at an altitude of 6,800 feet, where we found ourselves on an undulating plateau, with villages and, strangely enough, good drinking water only a few feet below the summit. At 10° (N.N.E.) we had a headland. Also, further back a prominent conical peak, with a wooded summit and brilliantly red base. To the north-west extended a spur from the long range we had crossed the previous day.

Yambo was the name of the village on the top of the mountain. At this place I received the sad news that an English traveller had died from malarial fever at the foot of the Abyssinian plateau, but I could not find out his name until later.

We remained at elevations of over 6,400 feet while passing over the undulations of the higher plateau. In the gullies we met swampy streamlets, always fairly troublesome to cross. We were now constantly proceeding through tall grass, now descending for a hundred feet or so, now rising again in the higher places, among *ghirar* trees, while orchids and innumerable parasitic plants grew upon the trunks and branches of trees. There were a few white and yellow flowers about, and many fire-trees with brilliantly-coloured red blossoms ; white and blue convolvuli were also numerous.

Not until the evening did we descend to a streamlet flowing north (5,800 feet). There we found lots of gigantic thistles and some charming snapdragons (*Antirrhinum*). Swarms of small butterflies of rich cadmium yellow and velvety black played about the vegetation, also a larger kind, of a pure lemon-yellow. There was a thick undergrowth of *bullyti*, a kind of soft-centred reed with white flowers, and masses of *sambalet*, a tall, reedy grass eight feet high.

Towards 3 p.m. we descended to the Goki river (4,550 feet), flowing north. There were any number of coffee bushes growing wild, and the berries made excellent eating. The coffee in this region was of delicious quality. I purchased great quantities of it, and enjoyed it thoroughly on my way across Africa. In flavour it was like the best Mocha. Jessamines were plentiful, and contorted vines hung in streamers and festoons from the highest branches of trees.

Half an hour later we were again climbing up an ascent of one thousand feet to 5,410 feet, where we found ourselves forcing a passage through high grass and *ghirar* trees. Every now and then when we had a peep at the surrounding scenery we saw thickly-wooded high hills on all sides, with hillocks quite close to us on the left and somewhat more distant ones on our right.

When we made our camp more patients streamed

in. These people had a way of always coming in before or during my meal-time. One bad case of leprosy was particularly repulsive. He seemed sad to a degree when I told him I had no power to cure him. I gave him some iodine, which would do him no harm. He was very grateful for it, and soon after brought in a load of fire-wood as a present.

There was a steep ascent from the river until we had reached Yayu, where we camped near the village. The natives said that there were many lions about the country, and it was amusing at night to see my Abyssinian soldiers keep well within a circle of blazing fires, which they kept alight the whole night in order to run no chance of attack.

Camp Yayu was 5,150 feet above sea level. From this camp we proceeded uphill towards the north along a wooded hill range, and kept at elevations between 5,600 and 5,850 feet for about an hour and a half, after which we gradually began to descend.

We met many Galla on the trail, all extremely polite. They uncovered their heads, over which they were wearing shawls ; they laid down their spears and doubled themselves up in a grand salutation.

All along the trail on our left stood numerous huts. To the south-west and west, after passing the terminal headland of the ridge we had been following, we saw, further beyond, another long, wooded range encircling us to the south-west, west and north-west.

On the previous two marches we had seen on the top of hills conical mounds some nine feet high, the graves of Galla chiefs. Similar graves were to be seen on the roadside, all with four pillars at the corners and one in the centre of the grave. Nearly all these graves were surrounded by a wall of stone, or else of matted reeds or sticks.

By nine o'clock we had arrived at the real Yayu market (5,333 feet), with a *uarca* tree some forty feet in circumference at the base, the roots and branches spreading out great distances from the trunk. The roots were used by the natives as convenient seats on market-day, and the upper portion of them was well polished by the numerous people who had sat upon them.

Perhaps my readers will be astonished to find a *uarca* tree in each market-place, but it is common in the Galla country to select a place with a big tree as their trading centres, not only because it supplies an ample shadow for the people during the hot hours of the day, but also because these gigantic *uarca* trees make easily identifiable landmarks in the country.

There were, of course, the usual sheds and a number of houses in the neighbourhood, especially below, as we commenced to descend rapidly after passing the huge tree. Many people were tilling the ground with oxen, and attending to their banana plantations near the huts. The country we were going through now was beautiful, with any amount of coffee, mimosas, palms, figtrees and vines of all kinds, including productive rubberlatex vines.

By a steep descent we arrived, towards ten o'clock, at the Take river, some twenty-five feet across, its crystal-like water flowing in a north-westerly direction in a tortuous channel. We were now as low as 4,620 feet. Half an hour later we came across another little streamlet, also flowing over a rocky bed towards the north.

The most common kind of mimosa in this part was

the one called *ghirbirra* by the Abyssinians. This particular mimosa, unlike others which are found in this and other parts of Abyssinia, had no thorns. Very common, too, was a cactus, with a three-winged leaf, these leaves in section forming a triangle.

At Gaji, or Gajima (6,050 feet), another big market on the summit of the range, we came upon lots of people, as it happened to be market-day. The type here was improving somewhat. Some of the women were striking-looking. They showed a great deal of character about the face, their lascivious lips being firmly closed and somewhat drooping at the corners. The fashion of dyeing the hair was here quite common, and most of the ladies preferred to dye their hair (which was twisted into little kinks) of a chrome yellow colour rather than to leave it of its natural glossy black.

Here, too, under a huge *uarca* tree and the usual low sheds, one saw hundreds of picturesque spearmen squatting upon their haunches, the women and children attending almost entirely to business transactions.

We only traversed this market, and soon after descended into a swamp, only to rise again to 6,100 feet, and proceed across grassy country, undulating in portions. In some places we met millions of gigantic thistles, eight to nine feet high, the feathery, white, dried flowers of which were fully four inches in diameter. On the third pass (6,150 feet) which we climbed that day stood a gigantic cactus fifty feet high, a tall stem, with a big ball of fat triangular leaves at the top. Early in the afternoon we came to a small stream, the estuary of the extensive marsh at the foot of a hill range, and here there was a great growth of flat-leaved water-plants and innumerable reeds. We went over the fourth hill

(6,200 feet), and as we went down its slopes there was a great village, with dozens of store-houses in rows, besides those within the lozenge-shaped enclosures outside the houses. We climbed a fifth hill that afternoon (5,700 feet), and we came to the Harafa village, also with a great number of these store-houses. In the neighbourhood of this place we found boundary fences made with long rows of gigantic cacti. Some of these fences were too extensive to mark the property of private individuals, and I think they must have been made to define the sphere of influence of each tribe or village.

By a steep descent among thick undergrowth and much tall, thick grass, most unpleasant to march through, as the blades constantly cut our faces and hands as we rode through, we reached another stream, the Sor, three or four feet deep, with a swift current, flowing north, and more than ninety feet wide at the fording place (5,300 feet).

It was about three in the afternoon when we reached the Sor, and, having taken us some time to cross it, we encamped on the western bank.

Scores of patients poured into the camp as the news had quickly spread over the country that I was not uncivil towards the natives. Several lepers came in for remedy—lepers were numerous in this region—one with legs much swollen, absolutely atrophied, and contracted toes. My servant was about to accept a present of edibles from this grateful patient, but as the sores on his hand were of a purulent nature, I forbade him to take them. To my dismay, a little later, on going out of my tent, who should I see squatting among my men but the leper handling my soup plates and enamelled dishes, which he seemed greatly to admire, and which he was offering to barter for the foodstuff that had been refused.

As we were getting near a big centre, cartridges could again be used as currency. Adem purchased two big chickens for one cartridge, and eighty pounds of barley for two cartridges. Marketing was certainly not dear at the Sor river.

I noticed in the neighbourhood several kinds of mimosas, one small, with minute leaves, a larger one some seven feet high, and then the *ghirar*, quite a tall tree, the most common of all, very spiky, with long, straight, whitish thorns. The giant cactus, with its triangular leaves, and with offshoots every foot or so, was still plentiful. Immense quantities of wild coffee shrubs were growing under the thick vegetation and apparently flourished in the stifling air. The leaves of these plants were of a healthy, vigorous, clean, dark green, with a beautiful glazed surface. The red berries in their ripe condition, which become black on being dried, were also in excellent condition, and when roasted and ground could be boiled into a delicious beverage.

CHAPTER XVIII.

MANY Galla passed near my camp carrying their spears, the *uarano*, over the left shoulder, and generally resting one hand upon the steel head in its leather sheath. Most of them came in to make their salaams ; others saluted and went along.

The men wore skin caps. Fur of a dark red, or else of a velvety brown, seemed to be the fashionable colours in Galla headgear. Other folks wore caps made from the skin of the *guresa*, a beautiful big monkey, which possesses a silky coat, black under the arms, not unlike a small "zouave," while all round the lower portion of the body the hair is equally long, but of the purest white. The face is framed in a white beard, and the magnificent long tail has a big white ball-like tuft of hair at the end.

One of my Abyssinian soldiers—these Abyssinians have the instinct of destruction in a marked degree— shot one of these monkeys one day, for which I severely punished him. The poor monkey was wounded, and fell upon the trail from its high perch on the top of a tree. In intense pain, the poor animal seemed just like a human being in its dying moments, and the reproachful expression of its face haunted me for days.

I do not believe that I have ever seen more beautiful monkeys than these *guresa*, and I could never restrain my admiration for their marvellous powers of jumping from one tree to another, and for their intelligence in using the swing of the branches in order to be propelled amazing distances through the air by the impetus. The skin of the *guresa* has a considerable market value in Abyssinia.

Abyssinia is a great country for monkeys of all sizes; but perhaps the *totos*, or dog-faced, long-nosed monkeys, are the most common. Irritable to a degree, ill-tempered and vicious, these brown bristly-haired brutes grow up to a good size. Although, like all monkeys, they can be amusing, they were always quite repulsive to me, as they were neither beautiful nor graceful.

One could not help being struck, over and over again, especially after the rudeness and conceit of the Abyssinians, by the thoughtful and grateful manner of the Galla. If one happened to answer their salutation— which I always endeavoured to do whether they were rich or poor—they beamed all over with joy and kept bowing profoundly until out of sight.

The nearer we got to Gori town, the more it seemed fashionable for the women to dye the hair and smear it with a chrome yellow-coloured grease. The hair was arranged in a tuft on the top of the skull.

Silver armlets were worn just above the elbow, and heavy brass bracelets, the *hamarti*, which covered the arm from the wrist to the elbow, were also much admired ; but, as a rule, only the richer people were so ornamented, as the poorer folks could not indulge in these valuable decorations. Yellow and blue beads, or else amulets, were frequently worn round the neck.

I do not think that the Galla are tree worshippers,

as has been written by some authors. The notion has originated, I believe, from the fact that they select the spots where giant *uarca* trees are found, to hold their weekly markets or to make their encampments. The principal reason they do so, as I have already said, is because these trees offer good shade, and are good landmarks for people to meet.

We find the Galla type of Western Abyssinia considerably different from that of the east. The people here have eyes *à fleur de tête*, almost bovine in their prominence, an effect produced undoubtedly by their connection with the neighbouring negroid races. The eyes are wide opened, but with little expression in them. The lips are fully developed, of good shape, and in their normal condition kept tightly closed. They show a good deal of character in their firm modelling. The lower lip is larger than the upper one and rather heavily formed underneath down to the chin. In profile the lips project considerably. The nose assumes greater proportions here than further east ; in fact, it is quite big and flattened, with broad nostrils, which make Galla faces better looking in the full face than when seen side face. The glabella, or supra-orbital, bone in the central portion of the brow, is quite prominent and extra-developed. The cheek-bones are high and prominent, the face tapering quickly under them and ending in a somewhat sharp chin. In women this characteristic is more marked than in men, as their faces are naturally more delicately formed.

Curiously enough, while negroid characteristics are more noticeable here among the Galla than in other regions, we find that near Gori the colour of the skin is lighter than the colour of the people we had seen

between this place and Tulidumtu. Also, these Galla
are lighter built and shorter than their neighbours in
the east between Adis-Ababa and Harrar.

Oxen are used by these people to till the ground.
They possess a few rudimentary implements. A small
pick is used instead of a spade. This pick is worked
dexterously, particularly in sowing, the ground being
so rich that the minimum of stirring is required to make
it produce anything. Bananas are grown in the enclosures of Galla villages.

One great industry in this country was the collection
of honey in cylinders made of tree-bark, strengthened
by basket-work all round, and enclosing the beehives.
Many of these cylinders could be seen suspended from
the most inaccessible top branches of the highest trees,
especially the *uarca*. The honey produced was quite
good, but dark in colour.

All the Galla in this region were Mussulman, but
although these people make their salaam to Mecca at
sunrise and at sunset, I did not come across a single
Mussulman priest and saw no mosques.

In the way of dress, the *kaldoh*, a sort of skin apron,
was worn by the women. Among the implements, the
uilli gaffa was probably the most interesting—a horn
butter-pot.

Our next march was through intricate, thick vegetation, that tore our clothes to pieces as we rode along.
We ascended to Batcho (5,950 feet), a small village on
the top of a hill range, the whole country around us
being hilly and thickly-wooded. We then went through
a regular forest of cacti. Upon the trail we avoided
several spiked pits dug by the Galla. The air as we
were going through this thick vegetation was stifling.

We met another troublesome little stream (5,650 feet), only six feet wide, but with a bottom of such soft mud that we had the greatest difficulty in getting across, the mules becoming scared as they sank deep in the mud and refusing to go on. I had to send some men to the other side, and by means of ropes we had to pull the animals over one by one.

On rising to another pass (5,950 feet), we came upon long rows of gigantic cacti, used as boundary lines between landowners' properties.

Later in the day we were still going through dense vegetation, but the trail was good and fairly wide. In fact, we were now upon the high trail again, the first part of the march having been made by a short cut. There were many mimosas here, with medium-sized leaves and long double spikes, white in colour and always in sets of two at an acute angle along its branches. The two other kinds of mimosas which we had found on our previous marches were also common here, and in the forest there were innumerable creepers and vines descending in regular streamers and festoons overhead.

We met many streams that day ; one, some thirty feet wide, flowing north, had fortunately been bridged over. Between noon and one o'clock we went across three more streamlets at an average elevation of 5,700 feet, with hill ranges between 6,000 feet high. The latter watercourses flowed southward, joining in a stream, with an outlet into a tributary of the Sor, which eventually ran in a north-westerly direction and then southward again until it reached the Baro river.

By one o'clock we had reached the top of another hill range, and we had before us a charming view of cultivated hillsides with dozens of huts. We were here in a kind of basin surrounded by hills, and when we descended in the centre of it for a couple of hundred feet we were in a swamp over which a rudimentary bridge had been constructed.

Before us, in front, was a high two-humped mount, standing between us and Gori. We climbed up at a steep gradient, and at the height of 6,600 feet we found ourselves upon a terrace in the plateau on which was an unpleasant swamp.

To the east we left behind the high headland which we had passed on our way, and north-east we had a beautiful view of the wooded undulating valley below us. To the south-east and north were hill ranges. The top of the range was two hundred feet higher (6,900 feet), and, just beyond, we reached Gori town (6,720 feet), a number of scattered houses being found upon the high plateau overlooking the magnificent undulating valley to the west. The principal portion of Gori town—if town it can be called—stood upon two humps of the table-land, the Governor's palace, a double-tiered structure, with a spacious verandah, being on the highest point. A big market-square was to be seen a short distance from the palace.

No sooner had I arrived and pitched my tents in the enclosure of Mr. Timoleon Armanxopoulo, a Greek trader of ability, than I received a long message of welcome from the palace, where two Vice-Governors were in charge of local affairs during Ras Tassama's absence. So little do the people of Abyssinia trust one another that no less than two persons are invariably left to look after the interests of their master.

With the message, gracefully delivered by a chieftain, came a string of some forty men, women and

children, all slaves—Masongo, Shankalla and Galla—
carrying with them a sheep, many chickens, eggs, native
breads, several pots of drink, Abyssinian soup, fire-
wood, Indian corn, barley, and loads of grass for my
animals. More, they said, would be forthcoming in
the evening and on the following day.

The women were quite naked except for a tuft of
verdure in front and behind below the waist.

These presents were a nuisance, as it was necessary
to return the compliment, so that in the end they
became three or four times more expensive than if one
had bought the stuff direct.

As soon as these people had departed, the chief of
the market—a leper—came in later in the evening,
when market transactions were over, and he brought
with him more presents—more chickens, more native
breads.

The market-place, situated on the western slope
of the plateau, had no particular interest, except
the usual pegs for tying cattle, the sheds with the
chief's shelter propped high upon piles, and a great
many shiny stone seats, where merchants sold their
goods.

The next morning, March 3rd, at 8 a.m., I rode in
state to pay a formal call on the joint Governors, who
came out of their palace to the third outer enclosure in
order to greet me. They led me by the hand into the
reception hall by an inclined plane made of wooden
sticks, so polished and slippery from the many naked,
greasy feet which daily trod on it, that it was really
quite impossible to go up with one's shoes on. There
was no railing at either side, and when I got half-way
up I saw every prospect of being precipitated some

twenty feet or so down upon a crowd of people who stood below. Still, as luck would have it, and being pulled by the arms from above and pushed by numerous hands from behind, I completed the ascent, and with a sigh of relief was ushered into a large audience room, beautifully clean, with Oriental carpets upon the floor, and an imitation European bed standing prominent in the middle of the room. Then there were a few cane chairs and a sofa.

The Governors sat themselves upon the floor, and Mr. Armanxapoulo, as well as Mr. Metaxaz, another Greek, interpreted for me. I was asked to sit on the bed, the place of honour, but I preferred a cane chair. *Tetch* was at once produced, and also a bottle of " crême de menthe " of the deadliest green, while a bowl of roasted corn was placed before me.

The higher of the two Vice-Governors, Agafars Indeilalo, who looked after the foreign relations of the State, seemed the more intelligent of the two, and had quite a pleasant face. They seemed anxious to know whether I had a pass from the Emperor, and when I duly produced it, they stood up on seeing the Imperial seal upon the letter, and immediately called in a third man to read what it was all about, as the Governors themselves could not read at all. When I handed the letter over to them, they first wiped their hands upon their clothes, then brought the letter up to the forehead and bowed. When the sentence was read that everything must be done for me to make my journey easy, and that I had the Emperor's permission to proceed in any direction I wished, the two Vice-Governors bowed themselves double. They said whatever I commanded they were ready to do.

Both of them seemed to pay more attention to drink and food than to serious conversation with any sequel to it, but they were certainly polite.

My soldiers and attendants were also called in, and were treated to salt coffee, as well as to two bottles each of wine.

The second Vice-Governor, Kaniazmatch Olde Gabriel, who cared for the household affairs, was perhaps not quite so attractive as his companion. His face could not be pronounced so genial; in fact, there was something mean about his features, which were, moreover, badly pock-marked. He was well known in Abyssinia as the official who was publicly flogged in Adis-Ababa at the instance of Sir John Harrington, the British Minister, for offensive and interfering behaviour towards a British officer.

In the evening there came outside my tent the official musicians, with their *malakat*, or elongated trumpets, not unlike those used in Central Italy on the eve of the Epiphany, except that the Italian ones were made of glass, whereas those of Abyssinia were of reeds, five feet in length, and strengthened by a leather cover sewn upon them. There was also a smaller trumpet, the *ambelt*, and both produced a tremulous, twangy sound, mournful to a degree.

These official musicians had come to offer the proper welcome by announcing to the whole country around with their unmusical sounds that a foreign visitor had arrived in the town. Having received the usual present, they eventually departed.

I was astonished to find so few musical instruments in a country like Abyssinia. Beyond the *nugara*, or drum, the small *baganna*, a kind of violin, and the *kherar*, all of which, except the drum, they play extremely badly, there were really no typical musical instruments of any importance.

The drum, curiously, is never played when the Emperor goes out, and in time of war the drummer always keeps near the Emperor, principally in order to convey signals of command.

CHAPTER XIX.

WE left Gori on a Sunday morning, March 4th, having done what marketing we could in the place. We descended quickly more than a thousand feet among spiky *ghirar* trees and a thick undergrowth. Two streams crossed the trail. One particularly was most picturesque, running in waterfalls over a rocky incline, and so swift that a bridge had been constructed over it, or else it would have been difficult to cross. After this we came to fairly open country near the trail, except in some portions, where we went through picturesque forest, with lots of coffee plants, and vines of great length hanging from the tallest trees. Tall, corrugated palms, forty-five feet high, with oblong leaves, were numerous, and also the high palm with a clean barked trunk and a top tuft of leaves like a large ball.

We had rather a hard march for the animals that day, as the country was mountainous, and we kept mounting and descending hundreds of feet. First, over a pass 5,900 feet high, then an hour later down to a stream bridged over and flowing north no higher than 5,550 feet. Then again we ascended over undulating country to an elevation of 5,800 feet, and by three o'clock we had arrived at a fair-sized stream, also flowing northwards, but only 5,300 feet above the sea level.

The country was now fairly wooded all along. After a continuous march of eight hours we encamped at a place called Abbiyu, where there was a good deal of cultivation and extremely pretty hills all round dotted with huts, especially to the west and north-west.

It was rather curious to notice here again all the men with their noses covered with their shawls, in order not to be upset by the corpse-like odour of a white man !

We left early the next morning, passing two small streams flowing north, and continuing up and down across very hilly country. On the top of a hill range we came to the Buru market, with many sheds. Then up and down, up and down again, all the time, our elevations varying between 5,800 and 5,900 feet.

In one spot we came to a cone of earth enclosed in a fence. Upon it was a flagstaff with a conical white top, from which flew a red-and-white flag, a mere handkerchief split in two. This was of course a tomb. The bier, or stretcher, on which the dead body had been conveyed to its burial-ground was still lying on one side of the conical mound.

The hills were well cultivated near here, and lots of cattle grazed in the meadows. Dozens and dozens of huts, each with a group of small store-houses, dotted the landscape, and fine *uarca* trees of great size were numerous. As we came further west in Abyssinia, it was noticeable that the Galla had thatched walls to their huts instead of mud ones, as was the case further east.

In the afternoon we descended to a stream (5,300 feet), flowing north, a tributary of the Birbir, which eventually flows into the Baro. The vegetation was not so luxurious as we proceeded westward, and we now had rounded hills with few trees.

In the population, too, we did not see so many Galla, but we occasionally met some of the giant Yambo, with their shrivelled-up women, who wore nothing more than a hide round the hips and a string of blue beads round the loins. Most of them had big paunches, quite a deformity, caused in great measure by the rudimentary way of tying the umbilicus at birth, also by intestinal derangements, which are frequent with most of the tribes living in tropical and semi-tropical Africa. I came across several cases of beri-beri, the legs having become much swollen.

The women usually inserted in their hair a brass or ivory ornament sticking upright at the back of the head. The children, who went about quite naked, wore a circular tuft of hair on the top of the head, whereas the rest of the cranium was shaved clean.

Bure, situated on the western edge of the plateau, was reached after hard marching for the mules and horses.

I stayed there one day in order to obtain fresh muleteers, as the Abyssinians I had taken from Adis-Ababa were terrified at having to descend from the plateau into the low fever country of the Sobat, and they refused to come any further.

Nagadras Biru, the Governor at Bure, a most intelligent and polite man, did all he could to assist me in finding other men, and, in fact, succeeded in providing me at once with exchange muleteers. At the head of them he placed a man who had been prominent in the war against the Italians, and who spoke Italian quite fluently. He was the brother of Tesfa Michel, who

Governor Biru, of Bure, and his wife.

was now official secretary and interpreter to the Governor, and who was at one time interpreter to General Barattieri during the famous battle which saw the defeat of the Italians. Tesfa Michel also spoke Italian fluently, as also did Ligg Cassa, another interpreter with the Governor. Both these men were from Tigré, and were quite superior people to those of the Shoa.

The Governor himself, a man of an extremely highly-strung temperament, was enterprising, and took the keenest interest in the commercial and agricultural development of his province. He was a native of Bulga, in the Shoa, and was thirty-nine years of age. He struck me as being, after Ras-Makonnen, one of the cleverest men I had met in Abyssinia. He was married to a pretty and most charming wife, with whom he lived happily in the palace and whom he treated quite in European style. She helped him in entertaining visitors, and for an Abyssinian woman she was indeed quite bright and pleasant.

From Bure to the country of the Yambos at the foot of the plateau, we should have to travel by a bad and steep trail, and my animals being tired, I hired a number of carriers to convey the loads upon their heads in order to spare the animals. A Yambo chief was called in, and the Governor demanded the carriers I required. The Abyssinians stand no nonsense on the part of these barbarians, and the men came forth at once.

These Yambos were most peculiar people, capricious in no small degree, great lumbering figures, with not a stitch of clothing upon them, but occasionally with a cap of *guresa* skin upon the head. Others had bleached the hair white, or else dyed it red with a peculiar composition they use, which we will examine later on.

They gave me a deal of trouble when they came to examine the loads. These people were superstitious. There was one box painted black which nobody would carry for no other reason than because it was painted black. In fact, although I got two men for this particular box, one to carry it and one to look after him so that he did not escape, this package was abandoned on the road several times, and I eventually had to cover it with a piece of canvas so as to avoid further trouble.

A distinctive mark of this tribe was the extraction of the four front lower teeth, which they removed with the point of a spear.

Before a chief, the Yambo make a deep bow on passing, keeping the hands behind the back, while the women usually kneel down. Abbazzalle was the chief of the Yambo who live on the top edge of the plateau, his brother being a sub-chief.

It was rather pitiful to find here at Bure a number of Greek traders extremely ill with malarial fever. They had contracted it at Gambela at the foot of the escarpment. They were terribly depressed, and their condition excited a good deal of compassion. I felt all the more for them, for on my arrival they had great expectations of obtaining medicine from me, and their hearts sank deep when they heard that beyond some carbolic soap, castor oil, caustic and iodine, I carried no medicines with me.

There had been a great rush of these Greek traders for Gambela when this western route of Abyssinia was opened from Khartoum. The results had not come up to their expectation, and all seemed dejected and discouraged. Not only had the trade proved not quite so good as was expected, but the climate, these men said, was so bad that it was impossible for any human being to live in the place.

Undoubtedly some day, if things are managed properly, this route *via* the Sobat to the Nile should become a well-beaten one, and Bure, owing to its geographical situation and the invigorating climate it possesses, ought to become the most important centre of traffic between Adis-Ababa and the Nile, much more so than Gori, the former capital. Bure, from a commercial point of view, is better situated, being nearer the Sallé and Motcha districts, where coffee, ginger, and a kind of scented onion are grown in immense quantities. I think Gori was selected by the Abyssinians as the capital of that district more with an eye to the possibility of trouble with the Galla than for the commercial development of the country.

Sheep and goat skins, oxen, hides, butter, honey, wax, rubber and coffee are plentiful all over the country near and about Bure.

Messrs. Gerolimato and Co., of Harrar, were endeavouring to develop the commercial possibilities of Western Abyssinia, and they had entered into partnership with Ras Tassama in order to see what could be done ; but I believe that they encountered many difficulties which they had not at first anticipated. Principal of these difficulties was the heavy tax imposed at Gambela of nine per cent. on the sale price (not on the trade value), and without any allowance whatever for damage to goods upon the journey. The expensive charges for transport by river as far as Gambela to Bure (one thaler, or two shillings, for every sixty pounds, and another thaler from Bure to Gori for the same weight) are prohibitive for goods which have to be sold at low prices to the natives. It also makes the price by that route too heavy for exports to be able to compete with those from other markets in the Sudan, Egypt and Europe.

Coffee, for instance, which can be purchased for three thalers (six shillings) a *faram* (thirty-seven and a half pounds), costs as much as two and a half thalers for carriage merely to Gambela, three to four days' journey. Thus it is that the coffee industry, which could be made extremely remunerative in Western Abyssinia, is now simply killed by the existing conditions.

It is difficult to transport machinery by the methods now at hand. When I was at Gori and Bure, machines for cleaning coffee were expected, but had been delayed at Khartoum, the Sobat river being navigable only for a certain period of the year, the merchandise accumulating so that the small steamers which ply to Gambela once or twice during the year have not sufficient carrying capacity to transport all.

Madappolam, Manchester drill, variegated white piqué (the *duriah*), *shash*, usually red, and American grey cloth are the principal articles in demand in the local markets. Manchester cottons had of late gained a good deal over the American, but, as we shall see presently, the difficulty of conveying these goods in safety from Gambela to Bure and Gori is great at present, as there are no sheds upon the trail where the goods can be stored in wet weather. Also, during the rainy season the rivers are dangerous for men and loads.

Even without reckoning the money for warehousing in Khartoum while awaiting transport by water up the

Sobat, the price of goods becomes prohibitive by the time they reach Gori. To push goods further towards Adis-Ababa it is necessary to send them by caravan, the lowest rate for the hire of mules being eight thalers (sixteen shillings) between Gori and the capital. The ropes for tying the loads, the sacks and strong packages which have to be made in order to convey the goods in some sort of safety, add a good deal to this price.

Then at least one hundred per cent. must be added for dues levied upon the road, such as one and a half thalers demanded by Ras Tassama on each six *frassels* (225 pounds); half a thaler which has to be paid at the Didessa river to Olde Gorghis for each mule in the caravan, and another tax of one thaler for each loaded animal levied at Anun after Gibti. Those three thalers have to be disbursed upon the trail, plus two thalers for each *frassel* ($37\frac{1}{2}$ pounds) to be paid on entering Adis-Ababa.

For instance, a load of wax which, purchased in Gori, costs seven thalers, has already gone up to twelve thalers at Adis-Ababa, without counting cost of conveyance.

In Ras Tassama's country civet cats are plentiful, and each chief is bound to bring a male civet alive, or in default pay to the Ras six thalers.

To hunt these animals people go about in couples in the forest until the creatures are tracked down. Some coarse nets are then spread and the animals are driven into them. If females are captured, the front paw is amputated and the animals let loose again, so as to save the trouble of hunting them again. If, however, a male is caught, it is placed in a wooden cylinder and brought to the chief of the town. Ras Tassama keeps a staff of regular men in his country residences to look after these valuable animals. At Gori and at Tchora, at Sallearga and Motcha the Ras has a great number of civet cats. Every eight days the perfume is collected from the perspiration of the animals.

The owner of a civet is always a chief, and no one but a chief is allowed to possess one of these animals alive, any more than they are allowed to keep in captivity a lion, a leopard or a panther. Of the leopard, mortals of a lower social class can possess the skin, but not that of a panther or a lion. When one of the latter animals is killed, the skin must be brought to the chief, and all the hunter gets for it is a *shama*, as well as getting his forehead smeared with butter in appreciation of the courage shown in the hunt. The skin is lent to him for four days, when he returns to his village, and everybody is expected to give him a present. Then he must hand over the skin to the chief, as the lion and the panther are emblems of nobility or rank in Abyssinia.

It is curious to notice that the wife of a Ras takes half the share of his possessions, and she occupies quite a high position in social life. She is held in great respect and she eats with her husband. Even in the case of the Empress, she possesses as much as the Emperor, for if he has soldiers, she has her own soldiers ; he has slaves, and she has slaves ; if he gives a dinner, she gives a dinner, and so on. Both the Empress and the wife of a Ras are allowed to possess land, as well as their own slaves and soldiers, who work for them only and cannot be interfered with by anyone.

In Harrar, for instance, the wife of Ras Makonnen shared for some months of the year in the customs receipts. The Empress had her own custom house in the palace.

CHAPTER XX.

Just before paying up the Abyssinians, who refused to come any further, an unpleasant scene occurred with one of my muleteers, who had been drinking considerably in the town.

A large crowd of Abyssinians had collected round my camp, the Governor and some of the other officials being also present. One of my men who was always troublesome—in fact, he was one of those whom I had to punish for fighting at Addis-Jebbo—for no reason whatever used offensive language towards white men, partly to show off, I think, before his fellow-country-men. He received there and then a good many lashes of the *courbash*, and was made to kneel down and apologize before everybody.

The Abyssinians are touchy about seeing their own people struck by foreigners, and I fully expected a big row. I, however, turned at once to the Governor and told him that I was sorry I had been compelled to strike an Abyssinian, but I would stand insult from nobody, and in a similar case I would have struck a man of any other country. The Governor at once said I was more than justified in what I had done, only I had not punished the man enough, and he would see that the offender should further suffer for his misbehaviour.

The other men in my employ received besides their pay a handsome present, and returned towards the capital.

All my loads borne by carriers and my empty animals went ahead in the morning. In the afternoon of March 5th, I took my departure from Bure, accompanied by the Governor and his two interpreters, who insisted on accompanying me, some two hours' journey, as far as Gomma, on the edge of the plateau. The elevation of Bure was 5,650 feet.

As we went along, Nagadras Biru gave a wonderful exhibition of accurate spear-throwing while galloping on his horse.

Upon the road we met Alimi, the son of one of the greatest Yambo chiefs. He was unpleasant.

As we went along, we obtained a beautiful view on our left of the Baro valley, with great cotton plantations. On the top of the hill, before we began to descend, we came to a guard-house, through which one was compelled to pass. In the grand company in which I found myself deep bows were plentiful as we passed, but I suspected that had one travelled in a different way the same reception perhaps would not have been given.

Among high, thick grass we began a descent, but only to rise again to 5,900 feet, from where we obtained a magnificent view of the valley below and the plateau and mountains towards the Kaffa country.

Towards sunset we arrived at Gomma (5,450 feet), where two sheds had been erected, quite on the edge of the plateau. Handsome cotton plantations had been made by Nagadras Biru at this place. I met here the German Baron von der Ropp, who was studying the geological conditions of that country, mostly for

A suspension bridge of vines over the Baro stream (Western Abyssinia).

mining purposes in connection with an important German firm.

We had a pleasant dinner-party that evening, the Governor and the Baron being my guests, and we had an interesting time.

The next morning the Governor came to the edge of the cliff to bid me good-bye, and I began a steep and rocky descent down the western escarpment, partly through forest, and then among singed leafless trees. Barren, rounded, horrid mountains formed most of the scenery. We came across several *jaga*, or cairns of white stones, erected by Galla on the tops of hills. Bits of cotton were generally attached to these cairns.

Three hours and a half after leaving Gomma we reached the Baro river, at an elevation of 1,900 feet, and flowing at this point towards the north. We had difficulty in taking the mules across, as there was a good deal of water in the stream, and we could not find a suitable spot to make them ford. There was an elaborate suspension bridge made of vines and over thirty yards long, but only foot passengers could use it. We had to swim our animals across further up stream.

We saw many Yambo, tall and slender and absolutely naked. Upon their bodies occasional ornamentations were to be seen, consisting chiefly of cicatrices upon the breasts. An ivory ring, either plain or with ornamentations of dots like the teeth of a cogwheel, was sometimes worn above the elbow of the right arm. Some had iron wire bracelets, and a few hung large iron earrings from both ears. When walking, these heavy earrings were passed over the ear, so as to prevent them

dangling and injuring the lobe. In its natural condition the hair of the head was woolly and short, but
they frequently dyed it. They had no hair whatever
on the face and body.

Rubber vines were plentiful. Some of these, two
and a half inches in diameter, were not unlike huge
polypi twisting round trees up to the top branches,
from which they hung down again, ejecting a whitish
glutinous latex when an incision was made. The
Galla call the rubber vine *areg*, and the Abyssinians
mostly used the word " elastic," which they have
borrowed from Europe.

Further down the Baro river we came to four Galla
huts, where gold-washers lived. I saw a number of
these men at work in the stream with water up to their
necks, diving and taking up the gravel and sand from
the bottom of the stream in a large wooden tray. Then
moving the half-empty tray backwards and forwards
on the surface of the water, they gradually washed off
the sand and collected at the bottom a few grains of
gold. Over one ear each man tied a small cylindrical
cane, wherein the grains of gold were stored. As far
as I could judge, a man working hard from sunrise to
sunset would, with luck, collect something between six-
pence and a shilling's worth of gold. Perhaps with less
rudimentary methods more might be gathered.

By five o'clock in the evening, being then upon a
height, we got a bird's-eye view of the Baro, which had
cut itself a wide channel in a warmly-coloured bed
of volcanic rock. We were travelling among high
rugged mountains, with yellow dried grass and a great
number of the stunted *arghesana*, with leaves of
a light green colour. To the north-west before us

was a high conical peak peering above a mountain range.

We had to cross the Baro a second time at a place where it was a hundred yards wide. At the fording place my men had water up to their necks. The local chief of the village at the ford, Jelo, despatched his men to take over my animals, and he sent also a rickety canoe, in which I crossed the stream. There were plenty of hippopotami.

We halted in the evening at the Yambo village only a short distance on the opposite side of the stream, not far from a two-humped peak to the north-west of us, which had a conical high peak to the right as we observed it.

The huts in the Yambo village had sharply-pointed conical roofs reaching down to the ground. They were thatched with grass, and each roof was ornamented with antelope horns. Extra long antelope horns were also placed on each post supporting the reed fence round the village.

Large crowds of naked natives assembled round my camp, and squatted down on their heels, remaining there the whole evening. Many of them were ornamented with blue and white beads round the neck. Others possessed coarsely-made wooden beads. Their faces were flattened, with the central part of the nose much developed, and the supra-orbital central bumps abnormally so. The broadest part of the Yambo head is at the cheek-bones, which are prominent, the skull being much elongated upwards at the forehead.

These Yambos seemed inveterate smokers, their pipes being built on quite scientific lines, with a bulb either at the mouthpiece in the long straight pipes, or

with a gourd sphere at the angle between the bowl and
the long cane mouth channel, the object of this hollow
spherical arrangement being to cool the smoke coming
into the mouth.

Yambo huts were particularly interesting. Few of
them were higher than seven feet, with low doors.
These *otto*, as they called them, were beautifully constructed, and in the interior upon a hard cement floor
were two depressions, in which the food was prepared,
one on each side of the hut. Each *kahl*, or enclosure,
was some twenty feet across, and was entirely paved with
the same cement which was used inside the huts, and
which was prepared with a particular clay, mixed with
ashes of selected woods and a certain animal liquid.
This preparation became extraordinarily hard when
baked by the sun and took a beautiful polish. The
pavement of the *kahl* was at a slant for drainage purposes.
Outside and all round each hut was a platform three or
four inches higher than the rest of the paving, in order
to prevent the water coming inside the huts.

Central Africa is certainly not a place where one
looks for art. It is seldom that one notices even rudimentary designs upon structures, on weapons or implements, so I was rather surprised to find on these raised
platforms and around the two depressions inside the hut
some regularly designed, waved patterns, generally of
three parallel lines.

The Yambo had not many articles of furniture, a
small tripod carved out of one solid piece of wood being
the most noticeable.

The people seemed fond of ornaments. Nearly each
man had an amulet hanging from a necklace. The
thumb, and also the first finger, were inserted into

Yambo.

silver rings, but the armlets were generally cut in ivory. They were worn both round the wrist and above the elbow. More modest people showed tight bands of a fibrous leaf on the upper portion of the arm and also on the ankles.

The formation of the skull of these Yambo was interesting. It showed several characteristic influences of the races to the west. The cheek-bones were not only well developed, but they were so padded that they had the appearance of being swollen. Although the lips were large and prominent, they were in their normal condition tightly closed, a fact which was partly due to the Yambo removing the four front teeth as a tribal mark. The chin protruded considerably.

When you ask the Yambo, or any other race in Africa, why they remove one or more front teeth, they generally tell you that it is done for beauty's sake, or to be distinguished from one tribe or the other. This is perhaps true to a certain point, but I think the custom originated, especially in cases when all the front teeth are removed, from the natural advantage of being able to close the lips tightly and breathe through the nose in countries where the climate and other local conditions make it imperative to keep the lips closed as tightly as possible in order to avoid fever. At sunset and at sunrise particularly this is necessary in the countries liable to malarial fever where these tribes live, as it is at that time of the morning and evening that malarial fever is contracted by breathing certain germs which do not seem to poison the air so much either during the cooler hours of the night or when the sun is high in the sky.

I have been a great deal in countries where malarial

fever is rampant, and I am not at all convinced by the mosquito theory. The older theory of the Romans was certainly the more accurate one ; but it should be added that food, especially vegetables, polluted water and milk are also mediums through which malarial fever is frequently conveyed.

Experiments have been made, the results of which are said to prove that by drying up marshes and swamps, and thereby preventing the reproduction of mosquitoes in a country, fever can be stamped out. That is quite so. Only it is not the mosquitoes which necessarily give or convey the fever, but it is the country in which the mosquitoes live which is in itself deadly to some human beings.

I think no clearer proof can be given than the fact that when mosquitoes sting you all over in a non-malarial country nobody ever gets fever at all. Again, when the blood is in a healthy condition, even in malarial countries, one can be covered with mosquito stings and yet not feel any ill effects from them. Personally, I have been stung thousands of times by mosquitoes in malarial countries, and did not suffer from malarial fever to any mentionable extent, although I took no preventatives, such as quinine, etc. ; but the only place where I did suffer from bad fever was in the Persian desert some years ago, where I did not see a single mosquito for many months.

Again, on this journey, as we shall see later on, I will give several instances when people got malarial and yellow fever where no mosquitoes were to be found at all.

I happen to possess abnormally acute senses, and I have always noticed the immediate poisonous effects as one breathed contaminated air. This I particularly noticed at sunrise and at sunset, when rapid changes in the temperature occurred. The foul air seemed to act quickly on the respiratory and principally upon the digestive organs, causing sometimes the temperature of the body to rise. Not only in my own case, but with my men also, in fact, I found that the quickest and safest cure for malarial fever was not quinine, as is popularly believed, which really does more harm than good to many people, but a strong purge, castor oil by preference.

CHAPTER XXI.

THE Yambo must be the offshoots of a formerly potent race. Let us examine their physical structure. Although the skull is low and flattened, we find, for instance, that for a black Central African race the ears are comparatively well formed, with finely-cut curves and with lobes generally attached. Often, of course, the ears are artificially deformed by several holes right up to the top, silver earrings, or else rings made of monkey or antelope hair, being inserted into the holes. Both men and women have small, under-developed skulls, the forehead being low and narrow and the central and lower portions of the face broad in proportion. I could not trace much beauty or grace of line in the women. On the contrary, they were ugly, and even at a comparatively early age had dried pendent breasts. Nearly all had big repulsive paunches swinging before them as they walked, like the women we had seen further up on the Abyssinian plateau. The hands, nevertheless, were fairly good, with elongated, almost refined, fingers, which showed that these people had degenerated from a stock vastly superior to their present condition.

I was delayed in this village. My carriers took a long time to arrive with the loads, and it was not till ten o'clock that I eventually departed through lots of small Yambo villages. The *kahls* (or *kraals*) were about

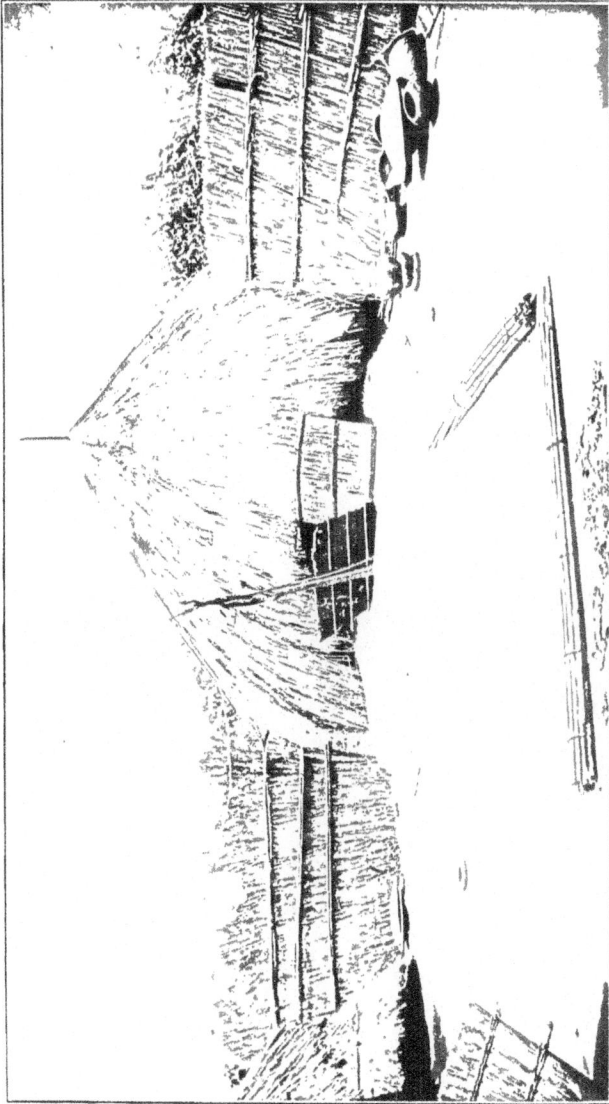

Yambo-huts, showing cemented court and platform.

fifteen feet in diameter, and had beautifully-polished cement floors.

We were now at an elevation of only 1,610 feet. The heat was stifling. The temperature in the shade rose to 108° Fahrenheit (42° Centigrade). During the night it had been extremely windy, with heavy clouds over-head and quite suffocating.

A hot march was before us along the flat, grassy, uninteresting country, and not till seven o'clock in the evening did we arrive at the trading station of Gambela, opened some two years before by the Anglo-Egyptian Sudan Government jointly with the Abyssinians.

This portion of the country for a few hundred miles further west actually belongs to Abyssinia, but the Abyssinians themselves never come down from their plateau, as they are too afraid of malarial fever, which is quite deadly in that region.

Gambela itself is situated on the right bank of the Baro, and it is the last point upon the river at which the small steamers occasionally despatched from Khartoum can float at high water. There are heavy rains from May 1st until November 1st, and sometimes during February there is what they call " the small rainy season," when heavy showers are expected and the river may suddenly rise as much as three feet. But it quickly falls again, so that it is only during the rainy and unhealthy season that the river is safely navigable at all. From January to June the country about Gambela is slightly healthier than during the rains, and the warmest months are February and March.

There are innumerable crocodiles in the stream and many hippopotami, while the banks are lined with birds of valuable plumage.

We were here in a country extraordinarily rich in game—elephants, giraffes, lions, leopards, ostriches, hyenas and antelopes being quite plentiful.

In some ways Gambela was conveniently situated within easy reach of the richest parts of Abyssinia. All the merchandize which formerly went from the west to Harrar, especially the coffee, ought eventually to find its way out of the country through Gambela. Then ivory, which is fairly plentiful in that region, may form a considerable item in the exports. Before the foundation of Gambela, a trading station had been established at Itang, and another earlier still at Kaig, a few miles further down the stream. These places were abandoned when Gambela was selected by Major Mathews and Captain Wilson as a more suitable site. The trading station of Gambela was founded on January 1st, 1904.

The entire trade of Sayo and Bure should drift this way from the north and north-east, where rubber is plentiful, and also that from Sallé, Motcha and Kaffa, to the south and south-east, where coffee of most excellent quality can be obtained, as well as wax, rubber and civet. In 1906, when I passed through Gambela, the Abyssinians had begun for the first time to send these goods towards the west instead of towards the east. It was satisfactory to learn that as regards the collecting of rubber, the natives were beginning to adopt more practical ways, and to tap the rubber vines, instead of destroying them wholesale as they had done so far.

As far as the Gori and Bure trade are concerned, it would perhaps be better were Gambela situated on the opposite of the stream (south). As things are now, the Baro, which makes a great détour, has to be crossed

Women's market in the Vambo country.

twice, and with difficulty, between Gambela and Bure. This puts a difficulty in the way of conveying goods by this route from Eastern Abyssinia, as well as from the rich districts of Sallé, Abigar, the Djouba country, and Yebelo, near the Pibor ; but, of course, on the other hand, the situation is convenient for the Sayo, Galla, and for the Anfillo, who are on the same side of the stream. Two bridges at the points where, under present conditions, the Baro has to be forded, would be of great assistance, and would make the present route quite practicable.

As things stand now, during the rainy season, when the steamers can occasionally come up to Gambela, it is next to impossible for the goods to proceed up country. The danger of crossing the river twice when it is swollen, in order to reach Bure, the bad state of the trail, and the heavy rains make it difficult to convey the goods to that place in fair condition. It would, therefore, be necessary to have sheds at Gambela, where goods could be stored until the more propitious dry season arrived.

Then another difficulty arises. When the trail between Gambela and Bure is practicable (during the dry season), there is not sufficient water for the steamers to come up to Gambela, and it is necessary to store the goods in Khartoum while they are waiting for the high flood to allow the navigation of the Sobat. So that the cost of warehousing must necessarily be added to other heavy expenses, and profits are proportionately diminished. Still, all this could easily be altered, or, at least, greatly modified.

The steamers which occasionally plied to Gambela were not by any means record-breaking vessels—except perhaps for slowness—and ran at the rate of something like three miles an hour when they ran at all. So it was really quicker to walk. Frequent stoppages had to be made to collect wood for the engines, and as wood was scarce along the Baro it was sometimes imperative to stop entire days in order to cut down sufficient fuel to get along. An attempt was made to endeavour to compel the tribes to pile up enough wood upon the river banks at certain spots, so as to avoid such delays, but all traders complained that the navigation of that river had so far been of little value commercially.

There was another more serious difficulty. An arrangement had been made between the Sudan Government and Ras Tassama, by which half the amount of trade dues received at Gambela for imports and exports, at the rate of nine per cent. on the "local selling price," was to be paid over to the Abyssinian Ras. During the twelve months previous to my visit they expected some £11,500 to be the share due to the Ras.

This tax came extremely heavy, especially on foreign imports, when all things were taken into consideration. If you add to the tax the damage done to goods in transit, porterage, warehousing, a heavy freight of twenty-five piastres per *kantar* (one hundred pounds) charged by the steamers from Khartoum to Gambela, etc., the extra expenses may be reckoned at not less than forty per cent. on the "trade price" of cotton goods, about thirty per cent. on that of *abukidir*, and about twenty-five per cent. upon glassware, according to their weight, market value and volume. The deadly climate of Gambela, too, must be taken into account, where even such people as Greeks, Armenians, Syrians and Egyptians, whose powers of resistance to malaria are great, are unable to live, and where high wages have to be paid to employees. Commerce so handicapped becomes prohibitive, although in Government statistics the returns may look extremely well. One has heard before of killing the proverbial goose which lays the golden egg, and that seems to be just what was happening at Gambela when I was there.

Practically all the trade of Western Abyssinia ought to come this way if things were made possible for traders, but the few who have attempted to do anything seemed to have little hope unless conditions changed for the better.

The receipts for trade dues in the year 1904 were only £1,000, but in 1905 they suddenly sprang to £10,000, the increase being mostly on imports, as the Abyssinians, so far, buy more than they sell.

I think that in order to develop this route quickly and satisfactorily, Gambela ought to be a free trading station until people have become accustomed to possessions, for the convenience of having which they would be eventually willing to pay a moderate tax. To establish a new trade route whose possibilities are at best but mediocre is hardly feasible under conditions so hampering.

There was an Egyptian official at Gambela, a *mamur*, called Mohammed Riad Effendi, an intelligent and pleasant man. He did all in his power to forward the interests of his Government and, as far as his orders allowed, to help the traders. He resided in a humble house by the river and his ten Sudanese policemen in another; but as this country was Abyssinian, and was merely managed by the Anglo-Egyptian Government, nobody seemed to have any absolute authority over the troublesome and unreliable natives of the district.

Riad Effendi's patience and tact with the natives and the traders were indeed wonderful. No better officer could have been selected for that post.

At the time of my visit, during the dry season in March, there were only three or four Greeks in the place, all ill with fever. They were connected with the Kordofan Trading Company ; with Angelo Capato, an enterprising Greek of Khartoum, and Tanios Saad, also of Khartoum. These people had themselves constructed three rickety sheds in a *zeriba* (or fenced enclosure), and in these they kept their goods, mostly cottons, silks, enamelled ware, and beads, wire, spearheads, etc., for purposes of barter. They traded chiefly with Sayo, Bure, Godjam, Walaga, Lega and Leka, Gouma and Kaffa. They seemed to think that the trade from the rich districts of Gouma and Kaffa had not properly started yet, and they had great expectations for the future if matters were facilitated. For the present their principal profits came from the north-east.

Godjam, Lega and Leka were as far north as the trade went in those days, and from those countries it was somewhat easier to bring the goods down to Gambela upon animals, whereas from Bure it was necessary to have them conveyed entirely by human carriers.

It is not for me to express an opinion on the advisability of giving the monopoly for rubber, coffee or ivory to certain companies. At the time of my visit a company had the monopoly of all the rubber, and Ras Tassama of all the ivory. There was a talk of someone else obtaining a concession for all the coffee. That makes it difficult for other people to compete, and it is only when there can be plenty of competition that trade advances in huge strides,

Yambo, the giant tribe of the Baro river.

Gambela, if things were managed rightly—as in due time they will be—would shortly become a big store for imports and exports, and would be the distributing centre for all the neighbouring countries.

The Abyssinian traders have an unbounded trust in the Sudan officers, as these are extremely conscientious with them. The Abyssinians, the *mamur* was telling me, always come to him to inquire the price of their own goods, as they tell him that they themselves do not know the exact value, and they beg him to establish a proper price, and, if possible, sell the merchandise for them.

The Yambo, too, the local inhabitants, seem much pleased with, but not very obedient towards, the Sudan officer. It cannot be imagined how kind and considerate this Egyptian was towards them. The chiefs of neighbouring tribes often came in while I was being hospitably entertained by the *mamur*, and he was indeed most patient with them.

These Yambo, although giants in stature, possess as much brain, or possibly less, than an average three-year-old child of any European country. They are capricious to a degree, independent, with an extraordinarily developed habit of nagging ; sulky at intervals, and suspicious at all times. Grasping by nature, they are quite unpleasant if they are not at once satisfied in their fancies.

Oghilo, the chief of Pinkio, a neighbouring village, often came in to spend hours with the *mamur*. He was over six feet four inches in height, and his brother was just as tall. There were many members of his tribe who reached a similar height. In fact, most of them were about six or more than six feet high. With no superabundance of flesh and well proportioned, with small heads, long legs, and perfectly naked, these men looked even taller than they were. They were indeed a race of giants, and they believed that in former days their ancestors were even taller than the people of the present day.

Oghilo himself was a great nuisance, as he had taken a fancy to a large mule-bell which was strung to the neck of my leading mule. For some hours he begged and entreated me to give him the bell, and as I could not spare it, he went on worrying me until I had to drive him away, promising that I would send him the bell when I had finished with it on reaching the Nile. He went away dissatisfied. The next morning the bell was missing. Happening to visit a village near by, I chanced to hear the familiar sound of my bell, and who should I see but my friend the giant Oghilo parading about absolutely naked among admiring natives, and with my bell attached to one part of his anatomy where no one but a Yambo would think of attaching anything.

Oghilo was a most unscrupulous scoundrel. He promised that in the afternoon I should get some thirty of his villagers to convey my loads for two or three days westwards towards Taufikia ; but when the hour came, not only could Oghilo not be found again, but all his men had disappeared, and no trace could be discovered of them.

I visited a good many of their tribes, as I did not travel by the river, but proceeded to march with my mules and a number of extra men, when obtainable, as far as the Nile.

I met many of these Yambo, and learned some of their customs, which were peculiar. For instance, mice and rats were what they relished most in the way of food, but they would not on any account eat crocodile meat, as my Abyssinians did. They were fond of hippopotamus meat when they could get it. They prepared themselves an intoxicating drink with Indian corn. When drunk, as they frequently were, they were disagreeable and troublesome.

It was interesting to see them in their hunts of wild animals. The entire village—men, women and children—turned out with their spears and javelins. The head of the javelins was made with the tibia of a giraffe, brought to a sharp point, and the rod was adorned with ostrich feathers at the other end. These throwing weapons were about six feet long.

I asked a Yambo one day how many wives he was allowed to marry. He put up his hand and let down one finger at a time, then the thumb, and then began with the fingers of the other hand, which I took to indicate unmistakably to be that not only bigamy, but polygamy on no small scale, existed among the Yambo. Not all, of course, have so many wives ; one, two, or at the most, four, being quite as many as most men can afford. They always marry in their own tribe, and rarely take wives even from a neighbouring tribe of Yambo. When the husband dies the eldest son becomes the husband of his father's wives, even of his own mother, which seems rather a disgusting state of affairs, and shows how low these people are in the human scale.

A girl can love any man, and it is only when an irregular birth occurs that she is taken to task and is compelled to declare who the father of the child is. The parents, armed with their spears and accompanied by friends, go to the responsible young man's village and pillage whatever there may be in his hut, besides appropriating all his cattle. If he should refuse to marry the girl, all his property is taken away from him, but if he can be induced to marry her, he only pays the usual ransom of one or more cows and sheep, according to his wealth.

As compared with the dances of Asia, I never saw among any of the tribes of Central Africa dances of any originality or grace. The Yambo, like all negroes, dance a great deal at their festivals, the men and women often joining in these dances ; the men opposite the women, who sing and clap their hands, while the men jump and hop about lightly with knees slightly bent. The tam-tam is not beaten with the hand but with two sticks, and as these people do nothing but play on the tam-tam all day and all night, they eventually become skilful at it.

The chiefs do not remove their front teeth, but all the others, both men and women, do. In their particular case, they profess that it is done in order to facilitate speech, as their teeth grow quickly at a peculiar angle, which makes it uncomfortable for them to close the mouth absolutely until the teeth are removed. Although this is the reason they themselves give, I think that their speech is only affected because their respiratory organs do not work as they should when the hot, fetid air of their region is inhaled in large quantities through the mouth, a fact which might certainly affect their speech also.

It is a curious fact that the Yambo who inhabit a region unmistakably deadly for all other people, as well as for tame animals brought there, are not themselves affected by malarial fever, notwithstanding that they are simply devoured by mosquitoes.

Yambo store-houses.

The Yambo women are prolific, but the children are not always as healthy as they might be, owing to complaints of the blood of the worst possible kind, including leprosy, being rampant.

The women think they embellish themselves by making large cicatrices on the middle portion of the body, while the men indulge in similar incisions on the arms and chest. Usually these take the form of elongated lines or dots. Most common of all are the four incisions on each shoulder. These incisions are emblematic, and they are supposed to have been caused in spasms of passion by their lady loves ; others upon the body are attributed to a similar origin. The Yambo seem very proud of these scratches. As a matter of fact, although few Yambo will confess it, these cicatrices are only made with the point of a knife or a spear when nobody is looking, either by a confidential member of the family, or even by a special professional man, like the *tachmish*, who is found in many parts of the Sudan, where this sort of ornamentation in various forms is deemed attractive. I have seen men whose arms were literally covered with these sets of scratches, arranged with wonderful regularity upon the arm considering the narratives they wanted us to believe.

It is curious to note that while such semi-civilized people as the Abyssinians think nothing of selling their children for a consideration, the Yambo, who are absolute savages, are most kind and affectionate to their young, and would rather be killed than part with them.

The Yambo are extremely clean, not only in their huts, but in their persons as well as their food. A few Yambo from Gambela, who had obtained cloth from the traders, draped the body slightly, and not always in the right place, but most of them, in fact nearly all, went absolutely naked.

Yambo are quarrelsome, and consequently cannot help being at enmity with neighbouring tribes. Although aggressive towards persons weaker than themselves, these overgrown people are in reality cowardly and weak.

In visiting some of their *kahls*, I found that the dead were buried in the centre of the enclosure. The raised portion marking the grave was then plastered over with the beautiful hardened cement of their own manufacture.

Before I started from Gambela, Shamo, the chief of the village where we forded the River Baro, who was absent hunting when I passed, came in with many of his followers to pay his respects. The young chief wore a red handkerchief festooned around his head and a felt hat upon it. Over a brightly-coloured sash around his waist was a cartridge belt with empty cartridge-cases, and all this finery was worn over a variegated shirt. His legs were bare. Two large mule-bells were attached to his right ankle, and one to the left ankle. Tinkling these bells, he walked solemnly in stately grandeur, followed by one rifleman with a long ostrich feather stuck in the muzzle of his weapon. Behind these two central figures came a lot of spearmen, with heads dyed of all colours.

The chief had heard that Oghilo was now in possession of a mule-bell, and evidently he had come to show that he possessed three. The MacMillan expedition had passed this way the year before, and no doubt the bells were obtained in the same manner to Oghilo's. He certainly impressed the natives very

General Gataacre's grave at Gambela (covered with thorns to prevent hyenas digging up the body).

much. They gazed open-mouthed at his adorned feet. A number of the men who came in wore as many as six earrings of beads attached to each ear, each one, as we have seen, in a separate hole all the way up the curve of the ear.

We did not go from the sublime to the ridiculous in the proverbial way, but instead from the ridiculous to the melancholy, when the *mamur* and I went to take a photograph of General Gatacre's grave. Whether it was that in countries where one does not see many white people one feels things more keenly than when you live among them, it gave me quite a *serrement de cœur* when the tragic death of this brave, if not always successful, officer was narrated to me.

Behind the humble bazaar and among a lot of untidy shrubs the unfortunate general was hastily buried in the middle of the night. The few sick Greeks and the *mamur* present had to keep some distance away, as the body was in a state of decomposition and falling to pieces when it was brought to the grave.

The poor man had died alone and unattended under a big tree at a place called Ideni, further down the river, unable to understand or to make himself understood by the natives. On landing from a boat near Ideni, he had proceeded to walk on foot without comforts of any kind towards Gambela, but a violent attack of fever had seized him, and he had to find temporary shelter under a solitary tree. He had despatched his Indian servants to Gambela, a journey which would occupy them two or three days, but unfortunately a few hours were enough to kill him.

The Yambo who had been watching him came to the tree when the General had collapsed, and, finding life extinct, for fear of being accused of murder, took the body in a canoe up to Gambela, where, owing to the intense heat, it arrived a couple of days later in a state of decomposition.

The grave of this well-known English general consisted of an improvised cross made with two boards of a broken kerosene box nailed upon a stick ; that was the only wood that could be obtained. A lot of thorns had been piled upon the heap of earth covering the body, in order to prevent hyenas and other wild animals digging up the body. Poor General Gatacre !

CHAPTER XXII.

I INTENDED sparing my mules as much as possible, and endeavoured to obtain carriers at Gambela. The *mamur* was obliging, and went to no end of trouble to procure men for me, but notwithstanding the promises of the various chiefs, no porters were forthcoming. One day was absolutely wasted waiting for these fellows. Policemen were despatched in all directions to induce men to come in.

Eventually, at noon on March 10th, a number of Yambo were brought up, and I was able to start on the long march towards the Nile. It was my intention to visit many of the interesting tribes on the north, and especially on the south, of the Sobat river. I should have to make great détours in order to see them. This would involve hard work, as most of this country during the rainy season was an absolute swamp. During the dry season—in which I was travelling—the mud became hardened, but was most uneven from innumerable deep footmarks of elephants, giraffes and other animals, and from wide cracks in the surface mud contracted by the heat of the sun. It was a severe strain for the animals to get along. The heat was intense and incessant. There were but few trees.

No sooner had I started from Gambela than I met upon the road a poor Yambo child, about ten or twelve years of age. He had wasted to a mere skeleton. His legs and arms were atrophied, the bones devoid of flesh; the knees, elbows, and all other joints much enlarged and seemingly calcinated. His head, too, was dried up like that of a mummy, merely the skin remaining tightly stretched upon the skull. The boy was absolutely blind and deaf. The greatest marvel to me was that the poor little fellow could live at all. The disease from which he was suffering was prevalent in that region in a more or less accentuated degree. Children appeared to suffer more intensely from it than well-grown people. It seemed to affect every portion of their anatomy; whereas with the older people the legs seemed to desiccate first, the knee joints hardening until they were unable to bend any longer, then the ankle becoming stiffened and the toes gradually atrophied. The arms were affected at the elbows in a second stage of the disease. I came upon many of these skeleton-like people. They were a pitiable sight.

We passed numerous Yambo villages along the stream. Many fields of Indian corn were cultivated by these giants. Near Pinkio there was a small lake on the right of us as we were travelling almost due west.

The Baro river, on our left at this point, showed an elongated island dividing the stream into two unequal channels, the right one being half the width of the other. In many places the stream was over a hundred yards wide. Some distance to the right we had a long range of mountains in the Afillo and Sayo regions, and nearer us were curious rounded mounds and humps.

We had gone but a few hundred yards from Gambela when most of the carriers made an escape, scattering the loads upon the trail. I had to send back to my

Yambo, on the Baro river.

friend the *mamur* to ask for a fresh supply of men. He rode out with a new lot of porters some time in the evening.

These Yambo were so unreliable and sneaky that I feared the new contingent might run away also. During the night I kept watch on them. We had an unpleasant night. The Yambo shrieked the whole night at the top of their voices in an orgy of their own, because, they said, the full moon was coming out, and they must give it a greeting. In the neighbouring village the tam-tams were beaten frantically all through the hours of darkness, and choruses of frantic yells could be heard in all directions. As a matter of fact, it was not the full moon they were welcoming, but, being of an extremely superstitious nature, they were endeavouring to keep away from their huts the evil spirits which they believe are the travelling companions of white men going through their country.

The damp heat was stifling all through the night—quite suffocating. Equally unpleasant was the concert of mosquitoes, which added greatly to our discomfort. We were stung all over. Notwithstanding that I had a thick mosquito net, these mosquitoes were so fierce that they could find their way inside with no difficulty. Also, as one's camp bed was necessarily not very wide, every time one's arms and feet came near the mosquito netting, they were instantly riddled with stings through the netting. Worse still, even the entire body was not spared right through the stretched canvas of the bed upon which one lay.

In the middle of the night I had to jump out and run barefooted after a batch of Yambo, who had suddenly bolted out of camp. I was unable to catch them again as I unfortunately trod on a bunch of thorns. The men got away, and I had to spend the remainder of the night in trying to extract the spikes from my aching soles and toes. For this a brilliant illumination of candles was imperative, and the light fetched around me swarms of ill-natured, buzzing mosquitoes quite fierce in their attacks.

We had encamped at a place to the west of Pinkio, quite a populated centre, where a ferry canoe was to be found. I was thus able to go to the other side of the stream to examine some of the villages.

The Yambo I had now in my employ were under a chief named Didon, an unscrupulous scoundrel, whom I took as a hostage, warning his people that if any of them took flight I would take their leader as far as the Nile. We had a grand row in camp, during which sonorous blows were exchanged, as they endeavoured to liberate their chief. I confiscated Didon's matchlock, which he valued very much, and in order to obtain its return peace was eventually restored. It was only after some time that we departed, travelling over flat country with many small plantations of Indian corn.

We passed a double-coned hill on our right, quite isolated upon this level land, and to the west-north-west a peculiarly-shaped mountain, with sloping sides at the base and a vertical walled rocky mass towering above it.

The influence of civilization brought up the river by traders began to be apparent among the natives. It took the form of skirts for the Yambo women. Only these skirts, made of strings of white and green beads, appeared to me too long to be short and a great deal too short to be long.

That day was doomed to small disasters. I had stored in one large case a bag containing some thirty pounds of powdered sugar, and next to it were placed several large bottles of castor oil. A bump! The case had tumbled off a pack! Sounds of broken glass, of course. Oil trickling out from the interstices. Two bottles of castor oil gone. *Dénouement*, the sugar absorbed all the oil and became so disgusting in flavour that it had to be thrown away. So, from that time, no more sugar in my coffee, no more sugar in my tea, no more sugar on anything, and it happened just at a time when, owing to the intense heat, I had taken a great fancy to sugar! Sugar is most refreshing and wholesome in tropical climates.

We halted under a cluster of small trees. After travelling all the time across a grassy and almost treeless country, we came to a tiny village.

The natives smeared their bodies and faces with white ashes, and dyed the hair on the scalp of a brilliant red or yellow colour. Others plastered the hair all over with a composition of white ashes and mud, and drew it into a point behind the head. When this preparation was removed, they elongated each kink in the hair with a wooden pin and gave it a fluffy appearance. The coiffure stood straight up on the head, and was of a brilliant yellow.

All these people were extremely vain—a quality universal among negroes. They thought of nothing except their personal appearance and how to improve it. Sometimes they added dabs of black and red upon the white-coated skin of their faces. Whether the vision of black people is different to ours or not is difficult to say. Their charming beauty seemed greatly admired

by the fair sex of their own country, but to European
eyes they looked perfectly ghastly.

At 10.30 on the night of March 11th we encamped
on a flat open space opposite Itang (alt. 1,300), on the
north side of the Baro, where ruins of the former trading
station could still be seen.

Further trouble was in store with the Yambo, notwithstanding the patience I had used towards them. They
now absolutely refused to carry out their agreement to
come as far as Kaig, or indeed to come along at all. I
was so tired of their company that I drove them away
from my camp, and loaded the mules again.

We next passed Ideni village, merely two or three
huts, inhabited by people quite different in appearance
from the Yambo. The men were slightly bearded. In
fact, we were here entering the Nuer country. The
women carried their children astride upon their backs.

I noticed some rather peculiar straw figures used as
scarecrows in their plantations of Indian corn. These
huge figures possessed plenty of anatomical detail—too
much, in fact.

Near villages in this neighbourhood there was usually
a high post, the stump of a *dum* palm devoid of leaves at
the summit. In this particular village, this post along
the stream had been dyed in sections of white and black
alternately ; but I think this was the work of hydro-
graphers rather than a characteristic habit of the population.

In front of my camp I witnessed an interesting sham
fight with javelins between young fellows and children.
I was astonished to see how accurately these people
gauged distances and calculated the parabolic curve of
their weapons through the air.

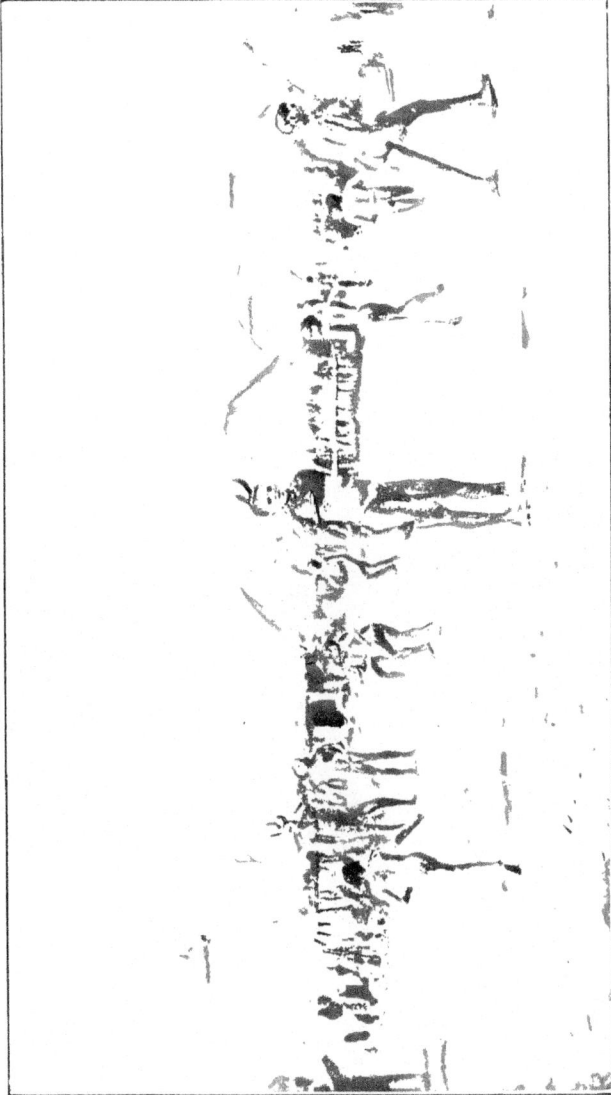

Nuer village.

This Nuer tribe had peculiar ways of doing the hair :
frequently in a long cone behind the head, with two
feathers stuck on the right side and another straight up
upon the head. They were thin and tall. All possessed
flattened faces, with long, prominent upper teeth sticking out beyond the upper lip. The nose was flat and
broad, and upon the forehead they had parallel incisions half an inch apart, from the brow as far as the
commencement of the hair. Many of them dyed the
nose of a different colour from the face ; others had
different patches of colour upon the cheeks. The younger
people plastered the hair down into a long, conical,
sharp point over the forehead, instead of behind the
head. The hair in its natural condition was black and
bristly, but after the dyeing process it became dried
and fluffy, and the kinks would become straightened
so as to give the people a fashionable fluffy head of
hair.

Sticks were passed horizontally through the ears,
and a huge brass ring was worn round the neck.
Numerous brass bracelets covered the entire lower arm
from the wrist to the elbow. A typical ornament, which
I noticed from this point right across as far as the
boundary of the French Congo, was the string tightly
fastened directly under the knee. These particular
people attached to it two pieces of wood on the left
leg only.

The favourite attitude of these tribesmen when
sitting was to keep one knee up and to rest the arm upon
it. The other leg was folded down and rested flat upon
the ground. Frequently they also sat upon the ground
with both legs bent up and the arms resting upon them.
But they never sat cross-legged as people in Europe

always imagine natives of any kind must sit, Turkish fashion.

An antelope skin, with a sort of strap attached to it, was worn hussar fashion by the better-dressed men as a mantle upon one shoulder.

At a place called Sham, near Ketch, I saw some spears of great length. They had an enormous elongated, leaf-shaped head with a high rib in the centre on either side, the section of the spearhead at its centre forming a quadrangle. Two throwing spears were generally carried by each man, as well as a war-club, some three feet long. When calling peaceably on friends, on sitting down the men stuck the heads of their spears into the ground. The war-clubs were cut from hard, heavy, but light-coloured wood, with a hemispherical or conical head at one end and a sharp point at the other.

Author's mules crossing the Baro river in the Nuer country.

CHAPTER XXIII.

AT Sham the inhabitants were again Yambo, but not of a pure type. Although their habitations were quite clean, they were not so neatly built nor properly looked after as those I had seen at Gambela. The roof did not show the same accuracy of construction. The door in the mud wall was only one and a half feet high and one and a half feet wide. It had a waved pattern over it. There was a three-cornered depression on one side of the hut in the interior for lighting a fire, and along the wall stood three or four earthen pots for storing maize. In the small paved courts facing the huts were large bowls of baked corn, the bowls being hemispherical, with decorations of the dot pattern and inverted waves filled in with dots.

In type these people had some of the characteristics of the Yambo and some of those of the Nuer. The lips, the most prominent of their features, were protruding and heavy, and they appeared out of proportion to the small, squashed, flat nose. The lips were usually wide open, showing the upper front teeth, which became of great length, the lower ones being removed at a comparatively tender age. Although the forehead of these people had sufficient height, it was abnormally narrow and lacking in character. If phrenology could always be relied upon, these people should be great mathematicians, as the bump—the only prominent one—of calculation was strongly marked ; but I rather doubt whether any of them could even count up to five, and this with the aid of their fingers.

In prowling about the village I saw a woman whose ears were simply riddled with holes, in each of which she had inserted a white glass bead. All the curves of the ear were absolutely filled with these white beads, each one sewn into the flesh.

The entire population seemed afflicted in a most alarming form by the terrible venereal complaint prevalent all over tropical Africa, and as they went about perfectly naked, one could notice the abnormal contraction of certain organs, or the undue swelling of others, not to speak of formidable-looking buboes of a virulent kind in the region of the loins. The blood of these people was indeed in a thoroughly vitiated condition. The muscles of their arms and legs seemed to undergo a process of desiccation which gave the knees and elbows the appearance of being much enlarged, and was evidently caused by the impurity and poverty of their blood.

The drinking bowls of these people were made of half a gourd. Prettily-coloured shells brought by traders from the coast were in great demand among these natives, who used them as spoons.

When we were proceeding on the march we saw numerous antelopes, and innumerable flamingoes with blue wings, white chest and long pink legs.

We crossed an immense grassy plain, where Ketch and two other large Nuer settlements of sixty or eighty houses in each were situated.

The walls of the huts were now made of heavy logs of wood, plastered with mud between, and much higher

than those of the Yambo—about five feet instead of two.
The door was somewhat narrower but taller than that of
Yambo homes, and in shape formed either half or an
entire oval. The method of closing the doorway was
simple enough. A mat was placed against the opening,
with logs of wood piled one on the top of the other
against it, and held in position by two upright sticks
parallel to the wall. The roofs, conical and of greater
height than in the Yambo country, were constructed in
superposed sections forming horizontal rings round the
hut. Some were as much as fourteen feet high. There
were also domed huts of thatch over a frame of bent
sticks, and only six or seven feet high.

The custom of dyeing the body and face white with
ashes was here quite general, the men sporting some
additional brown and red marks upon the face, the
ensemble of their wrinkled, rugged faces, with their few
hairs of beard, their overlapping brows and broad flat
noses being at all times quite repulsive, but more so under
their additional make-up.

I visited the villages of Buringhi and Bilunkul, and
in the latter village I found a six-stringed musical instrument, lyre-shaped, not unlike the one used by the people
of Kaffa. In this case, however, the sounding-board
was made of half a pumpkin instead of a wooden cone
with a skin stretched on it.

The natives were shy and suspicious. I had the
greatest difficulty in photographing them.

Before deciding upon a spot higher up stream towards
Gambela, the Sudan Government had established a small
trading station on the river at Ideni. We had left the
Baro at Itang, and we only struck it again at this place.

Owing to the grass being high, when we came near

the stream I saw and heard a great many women bathing and splashing in the river, but they had not perceived us. I stalked them with my best camera and managed to get quite close without being seen. When, however, I had to emerge from the grass in order to take the picture there was a general stampede with shrill squeals and yells, such as only frightened women know how to rend the air with. The bathing ladies fled at first in a body and then dispersed in all directions. But not, however, before I had succeeded in taking an instantaneous record of their flight, quite interesting, in a way, as it shows the extraordinary length of their legs and the curious angle of the body while running. A child —less rapid and more scared than her elders—who had also been taken for a refreshing bath, was abandoned by her mother in the water, and was fast getting submerged. Had I not hurried to pull her out—dear me, what lung power even the young possessed !—and deposited her on an improvised couch of weeds which I made for her on a small island, she would have certainly got drowned or seized by a crocodile. Perhaps the mother went to fetch her back when I had gone. I hope she did.

There were hundreds of cranes along the river and red gazelles on land.

The men in this region wore round their arms beautiful, heavy ivory rings, some as much as three inches broad, six inches in diameter and one inch thick.

At Bilunkul, where we halted for some hours in the middle of the day owing to the intense heat, the Baro was about fifty yards wide, with a great sandy beach at the river bend.

Towards two o'clock we continued our journey again

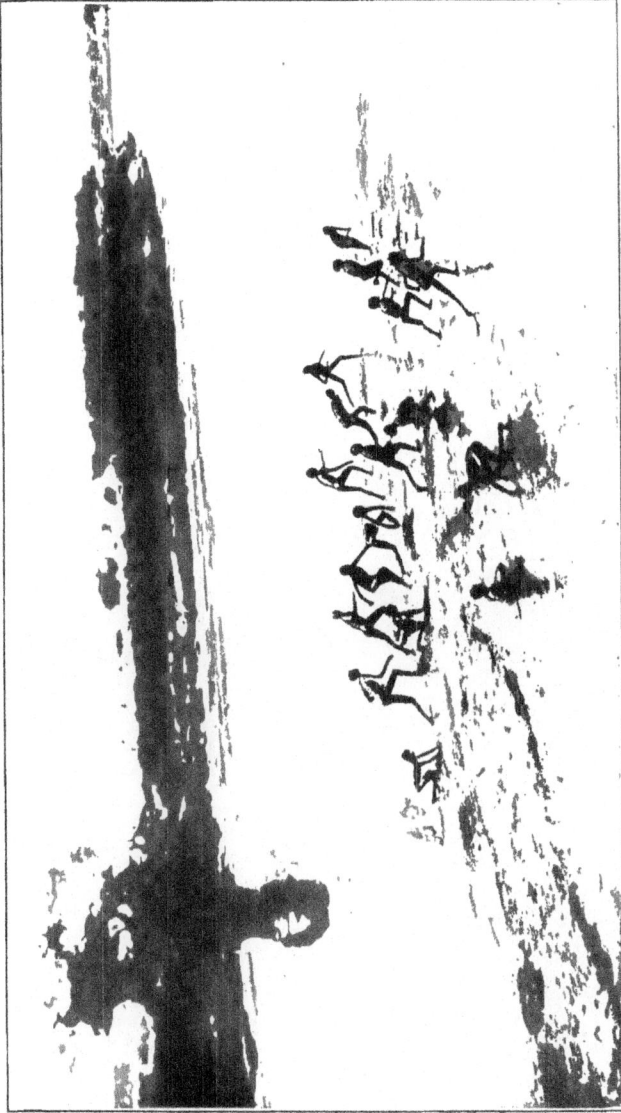

Stampeding Nuer Women (showing great length of their legs).

in the broiling sun over a grassy but treeless flat plain, with thousands of fine long-horned cattle belonging to the Nuer.   These animals disliked the sight of my mules, and whenever they perceived my caravan go through they took special delight in charging us—quite a formidable sight as they cantered in a body towards us. It took a deal of shouting to keep them at bay.

We kept pretty well at an elevation of about 1,300 feet, and after a long and somewhat tiring march for my animals, we arrived at and crossed the Jonkau stream, only five yards wide, flowing southward into the Baro. There was a village of Nuer near the place where we crossed the rivulet.

We encamped on the west side of the stream, where grass was plentiful. Curiously enough, although the heat of the day had been intense, the night was quite chilly, and we hardly heard or felt any mosquitoes.

I had with me an Abigar, whom I had employed as a guide to show me the various settlements of Yambo and Nuer.   He was a peculiar-looking fellow, shrivelled up with age.   He displayed a red fez, of which he was proud, as he had served in the Sudan police.   Over a shirt with only one sleeve he wore a thick winter waistcoat, which he had purchased from a trader and on which he had fastened four buttons, all of different colours and sizes.   While marching he bore a big bundle of spears slung upon his back, and his pockets were full of small articles which he had taken along, in order to do some little trading on his own account upon the road.   In one hand he carried, also for trading purposes, a small bundle of wire, and in the spare hand he conveyed for me a lantern, in which in the daytime were stored on alternate days tins of apricot and strawberry jam and biscuits, of which I eat quantities all day long on the march—hence the necessity of keeping them in an accessible place.

On March 14th we left camp at sunrise, and a mile or so beyond we reached the Baro, here about a hundred yards wide. I wanted to cross it in order to see some of the tribes on the southern side of the river.

After a good deal of bargaining with a local chief, who rebelled against taking us and the loads over in his dug-out, we came to an understanding with him and proceeded to take the baggage across. Money was absolutely useless in this region. To save myself the trouble of unpacking beads and brass wire, I offered this chief as much as four silver dollars which I had in my pocket, to take us across, but he explicitly refused to accept the money, which he threw upon the ground, saying that it was no good to him. He eventually consented to take us to the other side for something like one yard of brass wire, worth at the most threepence. There was a man with a good eye for business.

We had, of course, to swim the horses and mules across, and the canoe, being extremely rickety—absolutely falling to pieces, it was so rotten—it took us the best part of three hours to effect the crossing of the entire caravan. The scene was witnessed from both banks of the river by hundreds of admiring natives, smeared all over with white and quite ghost-like. They were sitting along the river banks with their knees doubled up, each one carrying two or more spears as well as war-clubs.

Good gracious! What a variety of headdresses these people were seen to have adopted when you looked at them. Some wore the hair plastered into a cone

Nuer, Showing curious coiffures and skin painted with ashes.

sticking out behind; others in a little cone rising up vertically upon the head; others still in an elongated cone projecting out in a graceful curve in front, several inches beyond the forehead. Some, more ambitious, had built a gorgeous aureole of long white and black feathers stuck in the back of the hair; others only had one feather stuck on one side of the head.

All the men had five or six parallel cuts upon the forehead, their special tribal mark, and many men and women showed the incisions upon the shoulders and chest recording love affairs, after the fashion we have seen among the Yambo. Some had a series of these cicatrices at the waist behind.

These people were rowdy, whatever we did or said causing a good deal of undemonstrative merriment among them. I never saw any of them laugh heartily; they seemed to take life sadly, not unlike the long-legged water-birds along the stream, whom they closely resembled. Nature has a wonderful way of adapting people and animals to local conditions. The country of these people was dry when we passed in the height of the hot season, but during the rains it is practically a swamp, and to get about involves being in water all the time. Hence the necessity of supplying the people with long legs, in order to keep the vital parts of the body protected as much as possible from the moisture. Nearly all the tribes of the High Nile valley, which go by the generic name of " Nilotic tribes," possess similar characteristics; but many paludal and riverine tribes of other parts of the world are also to be found with a special anatomical development enabling them to live in watery regions.

I proceeded to a village called Wau, and then to

another village with small domed huts, six to seven feet high. Nearly all these villages were now built at the sides of a square, in which stood hundreds of pegs for tying up goats and cattle at night.

These people possessed thousands of humped, long-horned cattle, which they would on no account sell or barter, nor would they dispose of milk, butter or cheese. At night, when the cattle had been collected in the central square, big fires were burnt all round to keep wild animals at bay—lions particularly, which were plentiful in that region. Drums were also beaten the whole night.

The men of these villages possessed a curious arrangement, which consisted of a large wooden cylinder, in which a hollow place to insert the hand was scooped half-way up. They explained that this was a weapon of defence against blows from the war-clubs, but I never was able to get them to give me a practical demonstration of how it was used. Of course, one could get a powerful swing with these heavy wooden cylinders, and anybody able to use them dexterously could certainly ward off any blow, and even disarm his enemy.

As we marched southward of the river, visiting several other villages, the heat was stifling. The short grass was burnt by the roasting sun. The scenery was wretchedly barren, and not a tree nor shrub was to be seen for miles and miles around. The country was absolutely flat.

In the afternoon we reached a place called Barakui, where the natives wore their hair long and dyed it a light brown colour. These people were independent in their manner, and rather inclined to be unpleasant. They were angry at my making a camp in the neighbourhood of their village, and insisted that we should move on,

In the Anuak country.

which, of course, I did not do.   We had to keep a sharp
look-out on all our possessions, as these people were unscrupulous thieves.

Here again we found the fashion of plastering the hair
with red mud, mostly into a long point in front, like a
clown.   The dwellers in this place had lovely ivory
bracelets of great thickness round their arms above the
elbow, and numerous brass wire bracelets covering the
arm from the wrist to the elbow.   They possessed
elaborate necklaces of blue and white beads, but their
entire dress consisted of a mere string of rope round the
loins, usually with one or two cylindrical pieces of wood
sticking up about two inches in front, or else with a well-
made knot at the waist behind.

These people coveted pieces of European rope, and
I had to keep men watching all the time over the ropes
with which we fastened our packs on the mules, as I
could read in their faces an inextinguishable desire to
intercept them.

All round the right shoulder-blade the men had two
semicircles of dots formed by incisions in the skin, and
also sets of incisions, generally in parallel rows, in the
umbilical region.

When these fellows perceived that I disregarded
their arrogance, and paid no attention whatever to their
threatening attitude, the chief sent over to my camp a
strange individual—a local poet and musician—evidently
a Nuer Mozart, with long hair held in by a white bead-
crown at the back of the head.   His features were
knobby ; his eyes mere slits.

I am fond of music, but I never place much reliance
in the honesty of musicians—less, of course, in that of
Nuer musicians than of other musicians.   When I saw

this unscrupulous-looking devil appear, I naturally took
some interest in his combination lyre-drum, which was
neatly made of a tortoise shell, with a skin stretched over
it, perforated in sixteen places, and of the usual triangular frame, with six strings attached to it; but I also
immediately wondered whether this genius of Nuer-
land had really come to give us sweet local melodies,
or whether his visit had ulterior motives. With him
came a friend of his, this one more poet-like. A poet and
a musician together. That looked rather bad.

While I pretended to be writing I kept a watch on
them by means of a small looking-glass. The musician
sat himself some little way behind me, strumming upon
the strings and making some ululations, while his companion, gazing towards the sky, walked about the camp
shoving with his feet—unseen, as he believed—any small
articles, such as knives, forks, etc., which were strewn
upon the ground about my camp. The musician, on
his part, seemed skilfully to combine thieving with improvising verses and music, and while charming us with
Nuer melodies with his dainty hands, he spread now one
leg and then the other to pick up with his toes—which
he could use like fingers—the various articles which his
friend and confederate had conveniently pushed near
him.

Interesting as all this was to watch, I could not help
wondering how these rascals would manage to take the
things away without my seeing them. Evidently they
intended sitting there until night came, the hour then
being two o'clock in the afternoon. Upon which, I
thought I would not wait so long, and proceeded in my
turn to charm them too—but with a different kind of
music altogether—and recovered my property, quite a

Nuer musician and poet.

good heap of it, on which for lack of pockets the illustrious minstrel was gracefully sitting.

Hot as I made it for my victim, we considered that quite a cool day as far as the temperature went. It was 120° in the sun and no shade of any kind existed except under the shelter that I had put up, where the temperature registered 100°. There was, however, a nice breeze, which gave us great relief, as we had been suffering a good deal from the hot, stifling air.

The skin of the Nuer possesses a strong natural odour, much resembling that of sheep. It could be easily detected in the pure air fifteen to twenty yards away if the wind blew in one's direction. Possibly it is intensified by their habit of sleeping among their sheep and goats. These people are clean in their habits, and they spend all their time between bathing and smearing their bodies with ashes. They think themselves very beautiful.

The umbilicus of children is so badly tied at birth —in fact, the umbilical cord is left quite long and a mere knot tied at the end—that one finds many children of five to ten years old with the umbilicus enlarged to the size of a large egg—quite a deformity.

We have a different type again in this particular tribe, influenced probably by their vicinity to the Anuak. They have a long and prominent upper lip. The forehead is large in proportion to the size of the head, but extreme weakness of character is apparent in the lower portion of the face, particularly in the small receding chin.

Many of these people were regular giants, as far as their stature went, many of them being above six feet four inches. Several men I saw six feet six inches in height. Most of the men were over six feet, and all remarkably long-legged.

The body and arms showed no strength whatever, the chest particularly being badly developed, narrow and weak. These people, unlike the Yambo, only remove one upper front tooth.

The women either shave their heads clean, which they do by scraping it with a piece of shell, or else they wear a coiffure like the men, plastered into a curly short horn. These people are absolutely hairless on the body. The women are only well formed when quite young, when they possess well-rounded and fairly daintily-chiselled limbs, with gracefully-modelled body and breasts, but when getting older they either become massive and un-shapely or else skinny and ancient-looking. They have five long cuts above the forehead as a tribal mark. A stick several inches long is generally thrust into the upper lip.

Men and women decorate the body with cicatrices of the parallel-angle pattern, the incisions being made with the point of a porcupine quill.

Men, women and children, when standing, often raise one foot upon the knee of the other leg, not un-like water-birds, and keep their balance steadily for a long time by resting against a spear or even without. These people are great fishermen, the entire village going out on fishing expeditions, when the noise of their shrieks while chasing the fish along the streamlets with their spears resounds for miles around. They generally send a canoe with three or four women in it up a small stream for a mile or so, the people in the skiff beating the water and chasing the fish in the direction of the crowd. All are waiting, spear in hand, and a regular pandemonium takes place when the fish arrive, and all the fishermen jump into the water, spearing to right and left with wonderful skill.

Huge crowds of fish are captured on these occasions, and when everybody has enough the fishers return singing to the village. Some also use a fish-hook made of bone, to the head of which a long line is attached, the other end being fastened to the fisherman's neck, but this is only used for the larger fish.

Nearly all the men wear two large ivory rings above the elbow, while the women are fond of wearing iron anklets on their lower extremities.

It was amusing to watch the excitement of these people one day when a crowd collected round my camp, and I was in the act of shaving. They thought that I was about to paint my whole body white when they saw me lathering my face, and their disappointment was great when I scraped off the soap again with a razor. There were many applications to obtain some of the soap for their own use, as they said it gave such a beautiful white. But as the bartering consisted of taking all the soap, and giving nothing in exchange for it, I was unable to satisfy their vanity.

In the evening the thermometer dropped as low as 65°, and my men felt the cold intensely.

The sight of Barakui village close by was quite weird at sunset. A great number of sharply-pointed huts stood against the low, brilliant, golden red horizon, above which delicate greenish tints gradually blended into the deep blue vault of the sky.

CHAPTER XXIV.

DURING the night we had a disaster which came near wrecking my entire expedition.

The fires which we lighted round our camp every evening had gone out owing to my men falling asleep. Towards midnight I was awakened by frantic neighing and braying, my horse and mules making desperate efforts to tear away the picket line.

We were encamped on finely-powdered, soft, alluvial soil. Not a tree nor a stone was to be found within a great distance. The pickets, although forced deep into the ground, offered but little resistance and did not hold. Before I was able to jump out of my camp-bed all the animals had stampeded in a body, and, as the night was dark, they were soon out of sight.

It was a disaster which could not very well be averted, but when I realized its likely consequences it gave me a great deal to reflect upon.

My men seized their rifles and ran after the animals, but they had gained such a long lead that they were unable to hear them or detect their direction. Still, they ran and ran like mad in all directions, trusting more to Providence than to personal judgment, as they, too, contemplated the plight in which we should find ourselves were the animals not recovered.

I remained alone in camp. On making a tour of

Nuer village.

inspection with a lantern, I discovered in the soft soil
the tracks of a lion. So in my mind I constructed the
entire explanation of what had happened. Evidently
the lion had sprung upon the mules and had been the
cause of the trouble.

The neighbouring villagers had been roused by the
noise in our camp, and I could just perceive in the
distance lots of ghost-like painted figures, spear in hand,
running to and fro near their huts ; while the distant
barking of dogs, towards the east, where the river was
about thirty miles away, made me suspect that the
animals had dashed in that direction.

I waited and waited for several hours and listened
for signals from my men. With the exception of suspicious cries from the native village, everything had
become quite calm again. In order that my men could
find their way back to my tent, which they could not
possibly distinguish at night, owing to its khaki colour
being the same as that of the ground, I fastened several
sticks together and hauled up the lantern, some height
above the tent, so as to form an improvised lighthouse.
I was rather anxious about them, as the natives round
us were not friendly, and although I was sure they
would not attack us in a body they might probably
intercept my men singly.

The morning came. Neither men nor mules had
reappeared, and when ten, eleven o'clock, and then noon
had gone by, and no one had returned, I began to feel
rather uncomfortable. No help could be expected from
the local natives. Quite the contrary ; now that they
saw me alone in camp they became threatening. I was
too far from the river to convey the loads there, make
a raft, and proceed by water, and this disaster, I quite

realized, meant that I must abandon all my notes, photographs, instruments, most of my rifles and ammunition, and make for the stream with only what provisions I could carry on my back. At best, this was not a bright look-out in such a hot, desolate country.

In the afternoon one of my men, with bleeding feet and half dead with fatigue, returned to camp with the sad news that he had lost his companions and had seen no signs of the animals. Two more men returned later, bringing a similar account. They, too, were worn and thirsty, as they had found no water the whole day.

At sunrise I had followed for some distance the traces of blood from the spot where the mules had been tethered, which left no doubt that the lion had jumped upon, and probably clung to, one of the animals as they stampeded.

The mishap could not have happened in a worse place. The only water we had at this camp was from an effluent of the Baro, and the stagnant water was swarming with large worms and black germs of great size. The air in the daytime was so hot and full of dust that one's face and clothes were black with it when a slight breeze raised clouds of it. There was no shade of any kind, and it was impossible to remain under the tent, as the moment one got under cover the heat was suffocating.

The sarcastic hilarity of the natives who came to laugh at one's misfortunes was irritating, and their absolute refusal to help us to carry my heavy baggage to the stream on any account whatever, did not add to my happiness. They rejected with scorn presents I offered them, and by the unabashed manner they circled round my camp in force I suspected that they were under the impression they would soon possess all I owned. To complete one's trials, a native musician with a lyre came to fill the air with incoherent and discordant notes like a morose child's three-finger exercises, improvising songs about us which created a good deal of mirth among his tribesmen. The temptation to smash this fellow's head as well as his tortoiseshell musical instrument was almost unconquerable, and it was only by some pieces of cotton wool which I stuffed tight into my ears that this man's life was eventually spared.

Also, luckily for him, hundreds of villagers—indeed, the whole population, men, women and children—brandishing spears and shrieking wildly, spearing fish as they went along, came rushing along the banks of the putrid stream, while a canoe in the water drove the fish towards the crowd in the manner already described in a previous chapter.

It was a picturesque sight. Only I was not quite certain whether this fishing expedition was not really intended as a blind in order to attack us unexpectedly. The two or three men who had returned to my camp seemed anxious and took to their rifles. I handed ammunition over to them, in order to be ready for any emergency. I, too, loaded two of my magazine rifles and kept them ready, carefully watching events.

The natives had decked themselves in all their finery to go on this particular fishing expedition, and it looked to me more like their war-paint than the attire usually worn when slaying fish. Some of the men had as many as a dozen white and black feathers sticking up straight upon the head, and small sticks thrust through the ears and in the lips. Among the few women who were dressed at all, some wore small fringes of hide in front of the lower portion of the body. Others, more elaborately dressed, donned a little skirt, three inches long, worn very low and going all round the body ; while one or two of the more stylish ladies were adorned with a leather triangular tail behind, reaching down to the knee. They seemed proud of this style of dress.

Whether because the people saw that we had taken to our rifles, or for other reasons—the fishing that day seemed to be only near my camp—after a great deal of excitement the Nuer returned to their village. Daylight had by this time waned. The sun was getting towards the horizon, but there were no signs of the mules nor of most of my men.

At last, after dark, a blind boy belonging to a different tribe from that of Barakui came into my camp to say that my mules had gone across the Baro. His village, he told us, was along the stream, and he had heard the noise of the animals galloping by and going into the water. There was irony of fate for you ! That a blind boy should be the only one who knew where the mules were. It all seemed so extraordinary to me that I did not at first believe him, and I suspected this to be a ruse to ambush us. I asked him how he had found his way to my camp. He told me that his village men had brought him close by, and were there still hiding. They were on unfriendly terms with the Nuer of the village near which we encamped, and if I chose to go out to them we could arrange to have the mules brought back. I sent two of my men with this boy, in order to get his villagers safely to my tent. In fact, after a long conference, they said they would endeavour to capture the animals on the other side of the stream and bring them back. A handsome present was promised the moment the animals were handed back to me, but not before. They all swore the animals had swum across the river and gone over to the north side, some thirty to forty miles from my camp.

The next morning another of my men returned, who had followed the tracks of the mules, and he had arrived at the spot on the river where they had crossed.

The entire next day elapsed, and I had already made up my mind to send for relief, either to Gambela or Nasser, when shortly after sunset my heart bounded with joy. In the distance I perceived two more of my men and six mules driven by a horde of Abigar. When they reached camp—the animals were in a terrible condition —I took them over again. The natives told us how they had captured them eight or ten miles north of the Baro.

In a moment of exuberance I offered the Abigar chief and his men a substantial sum of silver, about five pounds sterling worth, which they refused with contempt, as they said that was no present to offer, and they did not know what to do with it. I told them if they brought the other mules they should have as much again, but they refused.

What did they want ? I asked. I would certainly give it to them if I could afford it. Upon which the chief said he wanted two brass wire bracelets for himself, and one brass wire bracelet for each of his men, some thirty altogether. Not only did I give them what they demanded, but I gave the chief eight brass bracelets and two extra to every other man, with promises of giving as many again if they brought in all the other animals. They were delighted, and so was I, because in this transaction not only should I get my mules back, but I should save at least nine pounds ten shillings out of the ten pounds which I had offered as a reward, and as there is no way of replenishing one's exchequer in Central Africa, I needed all the cash I carried.

Shortly after, another mule was recovered in a worn condition close to camp, where it had found its way, and, later, another straggled in. I had now eight animals back, all so tired that they could hardly move. Two or three of them were badly wounded, as in stampeding and carrying away the picket rope they must have fallen, and had been kicked or dragged along by the others in their frantic flight.

On March 16th, the next day, long before sunrise, I was up waiting for more mules to come in. The horse and another mule were perceived at some distance straggling in towards the camp, and I was in hopes that some of the other mules would soon follow the horse, round whom they always collected. Later, an Abigar ran in to say that all the animals had recrossed the river to the south side, and the villagers were trying to capture them. In fact, towards noon, much to my delight, the remainder of the animals were led back into my camp. One of them had been badly mauled, evidently by a lion, a good portion of its shoulder having been bitten off. The animal seemed in great pain. Before the accident this was, of course, the best mule I possessed. I had not the courage to kill it. It, however, died on the march a day or two later.

There were great rejoicings in camp, and the Abigar could not restrain their happiness—they simply burst into boisterous rapture—when more than quadruple the

Nuer, the long-legged people.

number of bracelets they had been promised were handed to them, with an extra roll of wire to divide among themselves.

The natives of the Barakui village, a mixed population of Abigar and Nuer, used interesting harpoons for fishing purposes, the barbed head of iron being removable from the rod (some six and a half to seven feet long), in which it was fixed. To hold it in position there was a piece of leather at the top, while a string which went as far as the other end of the rod was attached to the iron head, where another string could easily be added. Straight, conical-headed fishing spears were also used by them, as well as vicious quadrangular-headed spears, used both for fishing and fighting. These quadrangular spears had as many as eighteen to twenty double sets of small corkscrew-shaped barbs, at the end of which two large barbs in a reverse direction were placed, which produced a terrible wound. It was really amazing to notice on what scientific lines these savage people constructed their spear-heads, in order to establish in them not only a vibration while being thrown, but a high revolving speed while going through the air.

The water was so foul at this camp, and the heat so intense, that although my animals were done up with fatigue I loaded them again in the afternoon. I recrossed the Barakui stream from the north bank, on which we had camped, to the south bank. A huge crowd of Abigar and Nuer—who had by now become fairly friendly—came to watch our departure. They were extremely timid and frightened at everything we did. Their fear of mules and horses was curious in people who are brave enough to go and attack lions and elephants with no other weapons than spears. No sooner had we moved away than these people pounced like scavengers upon all the empty tins, the pieces of torn paper and broken glass we had left behind.

We passed a large settlement—some two hundred huts—with neat circles of pegs to which the natives tied their cattle at night. We saw here a different architecture for the huts. Instead of the smaller *zeribas*, or kraals, enclosed within a fence, each abode was quite separate, constructed of cylindrical walls of reeds somewhat higher than those of the Yambo, six to seven feet high, with high roofs made of the sections of a cone, generally seven in number, laid over one another, and forming a series of steps in the grass thatching. Many of the better huts had a small circular fixed screen in front of the door, the only aperture in their structures. The doors were here much higher and wider than in the Yambo country. The long spears of the men were left sticking in the ground just outside the doors of habitations.

We marched over a wide, treeless, flat country, so trampled upon by elephants in the wet season that thousands of deep holes—their footmarks—covered the whole country, and were a great nuisance—in fact, quite a danger—for my animals. These holes delayed us considerably, as they were often covered with grass, and my animals were constantly tumbling into them.

We had no experiences worthy of notice that day, nor did we see much game, except two herds of large red antelopes and flocks of herons striding majestically about, with their red beaks, black wings, white chest and a long red bag dangling from the neck. In the heat of the sun they spread their spacious wings and kept the head under the shade thus produced. They remained in that position sometimes for hours, generally perched on the top of high sandheaps or anthills, thousands of which are to be found all over this country.

Towards sunset we halted by the side of the Dumbiorau water, stagnant and quite as foul as the Barakui river. This place was notable only for the peculiar whitish-yellow banks, on which footmarks of all kinds of wild animals could be seen. During the evening many antelopes came to the water and one or two lions. We left early in the morning, and along the water-course we saw hundreds of hippopotami and crocodiles. We had quite an amusing time with them. Some of the hippopotami were gigantic, and at one or two villages the natives ran after us, entreating us to fire on them, as they relished the meat considerably. When in the water they were not so easy to kill with the small calibre bullets I possessed. It was only when you hit them in the eye or behind the ear that the wound was mortal at all. However, we got some.

The river Dura, which we next met, flowed, where we crossed it, at a depth of about four feet, from east to west, and turned northwards near a village, eventually finding an outlet into the Baro. From nine o'clock, when we crossed the stream, we marched over flat, uninhabited country, but in the afternoon we arrived at Jhiun, a large village of domed sheds flimsily constructed of reeds.

The way they build these huts is by thrusting the reeds into the ground in a circle, and then bending over the reeds until they meet, where they are tied into a bunch.

I saw at this village a native forge, quite interesting

to me, as the double bellows typical of this region were identical with the primitive skin bellows used in Tibet in Central Asia. They were made of a skin with two parallel sticks, which formed an opening to let in the air, and were closed again, when filled, by means of the hand. The channels of the two bellows were, of course, joined, and when blown alternately, they produced a continuous draught. Long rudimentary pincers, a hammer and a dish of cold water, in which to temper the steel of their spear-heads after it had been subjected to heat, were all the implements used by the local blacksmiths.

Towards two o'clock in the afternoon we reached another large settlement called Tajao, on the east side of a big lake, separated by a narrow dune from the Baro. The Adjouba river, which at this point flows into the Baro, is usually called on English maps Pibor, which is a mistake, a mere mispronunciation of Pibaro, or tributary of the Baro. The Sobat is merely a continuation of the Baro. It changes its name west of the place where the River Akobo, then called Adjouba (Pibor), coming from the south, joins the Baro.

After an interminable stretch over burnt grass, which made us black all over with smuts and ashes, we arrived at Jungmir, or Ajungmir. The Baro here flows due west after passing the lake—or, to be accurate, marsh —on its south bank, separated from the river by a dune two hundred yards across.

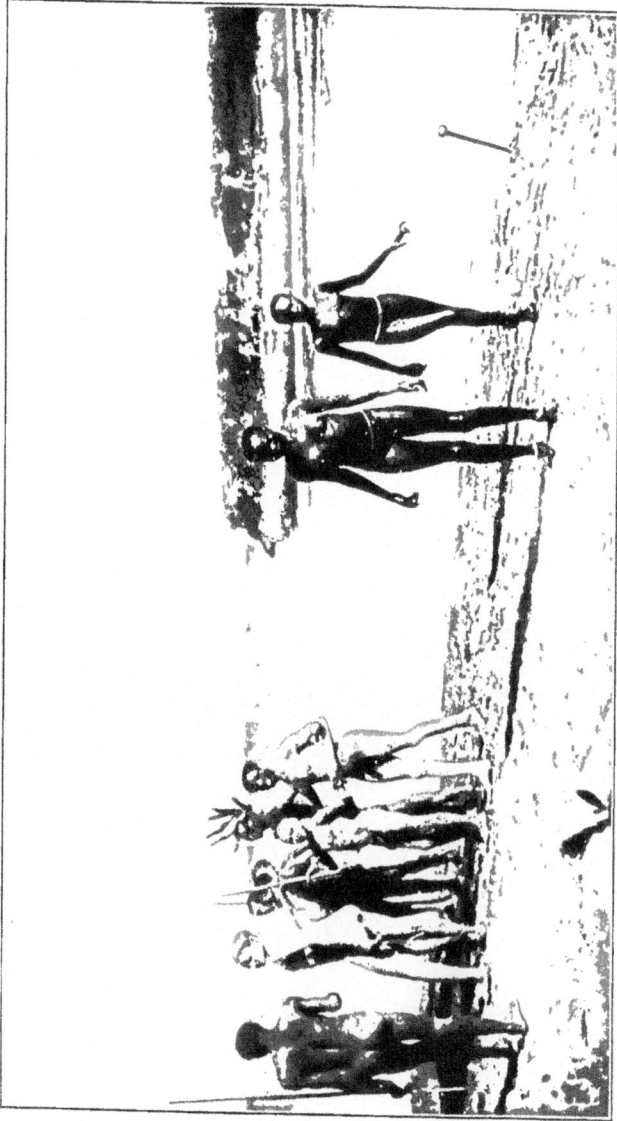

Nuer men and women.

CHAPTER XXV.

THE population of Jungmir consisted mostly of Abigar, a somewhat more powerfully built and handsomer race than the Nuer. Over the left shoulder and under the right arm the men wore a bandolier made of beads, or else of rope, with many amulets attached to it. Where beads were obtainable, they sometimes wore a mere string of black and white beads as a bandolier, and I have seen women wear two of these strings, one passed under each arm.

In the way of feminine attire, they attached to the waist at the back a small square of leopard skin, the triangular tail worn by the Nuer women not being at all fashionable in this portion of the country. One or two strings of white and blue, or white and black, beads were worn round the waist, or else a rope with a knot behind, the same as with the Nuers, with whom they have many customs in common. The cylindrical piece of wood attached to this rope and sticking out prominently in front was also to be seen among the Abigar. Some men wore a string of beads in the hair. Armlets of string, with pieces of wood attached to them, were carried as a preventive of disease.

The Abigars occasionally use a bow, but no arrows —which seems an astonishing statement, but is nevertheless true—the bows being of an elaborate shape, with two end coils, the entire bow, quite short and clumsy-looking, being wound round with an iron band, and the string itself not attached to the bow, but to two strings fastened across the two end coils. When I examined the bow, it showed no flexibility, nor did the man who possessed it carry any arrows, the reason being that this highly ornamental weapon has merely been devised in order to ward off the blows of war-clubs, and not to propel arrows—which are quite unknown to the Abigar —through the air.

The women here did not wear quite such long skirts of beads as in the Nuer country, the length of the skirts among the Abigar ladies never reaching a greater length than two inches. The women were greatly ornamented with cicatrices, especially from the umbilicus to the breasts, where I counted as many as twenty-four parallel lines in two sets of twelve each. Two double semi-circles were sometimes to be seen near the breasts.

The men were frequently ornamented with four lines of cicatrices in a curve, usually following the shape of the shoulder-blades, and six lines of heavy dots lower down near the waist behind.

These Abigar, although structurally better built than the Nuer, possessed badly-made skulls, much flattened on the top and elongated backwards, the foreheads slanting, and bumps lower down in the back portion of the skull quite abnormally developed. The development of the brow was considerable and the upper eyelid heavy.

These people had a peculiar way of ornamenting the ears, sticking seven elongated beads like small darts all along the outer circle of the ear and a small row of beads along the inner curve. Bandoliers were quite the fashion here also, as well as ivory armlets and heavy iron bracelets.

Half an hour after we had started from our camp we came to a troublesome stream, only five yards wide, but which gave us no end of bother. We had here again some of the soft sticky mud which we had encountered in some of the Abyssinian rivers. It was impossible to take the laden mules across, for they got frightened as they sank, and generally ended by throwing the loads over into the slush. So all the animals had to be unloaded, and each package carried over on men's heads, a labour of great difficulty, as the men, too, had a hard struggle to get across. It took us the best part of four hours to get over those five yards.

On the other side of this swampy stream we had a terribly hot march over burnt-up country. Thousands of birds were to be seen, especially near the river, and the caravan caused great excitement among them as we passed by. There were again large Nuer settlements, many of which had been abandoned and new settlements built in their vicinity. The huts had large conical roofs, and I noticed one or two the architecture of which resembled that of Galla houses, the walls being formed by solid wooden pillars close together, the interstices filled with mud. The walls of most of the smaller huts were of reeds, the door only being enclosed in a square erection of dried mud. The aperture itself was shaped like an entire oval.

The old military post of Nasser, on the south side of the Sobat, had been abandoned, and a new one called Torfot in a somewhat healthier position had been established further up the river.

The post of Torfot, where I arrived in the afternoon,

consisted of a number of thatched mud huts, with two small gable-roofed buildings for the thirty-one Sudanese soldiers and their native officer, by name Hamdan Effendi, who acted also in the civil capacity of *mamur*.

Letters from the Sirdar and the Governor-General of the Upper Nile Province had been waiting here for me for some months, and when I arrived I received a cordial reception from the native officer in charge.

The Sirdar most kindly placed at my disposal an iron boat which had been sent up the river, and also an escort of Sudanese soldiers. The Sirdar had generously offered me an escort of twenty-five men and a native officer to accompany me ; but I had no opportunity of availing myself of the offer, for which, however, I felt deeply grateful to the Governor-General of the Sudan.

Every possible kindness was showered upon me, owing to orders received from Khartoum, and my mules being extremely tired, and my men also, I accepted the iron boat in which to send my baggage and most of my men down the river as far as the Nile under an escort of a few Sudanese soldiers. As far as I was concerned, I continued my journey overland with my animals and only a few light loads, as I wished to visit several tribes both on the north and on the south side of the Sobat.

Torfot, although higher on the banks of the river than most other places on the Sobat, was swarming with mosquitoes of all sizes, insects of all kinds, innumerable flies, and after sunset with legions of moths and nocturnal aerial life of every description. This state of things was troublesome at mealtime. Drowning insects covered the surface of liquids in one's tumbler or cup, and one could not afford to throw away time after time what one possessed in the way of food and drinks. The insects gave the drinks a peculiar flavour, but this was preferable to the incessant dipping in of one's servant's fingers for the removal of the floating creatures. Of the food, too, one generally ate more than one thought or knew, in more ways than one. I was made quite ill at Torfot by crushing between my teeth a large fetid-smelling beetle which left a sickening taste in my throat and palate for some hours after. In breathing, too, even through the nose, and when one guards oneself against opening the mouth, mosquitoes and midges soon find their way in. At night, while having one's dinner, it was necessary to keep a light a long way off from the table. Insects would then be attracted in that direction and allow comparative peace.

The mosquitoes were so numerous and troublesome that even under a stout mosquito netting it was impossible to sleep at night. Although we were stung thousands of times all over the body, at this place and others upon the river, none of us got malarial fever. Yet these were the very mosquitoes which were supposed to be the great carriers of malaria.

On March 19th I rode away from Torfot with all my mules. My Somali boy, with most of my men, was despatched by river in charge of the baggage in the boat.

There were many tobacco plantations along the river banks, the Nuer going in extensively for the cultivation of tobacco. Thousands of crocodiles drowsed open-mouthed along the banks, and innumerable hippopotami stuck their noses and ears above the water. The natives, in order to prevent the latter from climbing up the banks and destroying their plantations, make scarecrows of straw, either representing human figures or else mere bundles of sticks dangling in the wind from posts on the highest point of the bank. I killed a large crocodile that day and one or two smaller ones.

As we were nearing Nasser, I came to a great many huts and villages on both banks, generally in groups of two or three fenced off within a reed enclosure. Again we had the conical roofs in parallel horizontal sections, here somewhat smaller and numbering from nine to ten steps in the gradation of cones. The reeds of the lowest layer projected far out, so as to prevent the rain striking the wall. Like Yambo huts, these possessed a small private courtyard, with a roughly-constructed shelf, whereon we deposited gourd vessels and grain pots. Large plaited baskets were used for grain.

A curious institution were the roofless summer huts. Many huts had the interior side of the walls plastered over with mud, and one of the chief characteristics of these particular Nuer tribes near Nasser was that the outer wall (five feet high) of their huts was plastered outside for only a quarter, or at the most a third, of the depth, from the top portion directly under the roof. This, they told me, was in order to prevent leakage in rainy weather from water which might come from the roof. A few huts, however, I saw which had the entire wall plastered over both on the interior and exterior faces.

There was a slight difference in the type of these Nuer, and they did not generally follow the custom of smearing themselves all over with ashes like the tribes further east. It was not uncommon, however, to see men painted white all over, except for a dash of grease upon the chest, which gave a beautiful black shine to the undyed skin, and a half moon by the side of it. The face and neck were painted of a brilliant red colour —quite a ghastly practice. Another fashion, common among these people, was that of smearing the body with butter when it was not dyed with ashes. The skin became then beautifully polished. The reason all these tribes plastered their hair into a point was merely to remove the natural kinks and curls and render it quite straight. Also, of course, to bleach it.

I arrived in the evening at the abandoned post of Nasser on the left bank of the river. Neat mud houses and huts had been erected—now abandoned—as well as some earthworks for the protection of the post. The place commanded the elbow of the river, being situated in the central point of the angle. It was an unhealthy post, the damp heat being quite suffocating even on the dryest days of the dry season. The river formed a kind of delta, with an elongated island in the centre just in front of Nasser.

We left early the next morning, at 5.30, passing the stream Uarkan *en route*, and towards 11.30 we passed a small island about three hundred yards long in the centre of the river, the course of the stream being extremely tortuous in this portion, and describing extensive circles. Along the river banks were high reeds. The country further inland was barren, but after a march of four hours west of Nasser we saw a few trees along the right bank of the Sobat.

A good deal of time was wasted that morning, as on the march I discovered that one of my best mules had strayed, and I had to detail four men to go and look for it the way we had come.

Naked natives ran about along the river banks,

greeting us with their typical salutation, similar to the gesture we usually make when we push people away, and calling out " bahve, bahve." These people were timid, and bolted whenever we got near. Only a few times were we able to approach them, but after they had got over their first fright they seemed jolly enough.

Like all other Nuer they smeared themselves with white stuff. Their type was finer than that of the Nuer I had seen further east, their features having greatly improved by relationship with neighbouring and more civilized tribes, such as the Adgira and the Fallangue, but principally with the Shiluk, a dominant race, formerly very powerful, and now found mainly along the Bahr-el-Ghazal and White Nile. This mixed type was more intelligent, and possessed a stronger physique than the purer Nuer we had so far met. As a tribal mark, these people displayed five cuts upon the forehead extending from temple to temple, and they wore similar ornaments to other Nuer.

Many of them had large swellings on the temples and at the back of the ears, where the lowest horizontal cicatrice of the forehead ended, and also on the shoulders and breasts, where cicatrices had been caused with a hot implement. These swellings, I think, were not intentional, but merely produced by poisoning of the blood in individuals suffering from leprosy or serious venereal complaints.

The people of the Adgira tribe on the Pibor river were in themselves somewhat repulsive, with faces extraordinarily flat, as if they had been compressed artificially into so ugly a shape. They possessed fairly long beards. Their shoulders and breasts were decorated with cicatrices in concentric arcs of a circle, going over the shoulders from the breasts to the shoulder-blades. These cicatrice marks had been made with a red-hot iron.

The most characteristic instrument of these Adgira was one which I noticed near the stream, a curious harpoon and bow combined, of great length, some ten feet long, with a barbed hook at one end.

The Nuer of this region were somewhat more hairy, the hair of the head particularly being much longer and finer in texture than that of the other Nuer, but in their case, too, it was dyed of a bright red colour.

The vanity of these people was amazing. I saw two men with brass bracelets so tight round the forearm that the circulation had almost ceased, and the hands had got swollen and almost atrophied. In two cases, which came under my observation, these bracelets had actually cut into the flesh at the wrist, and when I asked the owners why they did not remove them, as the hand was getting absolutely paralyzed, they said they would rather lose the use of their hands altogether than remove such a becoming ornament. They said it had been there from their earliest days and they would stick to it.

There is no accounting for people's tastes, and fashions in all countries are responsible for much idiotic suffering.

CHAPTER XXVI.

THE river was simply swarming with crocodiles. We had a heavy thunderstorm during the afternoon and another equally bad in the night. The rain came down in torrents. Late in the evening the lost mule was recovered and brought back to camp.

On March 21st I travelled over absolutely flat, barren country, the soil consisting of dried mud much cut up into huge cracks. There were only a few Nuer settlements, and isolated huts here and there with walls made of logs of wood plastered inside the hut with mud. Some of these huts had an additional porch over the door, so that a double aperture had to be gone through on entering the dwelling.

After four hours' marching we came to a lot of stunted *gherar* trees, their stems quite red, having been rendered so by the grass fires. My animals were faring badly, as away from the stream there was no grazing, the grass which had not been burnt by fire being absolutely dried up by the sun.

Outside the huts were frequently to be noticed heavily built platforms, where thatching straw and reeds were spread to dry, and where pots, pans and gourd vessels were kept. As we went along, the larger houses were built of logs of wood close together, well plastered with mud inside. The roofs were conical, and in the interior was a circle of pillars supporting the roof. Within this circle was another circle, with a raised edge, and within this third circle a fireplace, the ashes of which were carefully collected, to be subsequently used in the Nuer toilette.

We arrived at Shwai at four o'clock in the afternoon, after a long tedious march, with nothing interesting to see. We did not follow the river bank, as it made a great détour here. We cut our way across country, only touching on the stream twice during the whole march.

The doors of the huts generally faced west, but sometimes north. When facing north, a small peephole was generally found towards the west, especially in the bigger houses. These Nuer collect honey, but not in large quantities.

At Gogognar (Gouemiar on Marchand's map), about half way along our march that day, we found good grazing in a low land, with fine, fresh, green grass. Here there were hundreds of cattle belonging to Nuer.

In order to rest my mules as much as possible, I had sent all my provisions, as well as my tents and other baggage, by the steel *felucca*, and had fixed Shwai as the *rendezvous*, where we of the caravan were to strike the river again. When I had last seen the *felucca* early in the morning the wind was fair, and I expected that she would reach the place long before we did.

Unfortunately the wind fell, and we waited anxiously for the arrival of the provisions. Our eyes were strained to watch on the horizon-line for the white sail to appear ; but night came, and with it the usual swarms of mosquitoes to devour us, but no *felucca* was in sight. We were ravenously hungry, and we had nothing whatever to eat. We lighted a grass fire to while away the time and smoke ourselves so as to keep off mosquitoes. Once or twice we thought we heard voices upon the stream, but they turned out to be only those of natives fishing in their dug-outs.

We spent a wretched night, my men having eaten nothing for two days and I for twenty-four hours, during which time we had marched over forty miles on foot in the broiling sun, as the soil was so cut up by huge cracks that riding was uncomfortable, the animals continually tumbling down.

To make things worse during the night, we had a terrific thunderstorm, which blew down the only small shelter tent I was using, and which soaked us to the marrow of our bones.

It was not till March 22nd, at 8 a.m., that the *felucca* arrived. We immediately set about preparing a hearty meal, which we much needed.

From the spot where we had camped we saw a good-sized island in mid-stream about half a mile above Shwai, a little village of six huts or so. Another elongated island was also found further down-stream beyond Shwai.

I started again with my mules at ten o'clock, this time taking provisions to provide for eventualities. The country was, as usual, flat and uninteresting, with patches of good grass here and there, and some *gherar* trees. Any number of antelopes were to be seen. At 1.35 in the afternoon we came to Yakuaje (Marchand's Yakouetch), a village of about three dozen plastered huts belonging to a Denka tribe, the Fallanghe, as they call themselves. At this point we again encountered the stream, having left it at Shwai, from which place it described a great détour northwards. A small island stood in mid-stream in front of Yakuaje. The huts of these people were similar in construction to Nuer huts, only larger, with plastered walls upon an interior frame of wood and mud, and with a conical roof in eight or ten concentric sections. They seemed to have no special rule here for the location of the door, and it generally opened on the side found most convenient in their relations with the inhabitants of other huts. Each hut had four peep-holes around its walls, so that a view could be obtained on all sides from the interior. Each hut possessed a sort of fenced-off courtyard, subdivided into two sections, one where the out-of-door cooking was done, the other used as a store for building materials. Inside the hut itself, in the centre, were some wooden planks, upon which the people slept.

We were now one day's journey from Abwong, and we were in the country of the Aiwal tribe, people who in many ways resembled the Nuer, and who also smeared themselves all over with a mixture of cinders from sheep and cow dung. It is true that all these tribes indulge in this practice in part to protect themselves against mosquitoes, but I think that the primary motive is merely vanity.

Like the Nuer, these people use five parallel cuts upon the forehead as a tribal mark. The women plaster the hair on the top of the head with red mud, leaving curls at the side of the face. The men are fond of wearing a crown of shells encircling the tuft of hair at the back of the head. The temples and the greater portion of the skull are shaved. Heavy bracelets are worn, and, as among the last tribes of Nuer we had visited, these people wore rings and bracelets of an inconvenient shape, with two long projecting points sticking out in representation of the horns of oxen.

These people have a few primitive implements, such as a small shovel and an axe with a triangular blade. The primitive pipes, with a cooling chamber for the smoke near the mouthpiece, are also to be noticed.

Inside their huts there is nothing in the way of furniture, the few implements being stored under the small porch at the entrance of the hut. In the abode, when one becomes accustomed to the dim light, a central circle is visible where the white ashes for decorating the body are kept, and a raised border on which at night are placed two or more scooped-out planks of the roughest description, which they use as beds. Only in one or two huts did I see an oblong tripod with short legs used as a stool, and in another hut I saw a four-legged seat cut out of a single piece of wood. Outside, where the people spend most of their time, I noticed several arm and knee rests, which the people use in order to be comfortable while sitting upon the ground. The only other article of furniture which I could perceive in my search was a small wooden head-pillow, or rather neck-rest.

In this village I paid a visit to the blacksmith, a person who appeared quite *abruti*, as the French so exactly describe people who combine degeneracy, idiocy and rascality in their personal appearance ; he showed, however, some dexterity in sharpening spear-heads like razors by hammering them, although his only tools were a coarse hammer and an anvil.

Within the outer enclosure of each hut were numerous pegs to which goats and dogs—which swarm in Aiwal villages—were tied at night, as well as great numbers of oxen and cows.

Soon after leaving the village, next day, we were charged by three or four hundred of these half-wild oxen, and we had difficulty in keeping them at bay. These charges were a frequent experience in our march across the Nuer and Aiwal country, and I was always amazed at the pluck of my mules on these occasions. They never stampeded. When they saw the animals approach they formed a circle, placing their heads together, and using their heels freely and effectually upon the attacking animals when they came too near.

On the opposite side of the stream, only about two hundred yards from us, we saw a big herd of giraffes.

As the heat had been so great during the march, and as I had walked a great deal owing to the bad condition of the ground, I went, notwithstanding the crocodiles, to have a refreshing bath in the stream at sunset. It was a stupid thing to do, I know, and the consequences nearly turned out more serious than I expected ; but life would not be worth living unless one occasionally did stupid things.

I selected, of course, a place where the river was shallow, and it amused me to watch how sharp-witted crocodiles were. They waited till I had smeared myself all over with soap—especially the face—and whenever I stooped to pour water on my head, a number of them, eight or ten, quickly advanced in a semicircle round me, only just the tip of their noses being visible on the surface. They were getting nearer and nearer without making the slightest noise, and at a moment when a lot of soap had got into my eyes, and I was trying to wash it off, they had advanced to within two or three yards of me.

Crocodiles are timid brutes, and it was sufficient to

keep your eye on them or pretend to throw something, or shout, and they would duck under water and disappear. They soon peeped out of the water again and advanced once more, waiting for a moment when they could get you unawares. Within a few feet of the place where I was the stream was quite deep. When I had been in the water some minutes the number of crocodiles had rapidly increased. One can always tell by the bubbles of air coming up to the surface, and also by the series of angles quickly reproduced upon the surface, and formed by the nose of the crocodile, as it moves along, slightly below the surface of the water. I deemed it wiser to come out and finish my bath in a safer place.

When I got up on the high bank of the stream and looked down into the water, I fully realized how foolish I had been, as a regular swarm of crocodiles had collected. The river was simply full of them, and we saw hundreds and hundreds every day. In this portion of the river crocodiles seemed particularly numerous and of quite impressive proportions. They were, however, most dangerous to humans when out of the water, where they could strike and stun them with their powerful tail, and then drag them in.

Large antelopes were to be seen in great numbers, and elephants, lions and ostriches were common.

The Aiwal, perhaps, were not quite so tall as the pure Nuer, but they possessed finer features. They were slightly more intelligent, and certainly more friendly towards us than the tribes further east, although they, too, refused to sell anything whatever to us. It is possibly intermarriage with the Anuak or other tribes to the south which has somewhat benefited the type in this region.

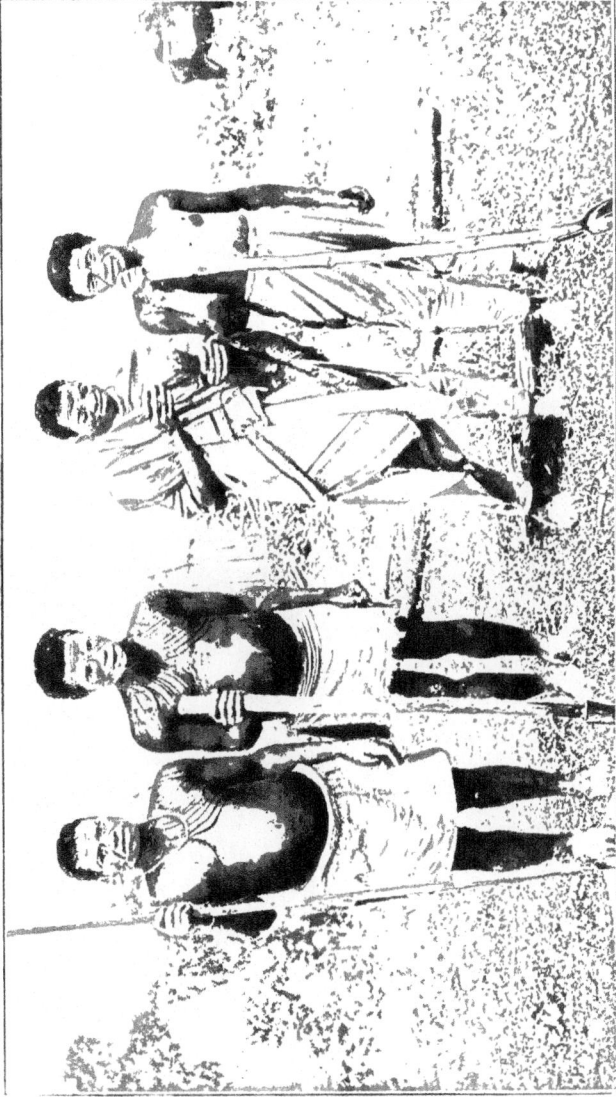

Anuak men decorated with cicatrices upon the chest and shoulders.

During the night we had another terrific rainstorm, which blew down my tent several times, and eventually smashed my tent poles. Rain came down in sheets, and we and our things got drenched. The heavy rain made travelling unpleasant, as the sticky mud made marching heavy for my mules, although most of them carried nothing on their backs. We covered great distances daily. We kept sinking in mud and slush up to our knees all the time. The country was barren, with no decent grazing for the animals ; only here and there were patches of *gherar* trees so close together that they tore our clothes when we forced our way through. Then we came to more interminable plains, with not a blade of grass. Several of my mules were taken ill, and the finest animal I possessed, which seemed to be in intense pain, collapsed, and we could not make him get up again. I left two men to take care of him, but they joined us again in the afternoon, bringing with them the severed tail of the animal as a proof of his death. Another mule also collapsed, and in an hour or so was dead.

The heat was so terrific that day that I had to halt for a few hours, and here again I had sufficient evidence of the cruelty of Abyssinians, my own men, of course. A pariah Yambo—a wretched leper—had attached himself to my caravan, picking up in camp whatever food he could get. I never had the courage to drive him away, and eventually the Abyssinians got the poor fellow to do most of the hard work for them. To my amazement and disgust, I found that my cook had entrusted him with the making of the paste of our daily bread, which he did with his cramped and sore fingers. Of course, the bread was that day thrown away, and my Abyssinians received a fine lecture. During the night, when I was lying down, I heard angry cries, followed by pitiful moans. Upon investigating the cause of the trouble, I discovered the poor leper lying helpless upon the ground kicked on the head and body by the cowardly Abyssinians. The Abyssinians were severely punished for it, and to prevent a revenge being taken upon the wretched Yambo, I had to keep him all night at the entrance of my tent.

Lepers, as you know, have a most peculiar, sickly, typical odour, which can be detected at a great distance. This new arrangement was inconvenient enough, as I could not sleep owing to the offensive smell. I was afraid to let him out of my reach, as the Abyssinians had sworn to kill him as soon as opportunity offered.

One day, as we were marching, the Yambo remained behind. The Abyssinians, seizing the opportune moment, pounced upon him. By a mere chance I suspected that something was up, and I went back upon my steps. I found the poor Yambo badly knocked about, and saved him just as they were about to cut his throat.

From that moment I never let him out of my sight. The poor fellow gave me endless pain. He was shedding bitter tears all the time, and was so depressed that he would eat nothing. He had made up his mind to die of starvation. Twice I had to rescue him from the river where he had thrown himself in order to get drowned ; although I must say that for a man who wanted to commit suicide he showed no reluctance whatever to being saved. I asked him why he let me take him out of the water so soon, if he really intended to die. He said that as soon as he had jumped into the water he was afraid the crocodiles would bite him, and

Author's three pet ostriches, and leper camp follower.

he was glad to be pulled out again. He did not mind
dying—oh, no !—but crocodiles hurt so when they bite !
After these baths he generally received a good fill of rice
and butter. He then forgot the idea of death by starvation ; indeed he did ! I noticed that his suicidal
mania was getting worse and worse, and there were
prospects of further plunges into the water, so that,
divining his thoughts, I seized him one day by the neck,
shook him violently, and made him understand that next
time he wanted to commit suicide I would see that it
was carried out properly, and that he did not come to
the surface again, which cured him once for all of this
bad habit.

Well, I had to be patient with him, but really he was
an infliction upon me that I did not deserve. With
moans and groans he would daily repeat to me the
history of his life—and heaven knows how many
histories of other people's lives I had heard before !
His was quite pathetic, what there was of it. He was
evidently an outcast in his own tribe, and had been
discarded by a young lady whom he loved dearly, and
who loved him much, he thought, but who married
somebody else who possessed more cows and oxen.

Such ways of young ladies have been known even
outside the Yambo country.

CHAPTER XXVII.

THE Aiwal are not unlike the Shiluk, whom we shall meet presently on our journey. They speak the Shiluk tongue, whereas the Anuak have a different language, although some tribes of the latter speak a sort of composite language of Shiluk and Anuak. They appeared to me a mixture of Nuer and Denka.

Near Abwong there is a local legend that the Nuer, the Shiluk and the Denka all came from one father, who was the happy possessor of one cow, a calf (female) and a boat. When the old man died, he left the cow to the Nuer, the calf to the Denka, and the boat to the Shiluk. The Shiluk was satisfied, and went away from the others ; while the Denka and the Nuer went to war, each son declaring that the father had meant the big cow to go to him ; and up to the present day those tribes are still more or less at war, the question not having yet been settled.

The Denka are sulky and sullen people. A Denka will not rise to salute you when you enter his hut, but will remain sitting down motionless and silent, and so will all the other inmates of the hut. After some moments, the words " Ba uti ? " are uttered (" From what village do you come ? ")—" uti " meaning " village," and " ba," " where." The answer a stranger gives is merely " Hehn." Then the host, after a long pause, inquires " Shinnin ? " (" In good health ? ") ; to which another answer of " Hehn " is expected, and this is all the conversation that takes place.

It is difficult to get information from these people, as they are suspicious and never speak the truth, but try to mislead you, or evade your questions. An ulterior motive is always suspected even in the most trivial matters.

The chieftainship among Denka is hereditary, and descends from father to son ; but there is a great deal of individual independence about these people, and, except in time of war, the chief has but a nominal power among them. More important than the chief with these people is the *baign*—a wise man, almost a human deity, who is well in with the gods above. He is a sort of magician and medicine-man, and provides remedies in the shape of peculiar roots and pieces of wood dipped in water. He is not to be confused with the *tiet*, a kind of medicine-woman, who makes incantations and supplies people with small pieces of wood worn as charms or amulets. The *tiet*, who is always a woman, prays to Denka deities by squatting down and murmuring words that no other Denka understands.

Quarrels and rows of any kind are referred for settlement to the *baign*. Like the chieftainship of the tribe, the title of *baign* descends from father to son. The *tiet* is consulted mainly on agricultural expectations, when she makes exorcisms during the full moon. If her prayers are answered by the gods, the people give her a present of food-stuff ; if not, she receives nothing.

The Denka attribute dreams to the presence of God during one's sleep for the purpose of giving one pleasure ; when the dreams are bad, they maintain that it is because God is angry at some evil deed the dreamer has committed. Lunacy they explain by the devil, *dyok*, entering the body of the sufferer.

These people, although possessing a god of their own, have vague ideas on what becomes of the soul after death, or whether transmission or transmigration of the soul into other bodies takes place. They firmly believe that once buried, everything is over, although they say that the spirits of the dead relatives sometimes come out of the ground and can be perceived in dreams.

When a man dies the relations cry spasmodically for one or more months. They sacrifice several cows in front of his house, making substantial meals out of them. For the loss of women, animals are sometimes sacrificed, sometimes not. More often not. When a Denka dies, he is buried in a sitting posture, upright, with arms bent upwards, in a small circular or quadrangular hole near his house, the head being not more than two feet underground.

In order to get married, a Denka of good position must pay from ten to twenty cows for a young healthy wife with no *impedimenta*, but for an older woman with children, four or five cows at the outside are deemed sufficient remuneration. The father of the bride, her brothers and uncles, divide the acquired animals among them. Denka often intermarry with neighbouring tribes. But if a Denka wants to marry a Nuer woman, he must be rich, because a calf a year must be paid for every child that is born, as well as one cow, so that if all goes smoothly after twenty years and nine months of married life he has to pay as many as twenty calves and one cow, which, added to the, say, twenty cows which he had to hand over on his marriage day, make the cost of these mixed marriages almost prohibitive.

There are curious laws regarding seduction. If children are born before marriage, the father of the girl is entitled to take possession of all the cattle of the youth's father. When uncertainty exists as to who the father really is, they go to the *baign*, who, with spear and ashes of dung in hand, receives the plaintiffs and accused. By these articles he swears all parties to speak the truth. He who lies will be devoured by crocodiles, lions or some other wild animal, or else be stung to death by a scorpion or snake. Plenty of varieties of death are offered to the offender. If one of the two or more suspected persons dies within a reasonable time, say, three or four months, or even up to two years from the date of the exorcisms made by the *baign*, the dead man is considered guilty, and all his father's property is seized and handed over to the young lady's parents. If, however, it can be satisfactorily proved that the young lady was in the wrong and seduced the young man, then nothing happens and the child is supported by her family.

Unlike married couples in Europe, who generally prefer to have boys, Denka parents always wish for daughters, as women are valuable assets in the Denka country, and bring in lots of cows at marriage. Unions are celebrated by a feast, when a cow is killed and large quantities of an alcoholic drink, the *mhau*, made from fermented Indian corn, are consumed.

Denka wives, they tell me, are faithful. Local laws allow the slaughtering of an unfaithful wife with no trial of any kind. The first wife is the important one in the family, and her husband cannot marry again without her permission ; but he can always do so, even if she were to refuse her consent, by having distant and separate households for each of his women.

Girls have no sexual connection until puberty. A father can buy a child for his son, if the latter cannot have children of his own, by paying so many cows, and letting the bride's father become the possessor of the calves which are born, as well as leaving to him the exclusive use of the milk from the cows.

The Denka are primitive people. They still light a fire by friction of two pieces of *andarab* wood. They make a hole in one piece and place dry grass upon it, and then obtain a fire by quickly revolving a vertical rod until ignition takes place. When *andarab* wood, which is the most suitable to obtain a fire rapidly, is not procurable, they use wood of the cotton tree, the *alaht*, instead.

The years are reckoned by the rainy season, which comes fairly regularly at the same time of the year, and the smaller subdivisions by the moon.

Like the Nuer, the Denka smear themselves all over with ashes of cow dung, the *arob*, which they say gives a cooling sensation to the skin. This must be so, as, if it does nothing else, it dries the abundant oily excretion from the skin.

They have little idea of the origin of diseases, all of which are put down to God's anger. Not so accidents.

If a Denka breaks his arms or legs, he has sufficient surgical knowledge to place the broken limb between wooden splints, and then bandage it up with the fibrous leaves of some aquatic plant. This is generally done by a man called the *atet*, which means " a clever man," the shining light of every village. He tries to force the bones back into their original position, and Nature does the rest.

Many Denka suffer from dropsy, and abnormal enlargement of the stomach is frequently noticeable. There is a special woman, a sort of midwife, who ties the umbilicus of children at birth, but it is done in no scientific way, and no doubt, as I have stated elsewhere, many of the enormous swellings of the lower portion of the body are due to the improper way in which this primary operation is performed.

The Denka are fond of using fire as a remedy for pains in various parts of the body. Occasionally they perform surgical operations with rudimentary knives. In amputating a finger, or the hand, they have sufficient sense to tie the limb tightly somewhat lower than the point where the operation has to be performed. No sooner is the portion of the limb removed than fire is applied to the exposed raw portion, in order to stop the bleeding.

Any number of lepers are to be found in the Denka country. Chest complaints are frequent and serious. All these people, in fact, are more or less weak-chested, or, at any rate, all are undeveloped round the chest.

When hungry, the Denka pull a rope tight round the waist. They call it the *wuien*. They are great believers in the evil-eye, and they carry, attached to their bracelets or armlets, a *uall*, a piece of wood which has counter-balancing effects against that superstition.

The Denka were at one time great fighters. Before going into battle they danced and sang war melodies and beat the tam-tam. Even to this day they fight with spears, and show great skill in handling them.

Their shields are made of giraffe, elephant or hippopotamus hide, sometimes of crocodile skin. In dances the men perform in the centre, the women in a circle around them. They hop about one after the other, first with the hands up, then with both hands upon the chest, men and women facing each other.

When the Denka hear thunder, they say it is God warning people that rain is coming, which shows some sense on their part ; but also they believe that thunder is caused by God fighting minor gods, whom they place in Paradise not unlike chiefs of celestial villages.

The Denka break the four lower front teeth root and all, as they say God wishes it. I think it is done mostly to promote respiration through the nose, and to allow the prominent lips to be closed, where they would remain wide open in their natural condition.

The Denka are good sportsmen. Entire villages go in a body after elephants. The owner of the first spear thrust into the elephant becomes the proprietor of the right tusk, the one who owns the second spear receives the left tusk, while all the other huntsmen are merely entitled to divide the meat among themselves. Covered pits are cleverly constructed both for elephants and hippopotami. They prize the meat of these animals. When pursuing hippopotami, they use barbed harpoons, with a long rope attached to them, the other end of the rope being attached to an empty canoe. In surveying the river one or two days after the hunt, they recover the canoe, sometimes dragged away for long distances by the hippopotamus, which is very much weakened, if not dead. In either case, he is easily captured, cut up into pieces, and the meat divided. More dangerous than either elephant hunts or hippopotamus hunts is their exciting chase of wild buffaloes, in which they show bravery. Fish they generally catch by making a *kir*, or dam of reeds, across a stream.

Canoes are scooped out of trunks of trees with a *hanish*, a small axe.

The Denka are fond of meat, but they seldom kill their tame animals, as they attach too much value to them. When cows, sheep, or goats, however, die a natural death, they are eaten with gusto, no matter from what disease they have died. Rinderpest has frequently played havoc amongst their animals, especially in the country further east, but, regardless of consequences, the meat of these animals has on every occasion been greedily devoured.

The Denka cultivate the soil merely with a pointed stick, with which they make a succession of holes, placing seeds in them. Nothing more is needed to obtain a crop, the soil being so fertile. When the ground gets exhausted, all they have to do is to go and make their plantations somewhere else, wherever best suits them. Their plantations of maize are, nevertheless, small and hardly suffice for their own needs. These people subsist almost entirely by hunting and fishing.

Among the musical instruments which the Denka possess is a stringed lyre, which they call a *rababa*, a word and an instrument adopted from their neighbours, the people of Kaffa.

The Denka have six long horizontal lines instead of five across the forehead, and these lines reach upon their shaved heads beyond the ears. These cicatrices, which the natives call the *tim*, are made by pulling up the skin until it forms a ridge, and then cutting the top of it with a blade, quite a painful operation.

With all these tribes I was interested in noticing how fast and weak was their pulse—one hundred and six to one hundred and ten beats in the minute were about the average in people not feverish. With nearly all these tribes abdominal breathing was prevalent both in men and women. The people bore exposure to the direct rays of the sun well, and they went about with heads uncovered without feeling any ill effects. When their bodies were not painted white, their perspiration seemed abundant, and abundant was also their salivation. They bore hunger fairly well, but not lack of sleep, of which they required fully twelve to sixteen hours a day. They had no great physical strength, especially in their arms, and absolutely no ability for lifting weights.

The women were physically stronger than the men, and could walk longer distances without feeling any ill effects. Although the men showed skill in throwing their spears, they could not hurl them to a considerable distance, like the cannibal people, for instance, whom I saw later in the French Congo and Congo Free State.

These long-legged Denka were lazy in the extreme, and although they could walk considerable distances for two or three consecutive days, I do not think that any of them could keep it up steadily for long periods of time, say, two or three months.

It was rather curious that none of these people had ever seen mountains; in fact, no such word existed in their language. I caused much merriment by trying to explain to them that other countries were not quite so flat as the Denka and the Nuer countries. Only one man said he had heard that to the east was a country like that, but no member of his tribe had seen it.

Some day the development of the navigation of the Sobat and of the country north and south of it will render Abwong an important place. When I passed through, there were only twenty thatched huts for soldiers and a larger one for the *mamur*, as well as another dwelling for an inspector, in old Abwong. In new Abwong, nearer the river, a large baked-brick house was being built for the *mamur*, with a *zaptia*, or Government office, of five spacious rooms. Within a year or so, twelve brick houses for the police were to be constructed, and one house in corrugated iron for the temporary British inspector.

The natives of Abwong itself were Denka, although in the district there were also some Anuak, and as one got west towards Taufikia some Shiluk.

Twenty native police, of whom only half a dozen were regular soldiers and the others irregular, were deemed sufficient for this station. It was found impossible to employ local labour, as the Denka were too lazy and stupid to learn anything, and also too independent, and could not be made to work. All labour had to be imported from Khartoum.

The *mamur* was absent when I was in Abwong, but I met there Ali Zaki Yonobashi, of the Department of Works, who showed me every possible civility during the few hours I remained in the place.

CHAPTER XXVIII.

From Abwong I made a détour towards the south, in order to visit some of the tribes in that direction. The country was flat and treeless, with occasional villages. Between Nasser and Abwong we had descended about one hundred feet, and we were now at an elevation of 1,250 feet. When we returned in a north-westerly direction towards the Sobat in the Denka country, we saw millions of small birds, and along the river flocks of black cranes.

In the afternoon of March 25th we once more crossed the Sobat. We found a single rickety canoe half full of water, but the natives of the village refused to ferry my loads across, so we proceeded to do it ourselves. My Abyssinians were pitifully helpless in the dug-out, and had it not been for the leper Yambo, who turned out quite an expert in canoe navigation, we should have been much delayed.

The river was swift, and as the canoe was not only narrow but let in a deal of water, it required infinite care to convey the loads in safety to the other bank. Hundreds of Denka had assembled with their spears on both banks, and they resented our using their canoe. One of them came forward and said he would work it for us. In fact, he got one of my loads on board and paddled steadily until he reached the centre of the stream, when he proceeded to make his escape, paddling away his hardest down the river.

This meant, besides being robbed, a delay of probably a whole day, with half my things on one side of the river and half on the other, and as my Abyssinians could not swim, and the river was deep at that place, I was rather in a dilemma as to how to take them across.

I shouted to the man in the canoe to come back, but he put on more speed, encouraged by the yells of the assembled natives on the river banks. Whereupon, after shouting many times for him to return, as he was decamping with my goods, including a valuable camera, I took a rifle and fired at the canoe with an expanding bullet, making a big hole in her. The man became so frightened that he immediately paddled towards the shore and we recovered the load. The thief received a good shaking, and after repairing the damage done to the canoe we continued to take men and goods to the other side of the river.

In this part of the country we saw thousands of beautiful cattle, but the natives would on no account part with them.

On March 26th we passed more Denka villages, and still travelled over flat, monotonous country with burnt yellow grass. Only here and there was a patch of fresh grass on which my half-dead mules could feed. My caravan, formerly of some thirty mules, was now reduced to about half that number, two or three more mules dying that day. I was marching fast towards the Nile, and as I had left the river and we were here in a waterless country, I intended reaching the military post of Taufikia at all costs that evening.

Before we left the river we saw an exciting hunting
scene, hundreds of clamorous natives running along
the banks brandishing their spears. They were dashing after a magnificent antelope, and eventually succeeded in surrounding her, all wildly thrusting their
spears into the exhausted animal. One of my Abyssinians, with sporting instincts, got among the crowd
and was about to fire through the animal's body.
Fortunately, I arrived in time to shove his rifle skyward, and the shot went into the air, or else not only
would he have killed the antelope, but the bullet might
have gone through several Denka who were crowding
on the opposite side.

Later on in the day we came across people of a
different tribe, the Shiluk. Their huts were of an
elongated dome-like shape, many with an extra point
at the top. The lower edge of the roof projected far
out, and the mud walls, four to five feet high, were well
made. Generally there were two huts opposite each
other in an enclosure of fascines of reeds and sticks
with matting between. Their boats, for lack of wood,
were also constructed of fascines of reeds tied together
so as to form a *felucca*. These boats—some of them
able to carry ten or fifteen people—floated beautifully
upon the water. They were easily constructed and of the
greatest use to the natives in navigating the river.

We were travelling over bad ground. During the
evening we unfortunately lost our way, misguided
by a light we saw in the distance and which we believed
to be the military post of Taufikia upon the Nile. We
made for that light and after marching for some hours
found ourselves a great deal north of the post and had
to return southward, passing many native villages

Shilluks and one of their boats of fascines.

before arriving at the post late at night. We did not find water all that day, and only a mile or so before we reached the post another of my mules collapsed and died.

We had marched some forty-five miles that day and all my animals were in an exhausted condition, having made a similar march the previous day. In fact, we had accomplished the entire journey from Adis-Ababa to the Nile—over 1,000 kilometres (some 625 miles)— entirely by land, in thirty-nine days, out of which we had only marched twenty-seven days, making an average march of about twenty-three miles a day—not so easy in such an inhospitable country and in such terrific heat.

At the mouth of the Sobat, Marchand had erected a post on the south bank, which has now been abandoned. A short distance up-stream was the American mission of the Sudan, an offshoot of the Egyptian-American mission. On a trip I made there, I found Mr. and Mrs. R. E. Carson in charge of the mission. For missionaries they seemed practical people. They had there some two hundred acres of land, which they intended using for teaching natives improved methods of agriculture. I believe they also intended establishing industrial classes.

The Sudan Government, in order to avoid the usual quarrels among missionaries, has wisely divided the country into various spheres of religious influence. To the American missionaries has been given the zone south of Fashoda and up the Sobat river. The English are at Bor, on the Bahr-el-Zeraf, and the Austrian Catholic mission in the Bahr-el-Ghazal.

Mr. Carson was hopeful of the results obtainable

in his region.   He told me that as soon as the mission was fairly started there would be two other missionaries established in the place, one a farmer, the other a man of mechanical aptitudes.   He believed that cotton could be grown profitably in that region, and he told me that two good crops had already been raised and pronounced of fair quality in Cairo.   A cotton gin and loom had been brought over for cleaning and working the cotton, and an improved iron windmill had already been put up for irrigation purposes.

Like a good American, Mr. Carson was busy teaching the natives the use and value of money.   So far he had encountered difficulty in getting them to appreciate the exact value of coins.   He seemed rather concerned at the custom of the natives, who would only part with their cattle in exchange for wives, but would not sell for any other consideration, and certainly commercial relations are likely to be restricted until some less cumbersome—if, perhaps, not so pleasant—article of exchange comes to be readily accepted.

Mr. Carson seemed an extremely practical man.   He told me that it was intended to construct two sailing boats for trading purposes on the river Sobat and on the White Nile, in order to teach the natives Western industrial methods.   He then proposes to teach the natives blacksmith's work, and means to go in thoroughly for the production of *sim sim* oil (derived from the well-known plant of the genus *sesamum*), which he believes will be remunerative and will contribute towards the support of the mission.

He was endeavouring to bring down the Shiluk from their proud idea that a man must never work, but he told me that he experienced difficulty in eradicating

"Sometimes small fish is caught on the Nile, sometimes not so small."

this well-rooted notion, as nearly all Shiluk have land and cattle and are quite satisfied with what they already possess.

The actual work of Christianization is only to filter in gradually when the natives are getting more civilized, but is not to be imposed upon them until they are quite ready to comprehend it. It is in the present programme of the mission to establish stations among the Denka, the Nuer, the Burun and the Yambo, as well as among allied tribes. A hospital ship is to be built, which will go up and down the river giving medical aid to the natives. Severe cases will be taken on board and brought down for special treatment to a central hospital. Mr. Carson, who is by way of being a doctor, told me with glee that there was great scope in the country for surgery. So like a surgeon!

I was somewhat glad to find a missionary who was rather against supplying the natives with clothes. In a climate like the one of the Sobat region, the less clothes one wears the better. Besides, the clothes in countries where infectious diseases are rampant only maintain and propagate contagion, as the people never wash, and often exchange their clothes, infecting one another.

Mr. Carson was telling me that the natives are suspicious, and cannot get over the idea that all white people are robbers. These people near the Nile have had unfortunate experiences with the Egyptians, with the Turks and the Dervishes, who killed many of their people and seized numbers of their cattle.

Taufikia itself is a military post with a large garrison of Sudanese troops. There are a few houses of brick and corrugated iron, and many tents and mud huts for the soldiers and their wives. Sudanese troops are well looked after—in fact, a great deal too well. They are provided with wives, with lavish food, portable hip-baths, water-bottles, and with all kinds of luxuries which they do not require. Perhaps they are dressed more with an eye to football matches than for military comfort, a brown heavy woollen jersey covering their chest, while their legs are garbed in tight khaki trousers, black puttees round the lower portion of the leg and heavy nonsensical leather boots, which get hardened after moisture and baked in the sun, so that the soldiers have to remove them when on the march, as they make their feet quite sore. The *tarbouche*, too, which in its natural condition is graceful enough, has been deformed into a sort of high cylinder wrapped up in a broad band of khaki, with a patch on one side on which the brass number of the regiment stands out.

A great deal of astonishment is displayed at the cleverness of native bands in learning European tunes, an astonishment no one who has spent a few days in a military post, I am sure, can possibly share. The musicians, who, it is quite true, do not know a single note of music, are placed under the cooling shade of a tree, and there for several consecutive hours in the morning and several hours at night they are compelled to practise two or three chords at a time of one tune or another, which two or three chords are continually repeated until the people in the neighbourhood are nearly driven out of their minds by the monotonous discords. When, after some weeks, two or three chords have been learnt, two or three more chords are added to them, and by the end of the year another easy melody out of the " Belle of New York," or such other classic, has been mastered, a Sudanese rhythm never being lacking in its reproduction.

My animals were in such a bad condition that they were quite unable to go any further. Even the horse which Ras Makonnen had given me was now so tired after his long march of about 1,450 kilometres from Harrar, that I had to leave him behind at this place. I endeavoured to make a fresh caravan of donkeys, which would be more suited for the country I should have to cross in the Bahr-el-Ghazal.

I sent back to Europe a good deal of my baggage by the Nile, purchased fresh provisions, and after a compulsory stay of twelve days—the most stupid, miserable and dullest twelve days I have ever spent in my life—I was ready to start further west.

There were three officers here, one, Major Lemprière, a perfect gentleman and most distinguished officer, who, unfortunately, went on leave when I arrived. The others seemed much affected by the climate.

In the river I discovered a good deal of gold in the sand, gold which undoubtedly comes down the Sobat and is deposited along the eastern bank of the Nile at this place.

I left Taufikia by river on April 8th, and passed the mouth of the Sobat, the water of which, being of a yellowish, creamy colour, was easily distinguishable from the greenish water of the Nile. The yellow line followed the eastern bank of the river. The country all round was flat and uninteresting, low and swampy to the south and somewhat higher on the north bank. Further west the south bank got a little higher, with slight undulations and with small accumulations of alluvial deposits around trees and clusters of grass.

Occasionally Shiluk were to be seen along the banks, all armed with spears and shouting out their friendly "Abhave, abhave." Shiluk villages were frequent on both sides.

It is impossible to imagine a more dreary, uninteresting landscape than that of this region. Before we got to the Bahr-el-Zeraf we saw to the south a hill, standing separate, the Djeb Zeraf, with three lower hills by its side. Soon after perceiving these low hills we came to the Bahr-el-Zeraf, which forms a short cut in the waterway from the White Nile to the stations of Bor, Lado and Gondokoro. Perhaps even a shorter cut might be made at no great expense, coming straight from Bor to the Khor Felus at the mouth of the Sobat. I believe indeed that Sir William Garstin contemplates a scheme of this kind, which would avoid the present détour of the river and would necessarily greatly increase the volume of water brought down for the irrigation of Egypt.

The Sudan Government is, in fact, giving great attention to these possibilities, and at the time of my visit had a small band of irrigation officers at work in the study of projects for increasing the volume of the White Nile from which Egypt draws practically the whole of its summer supply.

At Taufikia I met Mr. P. M. Tottenham, inspector of the irrigation works, who had been making a levelled survey over the line of Garstin's Bor-Sobat cut and also accurate surveys of the Bahr-el-Zeraf and through the marshes near Shambe. Some thirty gauges to record the movements of the Nile had been put up that year. Eventually the work of these devoted surveyors will make known with exactitude the intricate channels

Abyssinian horse presented to Author by Ras Makonnen.
(This photo. was taken after the horse had travelled from Harrar to the Nile.)

and branches of the Upper Nile, as well as the topography of the vast marshes in which the river practically loses itself. They had been able to free this channel through the unexplored marshes (which feed the river Zeraf) as far as the latitude of Shambe, when further progress was stopped by the *sudd*, a barrier of grass and decayed vegetation.

On the right bank of the stream we came to a Catholic mission near a Shiluk village. The fathers had begun building themselves a neat red-brick house. So far, however, they had merely a mud hut by the stream, with a little kitchen-garden which the monks were busy besprinkling with water in order to keep their vegetables alive. They prayed and watered the plants simultaneously. There is nothing like saving time. I was really sorry for these fathers when I saw them, as they seemed absolutely destitute. They had nothing except their vegetables, and they appeared worn and dazed from fever, with half-demented faces. Most of them were drawn from the farmer class and had but little education, but they were kindly disposed. Malarial fever was rampant in that region. All these men were suffering silently.

Away from the habitations lots of antelopes and water-buck were to be seen.

West of the Bahr-el-Zeraf we were again in a country inhabited by Denka. We had now entered a region of papyrus, which we had not yet seen on our journey. *Dum* palms were more numerous than the smooth-barked tall *ghuleb*, with its peculiar swelling half-way up its stem, which we noticed so frequently on the Sobat ; mimosa trees, the *gherar* of the Abyssinians ; and the white-green grass, the *talkh* (the *aglik* of the Arabs) were also to be seen in huge quantities, especially on the south bank of the river.

When we approached some village the natives, especially the women, received us with shrill ululations, a kind of falsetto tremolo, quite musical and weird at night.

We were here in the *sudd* region and saw a great many floating islands, some of which delayed us considerably until we could cut our way through. Nearly the entire river was in many places covered with vegetation and only a small channel left for navigation. Small islands often altogether blocked the congested channel.

On April 9th we came to Lake No, where quantities of papyrus clumps were to be seen on the south bank. The Bahr-el-Ghazal itself entered Lake No, describing a spacious curve. As a matter of fact, Lake No was formed merely by the flooding of the intervening country, where the Bahr-el-Djebel and the Bahr-el-Ghazal meet. The natives call it Mogren-el-Bahr, or " the mouth of the river." A well-defined line marks the two currents of the Bahr-el-Ghazal and the Bahr-el-Djebel (or Ghebel), the former a stream practically of stagnant water, the latter descending from Lake Albert. Directly in front of Bahr-el-Djebel to the north was the Eliri Mount, some days' journey from the river. Lake No begins where the Bahr-el-Ghazal is joined by the Bahr-el-Djebel. It would certainly be more correct to call Lake No " No Lake," as there is so much *sudd* floating about and thickly-webbed vegetation covering its surface that on travelling across it one sees no water at all except the small channel cut by the boats. In some places there were side channels, which suggested that

Escort of Sudanese soldiers and Author's Abyssinian muleteers returning up the Sobat river in a steel felucca lent by the Sirdar.

the lake might extend underneath the surface growths
for a width of from two to four miles, whereas the length
of the lake from east to west is calculated at about
eight miles. It is considered the largest lake in the
Sudan.

One tried hard to find something of interest as one
went along, but after passing the lake we had nothing
but swamp, *sudd*, reeds, papyrus and the *umshusha*,
as it is called in the Sudan (the *umsusa*), the tall grass
which covers the country.

Millions of tall anthills covered the flat stretch
of country as far as the eye could see. Occasionally
mimosas, few and far apart, slightly relieved the
monotony of the landscape. Towards the evening
hundreds of gazelles and water-buck were to be seen
close to the water-edge.

We were blocked on several occasions by quantities
of *sudd* in the channel. The stream nearly all the way
was over twenty-five feet deep, but it was difficult to
gauge its width owing to the *sudd* which collected near
the banks and stopped up the river almost altogether,
so that the boat brushed the reeds on both sides as we
went along. Marabu birds were numerous, and also
all kinds of long-legged, long-beaked water-birds.

CHAPTER XXIX.

BEFORE we proceed on the journey let us examine the Shiluk a little more intimately.

They were at one time a great tribe, much more numerous and powerful than now. The incursions of the Dervishes, the Egyptians and slave merchants have wrought havoc among them. They can be found now all along the left bank of the Nile from the 10° 30′ lat. N., from a place called Kaka, and as far south as Lake No on the White Nile. They divide themselves into fifty *podo*, thirty-seven of which are found on the White Nile, six in the interior on the river Kiro, and one on the Sobat, which we have already visited.

The influence of these Shiluk must formerly have been considerable, at least if we are to judge by the spread of their language, which, with certain variations, is understood and spoken by many distant tribes towards the east, such as the Yambo and the Anuak, and as far south as some of the tribes on the Victoria Nyanza. It is said that at one time the Shiluk extended as far as, and further than, the 12° lat. N., where they came in contact with the Baggara, with whom they were at war, but that they were eventually driven back to the place they now occupy.

They inhabit at present a thickly-populated zone

from ten to twenty miles wide, mostly along the left
bank of the river, the villages standing at short distances
all along. Especially south of Kodok (better known as
Fashoda to English people), the country along the stream
is literally covered with huts. Between the estuary of
the Sobat and Lake No the country is densely populated. The number of inhabitants has been estimated
at over half a million souls, but such authorities as
Father Tappi who have lived in their country for many
years seem to think that figure rather understates than
over-estimates their number.

The supreme chief of the Shiluk lives near Fashoda
and goes by the title of *Mak*, or more commonly *Ret*.
His title is hereditary, or, at any rate, the *Ret* is always
elected from among the Gnarets, the ruling family.
They are said never to die of a natural death, these
Ret being suffocated or strangled when ill or about to
expire, the tribe disliking the idea of their kings dying
like other mortals.

The Shiluk divide themselves into two great families :
the Quagnaret and the O-chiolla, the Quagnaret being
the noble, almost semi-divine, caste among them. The
O-chiolla people, of a lower social condition, are somewhat looked down upon by the Quagnaret, although the
O-chiolla are much richer and are really superior in
authority to their nobler tribesmen. It is possible that
the Quagnaret and the O-chiolla were in remote times
different races altogether, the Quagnaret being the
conquering race. In fact, we find some marked differences in the type. The Quagnaret are aggressive, proud,
and despise work ; whereas the O-chiolla work the ground,
look after the immense herds of cattle, and, in fact, possess
all the riches in the country.

The Shiluk, both castes combined, have had many vicissitudes even in comparatively recent years in their own country. They had severe fights with the Dervishes, with whom they afterwards made peace. Some were conquered, others would not submit and migrated from their country.

When Major Marchand came on his famous expedition to Fashoda they looked upon him as a saviour and even made a treaty with him. To this day they speak of this officer and his entire expedition in the most laudatory terms. For the Anglo-Egyptian officers they also have much admiration, mingled, however, with a good deal of suspicion, as they cannot imagine that white people go to the Shiluk country merely for the sake of protecting them. They fear that some day they will be pounced upon, their cattle seized and be robbed of whatever else they may possess. Their previous experiences in that direction with the Turks, the Egyptians and the Dervishes have certainly not been happy.

I believe they quite understand that for the protection afforded they must pay some sort of a tax, but I think they would prefer to pay it in kind with some of the produce of their country rather than get rid of their cattle, from which they are extremely loth to part. The affection of the Shiluk towards their cattle is quite pathetic. One never sees a Shiluk strike a cow or an ox, even under the most trying circumstances.

The Shiluk are terrified beyond words of British artillery, the accounts of what British guns could do at the battle of Omdurman having spread far and wide all over their country.

One Shiluk told me : " What can I do with my spear

Shiluk warriors.

with which I can only kill people near me, when you
have ' boom-booms ' "—by which name they call our
guns—" which can kill many, many men each time from
so far away that although we can hear we cannot see
you ? "

The *podo* into which the Shiluk country is divided
are districts, and each district is then divided into
helle, or villages. The chiefs of these villages are elected
by the inhabitants, although frequently the *Ret* gives
the position to members of his regal family. A considerable revenue comes to the *Ret* from the ivory tusks
of elephants killed by his tribesmen, from hippopotamus
skins and from cattle, which the various villagers must
pay to him on demand.

Then again the *Ret* has splendid opportunities of
increasing his wealth when murders or thefts occur,
on which occasions entire villages are pillaged by his
men. If the murderer happens to escape across the
river to the Denka, the innocent people in the village have
to pay for the offender and are robbed of everything they
possess. The person who has been robbed in the first
instance never recovers anything.

On the other hand, the *Ret* gets rid of a good deal
of his cattle for sacrificial purposes during festivals and
on great native holidays. Though his authority is
in many ways only nominal, his word is law on essential
points.

Every man of the Quagnaret caste is a warrior,
and always carries with him one or several *tong*, or war-
spears, and a large shield of hippopotamus hide. The
warriors are divided into so many contingents, one under
a leader for each district. Their navy—quite a formidable one—consists of an immense number of improvised

canoes made from fascines of wonderfully light wood, the *ambatch*, each boat being easily carried on the head of one man when on dry land, and accommodating two or three warriors upon the water.

Before a fight they all assemble at the sound of war-drums. On one or two occasions I got these men to show me their tactics, which were indeed extraordinary for such uncivilized people. Their spear-throwing was accurate, although they could not hurl far, the spears being too heavy to travel great distances through the air.

A number of these fellows became excited over their war-dances and sham attacks upon a position where I placed imaginary enemies. Having taken hold of a war-club and pretended to be the leader of these imaginary enemies, I came out of camp and went for the Shiluk, pretending to strike right and left. To my amazement, in a second I found myself covered by their spears round my head and body, so that I could not move at all. We had a great laugh over this, the Shiluk being certainly much more amused than I on that occasion. It was amazing how quickly they surrounded me and got the spears in position to strike at the most vital parts of my anatomy.

Some people think they can trace a resemblance between the formation of Shiluk skulls and those of the Fellah, especially in the projection of the nasal bones, but, personally, I believe this resemblance to be merely accidental, and it is dubious whether a real connection between the two races exists.

Naturally one frequently traces outside influences in their type, intercourse having taken place between Shiluk and neighbouring or conquering tribes. Perhaps

Shiluk hurling spears.

further north the tribes may show a greater resemblance to the Fellah than the tribes which I visited further south.

The anatomical structure of the Shiluk leads one to believe that these people have been specially built by Nature to live in marshy regions. Tall, long-legged, the Shiluk, in common with many other riverine tribes, possess many of the habits of water-birds. Often one sees them along the river banks or in their villages standing for long periods of time upon one leg, not unlike flamingoes, the other foot resting upon the knee of the extended leg. One peculiarity of the Shiluk race, as also of the Denka and the Nuer, who, as we have seen, are closely allied to them, is the extreme flatness of their feet and the abnormal prolongation of the heel.

We find among the O-chiolla the custom of removing the four incisor teeth of the lower jaw, but the noble Quagnaret do not indulge in this practice. The tribal mark is generally two incisions on the forehead, and these are made when young men come to the age of puberty.

It is curious to notice that some of the harpoons used to-day by Shiluk for killing hippopotami are similar to those represented on the monuments of the Pharaohs. It is possible that these people copied these weapons from the people of Eygpt. There is no doubt that the people of the Upper Nile Valley, in the entire region of the Bahr-el-Ghazal, as well as in the valley of the Sobat, the Denka, the Nuer and the Shiluk, all belong to the same great family, although local conditions and various outside influences from neighbouring tribes have caused slight variations in the type of various districts.

Both the Shiluk and the Denka gave versions of

one common legend of two brothers, Guacango and Dengo, who were made specially by the *djuk*, the god of the Shiluk, in order to populate this formerly uninhabited country. These two brothers, according to the Quagnaret, were the first of their race who appeared in the land. Dengo, having quarrelled with his brother, crossed the Nile with his cattle to the right bank, where he settled. The Quagnaret evidently originated from Guacango and the Dinka from Dengo, the word Dinka having been subsequently modified into Denka.

The Shiluk are to this day more or less at war with the Denka, in order to capture the cattle that Dengo took from them.

The Nuer are unmistakably akin to the Shiluk, but perhaps more warlike in their temperament. The Anuak show resemblance in their type to both the Nuer and the Shiluk.

The costume of all these people is simple, as we have already seen, the men going about absolutely naked, the women occasionally, but not frequently, wearing a small apron of skin, or more frequently a tuft of fresh grass.

We find among the Shiluk elaborate ways of doing the hair, which is sometimes matted into a sort of thick felt in the shape of two large elephant's ears at the back of the head, sometimes into a comb or a fan on the top of the skull, sometimes into parallel combs either longitudinal or transversal upon the top portion of the head. Generally these arrangements are suggested by animal forms, although the natives themselves say they are not. Like the Nuer and the Denka, they also smear the head for two weeks or so with a composition of ashes of cow dung, which has the property of colouring the hair red. The hair of the body and face, what there is of it, is plucked out when individuals are quite young.

The Shiluk have comparatively small heads in relation to their height, and somewhat out of proportion with the length of their legs. The Quagnaret are finer people than the O-chiolla. Some of the men have well-developed chests, but they are somewhat deficient in size and development of the thorax.

The Shiluk have religious ideas of their own, suggested, I think, by their contact with the Dervishes and the ancient Egyptians. They speak of a *djuk*, a kind of god, to be propitiated when they need rain or sunshine or to be freed from pestilence. Prayers are also offered to Guacango, a semi-deity. Many villages have a special hut, a place of worship, decorated with charcoal, in which, when the chief of the village dies, he is buried. Public prayers are offered sometimes, especially for a change of climatic conditions, and Guacango is specially appealed to under the endearing name of " Guacaio," or river god, when fish gets scarce in the river and he is wanted to supply more. A priestess called the *bared* acts as intermediary between the Shiluk and the deity, and after listening carefully to the prayers of the people transmits them to the *djuk*. This *bared* visits the people when they are ill, and makes exorcisms and incantations to drive away the evil spirit which is supposed to have entered the body of the invalid.

Sheep's blood is frequently used in these exorcisms, and is sprinkled all over the hut and the patient. The possessions of the sick man are scattered all over the village, especially upon trails, the people who tread upon them unawares being supposed to contract the illness and so deliver from it the person who has it already. The Shiluk believe that illness goes from one person to another, and that when one person gets rid of it, it is only because another person has contracted it. This belief exists not only in Africa, but also in Europe, not far, even, from good old London town.

In popular speech, Shiluk of a less noble birth can die, but not the *Ret*, who, after death, is merely spoken of as having gone " out of the village," or "out of the country " ; he is never spoken of as a " dead man."

The Shiluk know little about the soul, but they are inclined to the theory of the transmigration of the soul into other individuals upon this earth. Their god is upon earth, and not in heaven, as with us, the idea of an aerial deity seeming extremely ludicrous to them.

The Shiluk are noisy people when excited, and particularly boisterous at funerals. Their burials are quiet enough, the body being deposited in a deep grave amidst general grief. If the deceased be a chief, as we have seen, he is deposited in the sacred hut, but simple mortals are buried just outside their former residence. A hide is placed at the bottom of the grave, and the hollow is then filled tight with earth and flattened on the surface so that no one can detect where the grave is. Eight days later the parents and friends in the village come with spears and shields and dance and make evolutions round the grave, sacrificing and eating one or more oxen according to the wealth of the deceased.

Ancestral worship is in a way practised by the Shiluk. They believe that the dead linger about the living and look after them, and they firmly believe

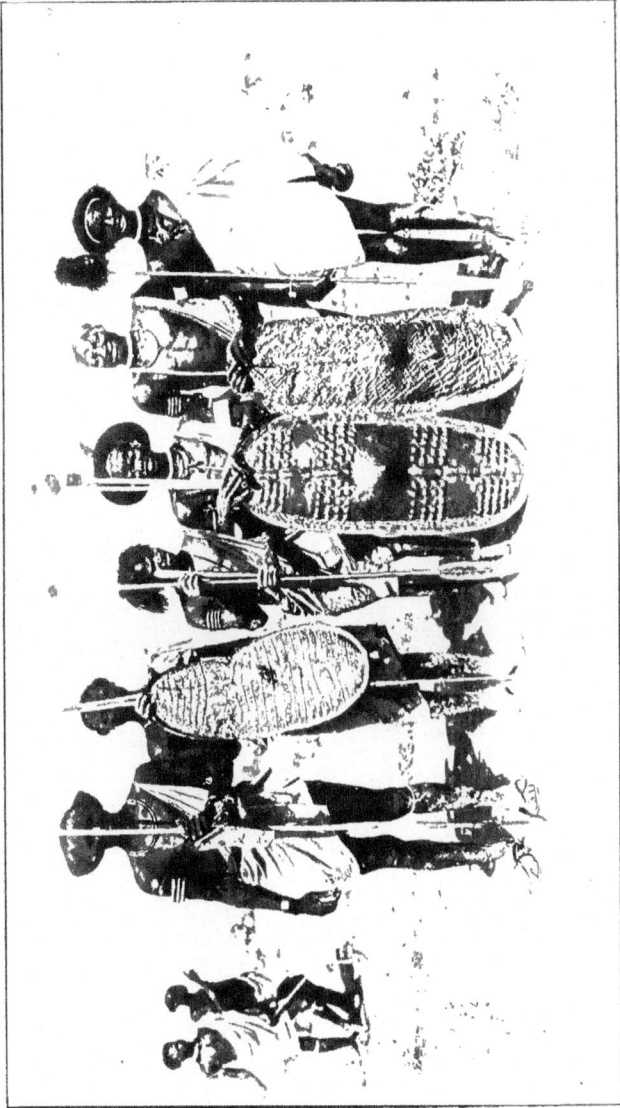

Shiluk warriors.

that communication can be established with dead people in dreams.

Shiluk are believers in the evil-eye, and attach much importance to the way one looks at them.

The Shiluk language is comparatively rudimentary. For instance, there is no inflection to mark gender or number. To indicate males it is necessary to add the word " gialo " ; or for females, the word " dacio." The plural is made by the suffix " ghir," which means " many."

Counting, as with most African tribes, is done on one's fingers, and is limited to five. Few people can count beyond. The number " six " is " one hand and one " ; " seven," " one hand and two," and so on.

In the Shiluk language we find no word for " mountain " or " hill," the nearest being " *kiddi*," a stone, which may also be another indication that these people have always lived in flat, marshy regions.

They have an extensive vocabulary for cattle, *daduk*, for instance, being a yellow cow ; *nyading*, a red and white cow, *dittang*, a black cow, etc.

CHAPTER XXX.

MARRIAGES in the Shiluk country are of the simplest description, although certain general rules are adopted here and there. For instance, the Quagnaret and the O-chiolla only occasionally intermarry. A Quagnaret woman, on getting married to an O-chiolla, loses her caste. Monogamy is prevalent in the Shiluk country, as it is seldom that a Shiluk can allow himself more than one wife, women in the Shiluk country being an expensive luxury. The near relatives of the girl expect in exchange for her value no less than three or four oxen or cows, or at least forty sheep or goats, besides sundry spears and cooking utensils. Only after payment of the amount is she handed over to the prospective bridegroom.

Moreover, when a Shiluk goes to bargain for his wife with her relatives, he has to drag behind half a dozen or more goats and sheep, and to present one to the father of the girl, the others to the assembled members of the family. By means of pieces of straw laid upon the floor the number of oxen, cows and goats is agreed upon, while the ladies of the house produce pot after pot of *merissa* in order to cheer up all present. The business part of the transaction being over, if the girl consents, she is presented with a bracelet of brass or ivory, which is passed over her wrist. That is all there is of the Shiluk marriage ceremony.

Fellows have been known to take a wife on credit, but these rash individuals heavily mortgage their happiness, and even run the risk of losing their better-half should a wealthier person present himself on the scene prepared to pay hard cash.

Shiluk do not frequently intermarry with other tribes. They generally go and select a wife from a distant village, but nearly always from members of their own tribe. When a man marries more than one wife, he must provide for each of them separate fields and huts, and keep each household divided.

When a man dies and leaves several wives, these usually marry his sons. For a consideration a Shiluk can marry his widowed sister-in-law, or even his aunt, as women are paid for at the rate of valuable animals and must remain in the family.

When the children are small at a man's death, his brother takes possession of the widow and of the cattle ; but on the children getting older the property is divided equally among the children, the wife, too, being handed back, if desired, to the eldest son in the family.

Adultery is not frequent. When it does occur, if the woman will not accuse the seducer, she is assured that she and her offspring will die within a year. She generally confesses.

The men are extremely lazy in the Shiluk country, and leave the women to do all the work. Indeed, the Shiluk woman has to cook, she has to fish, she looks after the animals, she goes to fetch water, she tans the leather in a primitive fashion, when necessary she brings loads of fodder and does what little agricultural work is to be done in the country.

They cultivate some *dhura*, some maize, *batick*,

pumpkins, lupins, etc. The *hibiscus esculentus (bamia)* grows wild, and produces an insipid fruit. It is only possible to raise crops from May to November, the rainy season ; they sow the seeds when the ground is softened by the rains, the man walking in front making holes in the ground as he goes along with a pointed stick, the woman behind, placing a seed or two in each hole and filling the aperture with earth with her foot.

The Shiluk country is cut up into numerous natural canals. There are many deep depressions in the ground, which during the rainy season fill up with water and form lakelets. The variation between high and low water in the river is from three to four feet. The land during the rainy season is thus divided into so many islands, the canals supplying good fish for the natives.

The entire village takes part in all the larger fishing expeditions, but the usual fishing is done either in their wooden canoes, the *yei*, or else in the *abbobo*, or raft of *ambatch*, the men spearing the fish with a kind of spear and bow combined, about seven feet long, such as we have already seen in use among the natives of the Sobat river. More generally, though, the natives dam the narrow canals, and capture the fish in large quantities in basket traps fixed in apertures of the barrier across the stream.

The *polypterus bichir* are common in these waters. Also, the *siluridæ* family is strongly represented. The *lepidosiren*, a salamander-like water inhabitant, which the natives eat, reaches sometimes a length of four feet.

The fish, when captured, is cut up in strips and dried.

In the streams the natives often hunt hippopotami

with harpoons, when they surround the animal and riddle him with spear-wounds. When the animal is worn out and has lost a great deal of blood, he sometimes makes for the bank of the river, where the natives kill him. If he dies in the river, he sinks, and will only come to the surface again after twelve hours or so, when decomposition has begun.

Guinea-fowl, crowned storks, and other large birds are plentiful in the country, and the natives kill them with sticks or catch them in traps.

Shiluk cultivate tobacco extensively for their own use. They keep regular nurseries of young plants, which during the proper season they remove to the banks of the stream. Their crop of tobacco is, however, not sufficient to supply local needs, and most of them indulge in smokes of charcoal.

Until a few years ago they cultivated cotton, but now they have ceased, as they did not find it profitable.

The north-western part of their country is sandy, and, under present conditions, quite useless for agricultural purposes. The only portion which is fertile is that with alluvial deposits from the inundations of the river, the zone inhabited by the Shiluk practically not extending further than ten or twenty miles from the larger streams. Two or three crops a year can be grown with no trouble in the latter zone.

The country, as we have seen, is a vast plain, smothered in grass and reeds during the rains. The climate is unhealthy—one might say, deadly—for men and animals, especially such as are non-indigenous. October and November are possibly the worst months, when the grass and reeds begin to putrefy under the great heat of the sun and exhale a pestilential odour. August is, perhaps, the wettest month, with terrific thunderstorms daily, and flashes of lightning so violent that it is difficult for people who have not been there to imagine their force. The sky during these tornadoes is lighted all over continuously by myriads of electric discharges.

From November the north winds begin, and the level of the Nile gets lower. The water in the marshes and lakes quickly evaporates, leaving reeds and grass to dry and tumble down. It is at this epoch that the natives set the country ablaze, and this is probably the reason that in many parts we find few trees, as these grass fires interfere considerably with their growth.

At night the entire country is lighted by these fires, which make a weird scene. In the daytime swarms of hawks, grey falcons and eagles, the *haliætos vocifer*, with their peculiar shriek, describe circles above the dense smoke arising from the fires, waiting for propitious moments to pounce down upon frizzling rats, snakes and tortoises.

The channels, when empty during the dry season, are useful to the natives as trails, and also for places wherein to hide their canoes.

December, January, February and March are hot months, March particularly, the month when I was there, when the thermometer was often as much as 40° Centigrade (104° Fahrenheit).

Near the ponds, canals, and on the river, thousands of birds can be seen either flapping their wings above the water, or placidly resting perched upon one leg along the banks. Some were of a brilliant carmine red, or of beautiful gradations of yellow and blue. Others, such as the *plotus melanogoanastu*, a fish-eating bird, were dark-coloured. Then there were the marabu storks, with their valuable plumage, and the *balæniceps rex*, with its disproportionate head and sac-like broad bill, a bird of most retiring habits, something between a pelican and a heron. Sparrows were innumerable, and probably one of the most common birds was the *parra africana*. The white-breasted Abyssinian raven, not unlike a magpie, was frequently met with, particularly in the yards of the villages.

Perhaps, however, the Bahr-el-Ghazal is particularly noticeable for the abundance of reptiles of all kinds, all holes, angles and fissures being full of them. Poisonous snakes are numerous and the natives suffer a good deal from them.

Possibly the most destructive living thing in that region is the *termix voratrix*, the white ant, which undermines the ground and eats up everything everywhere. The huge heaps, sometimes eight or ten feet high, made by these ants, are constructed so that they can protect themselves by climbing on these high places when the country is under water. These little brutes devour the grain, the baskets, the utensils of the natives, and even the wood of the rafters in their huts, unless the inhabitants keep a sharp look-out for them, and frequently tap the wood, the concussion as they believe stunning and even killing the *termix*.

Mosquitoes naturally swarm in such a marshy region, and are tantalizing to men and animals alike. Fortunately, one never sees them while the sun is above the horizon, but from sunset to sunrise they make life quite unbearable.

The Shiluk fumigate their huts with dense smoke, so as to protect themselves from the mosquitoes, and they also sleep on a layer of white ashes from cow dung, which is really a greater protection than sleeping under a mosquito net, although the remedy seems to be far worse than the evil itself. Even when sitting out of doors they sit on skins or on mats of *ambatch*, burning near them heaps of cow dung which produce clouds of dense smoke.

Shiluk huts are generally conical, or of a slightly flattened dome shape. They have but few things in the interior of their dwellings, with the exception of the hides or mats on which they sit or lie. These people are vain, and as long as they possess sufficient cow-dung ashes and fluid direct from the bladder—two essential articles in their toilette, as well as in their culinary arrangements—they are as happy as possible. Their cooking pots and milk vessels are always washed with cows' water, probably in order to counterbalance the lack of salt in that region.

The Shiluk are extremely kind to their animals, especially their oxen and cows. After grazing, when they bring them back to their villages, they make them walk between fires of reeds so as to free them from mosquitoes. Big fires are kept up all night around them, in order to protect them as much as possible from the stings.

Besides the oxen, sheep and goats, the Shiluk possess a good deal of poultry and innumerable dogs, not unlike greyhounds, with hair of a reddish-brown colour and a much elongated muzzle.

There is little wood in the Shiluk country—in fact, practically none, if the *dum* palm, scarce, is excepted, of which one sees one or two here and there near Shiluk villages, usually in the centre of the village, where their war-drums are generally fastened, so as to convey signals of danger, or of hunting or of fishing expeditions. The Shiluk possess quite an elaborate code of signals upon these drums.

The *higlig*, or *balanites ægyptiaca*, and the *deleb* and *dum* are, indeed, about the only fructiferous palms in the Shiluk country.

The flowers on land are few and ugly, but not so upon the water, where lotuses and water-lilies of white, blue and crimson, the *nymphæa stellata* and the *nymphæa lotus* are to be seen. The Ethiopian *vallisneria*, with its spiral peduncles, rises upon its coiling stalks some six feet up to the surface of the water, and is most remarkable for its sexual development. The *adenia venenata*, a creeper with a fairly pretty flower, possesses poisonous leaves, used by the natives for producing blisters. Animals are frequently poisoned by this plant, which is extremely common in the Shiluk country.

The water-fern, the *azolla*, and also the *pistia*, are common enough in the papyrus region ; also masses of *trapa*, a water-nut, and the yellow *ottelia*, not unlike *sesamum*, producing a gelatinous liquid said to be good for indigestion when dried and pounded into powder.

There are also innumerable weeds, which form the great grass barrier, *el sett*, usually miscalled in English, " *sudd*."

The *ambatch* is plentiful, and more plentiful still the *umsusa*, technically *vossia procera*, a most troublesome grass, with its leaf sheaths covered with hair-like adhesive bristles, which when touched produce most tiresome itching and irritation.

There were a few clusters of gummiferous acacia, and further back inland a number of tamarind trees, with dark-coloured leaves. The tree-like *euphorbia*, with its candelabra branches, which belongs to the *cactaceæ* order, and is similar to the *euphorbia* of Abyssinia, is also frequently to be seen. It reproduces itself with wonderful facility and rapidity, and is at all times difficult to kill.

Beyond Lake No we were in the Denka country. Thousands of cattle could be seen to the south of the river belonging to the inhabitants of this region. Then came more flat country of mud and slush. Flamingoes of various families stood pompously about, most of them black, with long, arched backs, and a larger kind, grey, with black wings and tail. Further back on dry land were thousands of cattle.

The *euphorbia candelabrum* could be seen here and there; the milky-white substance discharged by it when an incision is made being poisonous. It is used extensively by the Denka for poisoning their spear-heads. They make the steel red-hot, and dip it in the white sap, which is absorbed and retained in the closing pores of the metal during the cooling process. This is a similar cactus to the one common in many parts of Abyssinia, especially near Harrar, where we have seen the Galla make hedges of them round their kraals, and also in Western Abyssinia, where regular forests of them are to be found. Here in the Bahr-el-Ghazal there were only a few, and the tallest I saw was not more than twenty feet high. The branches and leaves were not so fat, but they seemed more numerous than those of the kind found at greater elevations in Abyssinia.

We then came to a portion of the country slightly more wooded with mimosa trees. The banks of the river were here somewhat higher, about four feet above the river level, and the stream itself was comparatively free from *sudd* and floating vegetation. It had here a width of clear water of forty to fifty yards. Beyond this region we came to a few thatched huts, where we found another tribe of Nuer again, who varied little from the Nuer we had found on the Sobat.

These people had almost aquiline noses, much elongated at the base, and big, prominent lips disclosing long, white upper teeth. The four lower teeth had been removed as with the other Nuer. Long-legged, with high square shoulders, they were like the others, thin-bodied with somewhat disjointed supple-looking limbs, the arms appearing too short in proportion to the legs. The ears of these people were badly formed, coarse and placed somewhat higher on the cranium than the position in which the ears are generally found in most races.

The outer rims of the ears of one man I saw were simply covered with brass rings, each ring being inserted into a separate hole.

The length from the nose at the nostrils to the chin was much greater than from that same point to the top of the skull.

The hair was dyed red and tied into a knot behind the head, or else left fluffy and flying in the wind.

Here, too, their hands were almost atrophied, or at any rate much swollen, by wearing tight bracelets which had never been removed from youth up.

Further west we came to the Bahr-el-Arab, which had been explored, for the first time, only a few months before I went through, by Lieutenant Walsh, of the Royal Navy, in the employ of the Sudan Government.

We were stopped several times by *sudd*, until we were able to cut a passage ; then on our right we came to the Djur River, most difficult to perceive owing to the water vegetation blocking the entire mouth of the stream.

The Bahr-el-Ghazal, on which we were, was here quite narrow and overgrown on either side with papyrus and reeds. We observed occasional patches of trees in the distance, and a higher cluster of trees stood now before us, now behind, or at the side. Each time we looked at it, it was in a different direction, as the Bahr-el-Ghazal described a most circuitous course.

We had quite an exciting moment on board, as we carried a large quantity of dynamite for the military post of Wau. Through the carelessness of a native, who upset a can of petroleum and set it on fire, we had the delightful prospect of a little explosion.

It took us several hours to go the last few yards towards our destination, the " heavenly spot " of Meshra-el-Rek, as we got stuck many times in the pestilential, putrid water, stirring up black, stinking, decomposed vegetation from the river bottom as we tried to shove along.

We arrived in Meshra harbour, thirty yards long by ten wide, a sort of *cul-de-sac* of stagnant water, in the afternoon of April 11th. If an international competition were arranged to give a prize to the most unhealthy, dreary, inhospitable, hot, poisonous place on the face of the earth, I am certain Meshra would win it easily.

CHAPTER XXXI.

YES, Meshra was a musty, mouldy, fetid hole, in which the natives themselves refused to live. There were a few traders, one or two officials, and some Sudanese soldiers, all ailing with fever and in a pitiable plight. The *mamur* himself was ill.

No means of transport of any kind could be obtained, and even goods for the Governor and Government officials in the capital at Wau had to remain in this place for lack of porterage.

The place consisted of four small corrugated iron buildings and a sort of walled enclosure—a fort, it is called—a mere mud shelter for military stores.

Twenty Sudanese soldiers and a native officer were stationed here, and there were two Greeks, one the agent of Angelo H. Capato, the enterprising merchant of Khartoum. Their business consisted mostly in forwarding to Khartoum ivory purchased further inland ; they also carried on a little trade in tinned provisions with the few British officers in the capital of the Bahr-el-Ghazal.

Meshra, with an area of only a few hundred square yards, is situated on a small island, in a sort of lagoon. A few wells have been dug, the water of which is not quite so deadly as the pestilential ink-like fluid from the lagoon.

The Tonj river enters the Bahr-el-Ghazal near this

cul-de-sac, just before reaching Meshra. The mouth of this stream is always so blocked with papyrus and reeds that it is not possible to discover where it is unless one knows its exact situation. No current is noticeable. In this pool, in which we anchored, we heard at night many hippopotami, and one of the officers on board killed a couple of crocodiles.

A flat circular-leaved, long-stemmed lotus plant with white flowers was extremely plentiful in the water.

The Government officials seemed perplexed in this place, and I think that orders from headquarters made them even more helpless. It would be unsafe for a traveller to go into that country unless quite independent of everybody, as credentials from the higher officials, including the Sirdar in Khartoum, seemed of little help in that region.

As I had my own animals, to which I added a few more which I was able to obtain from good Father Tappi, who was returning to Europe, I proceeded, on the day of my arrival, towards Wau, the capital of the Bahr-el-Ghazal. I had now only five men with me to look after my new caravan of donkeys, and when I came to start at sunset four out of the five were dead drunk. The Somali, the only sober one of the group, and I, also quite sober, had to pack all the loads upon the animals.

In order to reach *terra firma* we crossed the long tumble-down dyke made across the ugly swamp, through which it was formerly necessary to wade, with mud up to one's neck, for over a mile. As I travelled in the evening, my donkeys, not properly looked after by my drunken men, went all over the place, and the

loads were constantly getting scattered upon the trail.
A storm came on. Storms always did when you least
wanted them. It got pitch dark towards eight or nine
o'clock in the evening, and at a moment when I had
stopped to pack up the loads on one rebellious donkey,
thunder nearly deafened us and rain came down in
sheets. The other animals got ahead and strayed away
from the trail and I lost them all. It took the Somali
and me the best part of the night to find them again
and to recover the loads which were strewn all over
the place.

On April 13th I arrived at Amien, where a Denka
village and half a dozen *tukles,* or shelters for officials,
stood on the left of the road. There was a deep well
here, but this being the dry season there was no water
in it ; the only water we were able to obtain at the place
being rain water from filthily dirty holes, and, in appearance, not unlike milk gone bad.

The Denka country, roughly speaking, extends all
over the low, perfectly flat plain of greenish-black
alluvial clay and rock that lies between the Bahr-el-
Djebel and the eastern limit (marked in that region by
the River Djur) of the enormous table-land of ferruginous
soil and rock, with isolated mounds of gneiss, and extending westwards.

These Denka resembled, with variations, those we
have met further east. This particular tribe indulged
in four cuts on both sides of the forehead, these cuts
converging downwards. Like other Denka, like the
Shiluk and Nuer, these people were long-legged, and
their shoulders were high and square-looking, but not
broad.

Nevertheless, although it was plain enough that these

Denka were allied to the Shiluk, they were neither so tall, nor were their legs quite of such abnormal length as those of the inhabitants of the White Nile and Sobat. Few of them, if any, reached six feet in height, although their average height exceeded, I think, that of Englishmen. A somewhat elongated neck, great breadth of jaw and prominent lips, were again noticeable. The skull was flattened and narrow. The scanty hair was usually closely shorn, hence the prevalent use of wigs or caps of basket-work or beads. The women, too, shaved the hair close. Cow's urine, as well as dung and ashes, were much used by the Denka in their toilette, particularly in order to dye the hair of a reddish tint.

As we have already seen on the Sobat, the Denka never use bows and arrows, but are skilful enough with their spears and war-clubs. The latter, perhaps, made either from the *balanites ægyptiaca* or from the *drospyrus mespiliformis*, the local ebony, are the most characteristic weapon of the race, as well as the cylindrical or half-cylindrical arrangement for parrying the blows of clubs.

There is also another instrument somewhat like a bow which is used for a similar purpose, and which we have already seen among other tribes.

Like the Yambo and the Shiluk, but unlike the Nuer, these Denka were extraordinarily clean people in their food and in their dwellings. No vermin was to be found inside their huts, but snakes were plentiful in the thatch of their homes. These, however, were not poisonous, and of no great size. The commonest kinds were the *ahætuella irregularis*, and the *psammophis sibilans*, the latter so called because of the hissing noise it makes when attacked.

I was told that many large pythons existed in the country, but I never saw them. Both the Denka and the Shiluk—although they can hardly be called snake worshippers—seemed respectful to snakes, which they never killed. I believe this is partly because these reptiles kept their huts free from insects, and therefore they were made practically into pets.

Most Denka huts—more spacious and durable than those of other tribes—and villages are encircled by fields of *dhura,* and the inhabitants own a considerable number of cattle.

The *dhura* and grain of the *pencillaria* are pounded and sifted into fine meal and are quite good to eat— indeed, the *cuisine* of the Denka is not only clean but elaborate. The *arachis* is cultivated, as well as several kinds of beans. They do not eat dogs and snakes and putrid meat, like tribes we shall find further west, but are most particular in their selection of animal food. Hares and wildcat, tortoises, gazelles, and ante- lopes they dearly like.

The Denka have large herds of sheep—a typical breed of their own, short-haired and with a mane— somewhat resembling the breed to be found in certain parts of Morocco. Their goats resemble those of Abyssinia ; only those of the Denka are larger. These goats are great climbers in regions where they can feed on leaves of trees.

Owing to the great moisture in their country and the fetid quality of water in the rain pools—simply a living mass of germs—their cattle and sheep suffer a good deal from intestinal worms. Leeches of various *genera* are to be found in immense numbers, and cause the animals a good deal of suffering. I think that it is due to these leeches and the immense amount of blood they suck from the stomach and arteries that the animals in the Denka country never possess any fat. There is one kind of leech in particular, a repulsive little oval bag of a greenish colour, which swells out when full of blood to the size and shape of a sparklet cartridge. I have sometimes removed dozens of them from the legs of my animals. Between the legs, behind the ears, under the lips and neck, were favourite places for these parasites.

Although at Meshra mosquitoes swarmed in millions, at Amien, only eleven miles further, we were able to sleep undisturbed without mosquito nets. We left this camp in the afternoon, and marched through flat country with only a few trees here and there.

All this region is swampy during the rainy season. The long bridge which had been made across the worst place had now collapsed.

Ten miles further, towards 8.30 in the evening, we arrived at Medal, where we fortunately found a good well. Here I had another disaster, which in a way afforded me pleasure. I had a large tent with a bath-room attached to it of khaki-coloured waterproof. This stuff, smeared over with a rubber preparation, was highly inflammable. The sparks from some lighted wood carried by one of my men set it ablaze, so that in a few minutes the tent was rendered useless. I had reluctantly kept this heavy tent because the rainy season was now coming on and I thought I might need it. I was glad I had such a good opportunity for discarding it as it was heavy to carry.

We experienced steamy hot, quite oppressive, weather on our next march across flat, uninteresting country.

We saw a lot of giraffes near the road, but I never fired at these animals for two reasons. First of all, because it was forbidden by the Government ; then because they were too tame and their skins useless.

There were beautiful birds flying about, small green parrots in quantities, and tiny blue silky-coated humming-birds. Upon the ground crawled a great variety of beautiful lizards and chameleons of wonderful gradations of tints, from the richest and warmest cadmium yellow to the deepest ultramarine blue.

One beautifully shaped smooth-bodied lizard in stripes of yellow and dark brown was also noticeable, the yellow blending into a faint blue which gradually got darker until it became deep and rich towards the end of the tail. The most common chameleons possessed bright yellowish heads, dark blue bodies, and a yellow ringed tail of light blue with a black tip. There was then another kind of rough-skinned chameleon in all shades of vivid browns and greens. Dozens of them played around me at the "*Gemaiza*" tree, where I had stopped for my lunch.

There were three wells here, thirty to thirty-five feet deep, with putrid water that stank as we brought the bucket up to the surface.

In three more hours' march that day we arrived at Gedain, where another beautiful tree was to be seen and a number of *tukles* in course of construction.

More Denka were to be found here, all with four cuts on each side of the forehead ; men and women adorned with a pointed leather tail behind. Some wore quite a large tail, not unlike that of a modern dress-coat. Most of these tails were made of tanned leather, but many people wore tiny tails of antelope or water-buck. Several women showed broad bands of small white and red beads with a fringe of rope just over the loins.

Young men displayed two rows of parallel dots upon their skin running down each side of the body from directly under the breasts to the genital organs, and eventually forming an angle. All the men shaved the greater portion of the skull, leaving a circular tuft of hair at the back of the head, into which they stuck porcupine quills or ostrich feathers, as the fashion of the day prompted them. The women shaved a good portion of the side hair and also part of the top of the head. They plaited what remained into tiny tresses, which they often smeared with butter and red earth.

Although we still found a few men who covered themselves with ashes, the custom was not so general here as further east.

Denka houses had a narrow mud wall four feet high. A thatched roof, constructed separately, was placed bodily upon this wall when completed. A small open porch adjoined the front of the house, and several small peepholes were to be seen around the wall of the hut.

The fashion of wearing many rings in separate holes all the way round the curve of the ears was common among these people.

We fared badly for water, as there was none on the road, except at these wells, or in the small pools which had been dug by natives or by the Government. Some of these pools were only ten feet or so below the level of the ground in sandy soil. They contained a few inches of water, possibly as much as a small wash-basinful.

After the hot marches, when we arrived anywhere

insatiably thirsty, especially in the evening, we generally found natives sitting in these pools washing their limbs and body. As this was the only water we could find, it did not make us particularly amiable towards the local residents, and we had to face the problem whether we would resign ourselves to die of thirst or use it as best we could. I do not know that boiling it improved it much. We generally disguised it into strong coffee, but there was so much lime in many of these wells that even the strongest coffee we brewed was hardly less white than pure milk. It generally hurt one's gums and palate considerably, as it burnt to no trifling extent.

From Gedain the trail was good, sandy in only one or two places. Mimosas of the *gherar* type were to be found here also, but were not so luxuriant as those we had met in Abyssinia. We were now getting into somewhat thicker forest, with many fan palms of great height and a fruit palm, the *deleb*.

At a place called Bir-el-Gherad, sixty-two miles from Meshra, we came on two more pools of filthy milky water, ten or twelve feet below the surface of the ground, and also a deeper well equally filthy but of a slightly better flavour. Here, too, the strongest and blackest coffee that could be made really looked like *café au lait*, with two-thirds of it milk.

I made a wonderful purchase from some natives of thirteen eggs at a cost four times higher than the best new-laid eggs in London. When I came to eat them twelve had chickens in them ready to come out—if they had not been boiled—and so much gas had formed in the thirteenth, in its putrefied condition, that it exploded with a loud report when I tapped it. The smallest and most skeleton-like chickens fetched one shilling each in this country, and at best were unfit to eat.

My animals were suffering a good deal, as at most of these places there was just sufficient water for the men, but none could be procured for the animals. I generally marched early in the morning and late in the evening, as the heat was intense for my donkeys, who were much overladen and suffered from thirst as well as from lack of good food.

Some miles from this last camp we reached a place called Dug-Dug, where we had expectations of finding a good well.

" Oh, monsieur," exclaimed my faithful Somali, as he quickly pulled out half a bucketful, " this water is very good, monsieur. It is just like milk."

In fact, all the water of all the wells contained so much *calcium* that it resembled a white, syrupy cream when it was clean, but generally took bilious deadly green and yellow tints when it was not quite pure. Hence the exclamation of my attendant when he saw water of such pure white.

Since leaving Gambela on the Sobat I had with me three small ostriches, which had become quite tame and were following me about like dogs. These poor little friends of mine suffered so much from drinking foul water that at one time they disappeared and I was unable to find them again. It seemed as if they rebelled against coming any further. However, late in the evening they returned to my camp, but they appeared ill. One of them was taken with a violent colic and died. Another died shortly after.

The Denka of this region wore a high pointed cap made

of basket-work, not unlike a huge wine funnel upside down. In the pointed end they stuck either one or more ostrich feathers or highly-coloured feathers from other birds.

We left Dug-Dug in the afternoon, and passed the well of Deleba, from which point the country became slightly more interesting. There were great numbers of smooth-stemmed *deleb* palms of great height, with the usual swelling half-way, and also some of the shorter *dum* palms with forked roots, and beautiful fan-shaped leaves all the way up the stem from the ground.

At Higlig, further on, there was merely a pool of pernicious water. During the night the dew was heavy, the damp saturating everything with moisture, and the air so stifling that it seemed a typical place to get malarial fever. Everything was soaking wet in the morning, although we had had no rain at all.

By making an early start on April 17th we soon reached Ayum, thirty-six miles from Bir-el-Gherad, and here there was a good well some forty feet deep of quite drinkable water. We found some *gemaiza*, or fig-trees, producing fruit quite good to eat.

We heard the roaring of lions next night. They came quite close to camp. So much so that all my donkeys broke loose and stampeded. A tornado was raging at the time, and the rain came down in torrents. What with the lions roaring, the thunder and flashing of lightning, the fierce braying of the donkeys, and the shrieks of my men, it was a regular pandemonium.

The trail which has been made by the Government was here excellent and made travelling comparatively easy. There were lots of *abil* trees, *sasaban*, and mimosas of great size, many of which we found on our way to

Moyem, twelve miles further on, where I halted for the
night.

Here there was a well of good water at the resting
sheds.   These rest-houses were generally looked after
by ex-Sudanese soldiers employed as police.   At this
place the policeman was an impudent rascal, who,
instead of seeing that the laws of the country were
obeyed, was the first to infringe the regulations.   He
had killed a large giraffe, and had asked his friends to
come and share its meat that evening.   Large pieces
of the giraffe were being brought over by natives, and
great was the annoyance of this policeman when I
arrived on the scene unexpectedly.   Owing to the great
heat the meat was fast decomposing, and the stench from
it was such that it was not possible to approach the
wells.   I asked the policeman to remove it, as any white
traveller has the right to use these sheds.   As travellers,
however, never go that way, and as I did not wear a
khaki helmet nor a brass-buttoned uniform like military
men, but had merely a lounge suit and a straw hat, this
policeman was extremely insulting.

I noticed that many of these policemen seemed
an unruly, disorderly, drunken lot, without any manners,
and dishonest to a degree, except towards their officers,
who, in a way, are responsible for their conduct, as they
try to impress on the soldiers that any one who is not a
military man is equal to dirt.   This man was reported,
of course, to his superior officers, and it would be
interesting to know whether he was punished at all
even for his crime of killing a giraffe, for which white
men are punished, I believe, at the rate of £100 fine
or three months' imprisonment.

Between Ayum and Makot the road was excellent,

and the landscape wooded with fig-trees and mimosas. At Makot we were glad to find a well of fairly good water and a couple of *tukles*.

On leaving again in the afternoon, we went through a forest of mimosas and fig-trees, but we saw no more palms. We met occasional shrubs of the *luni*, which produce an edible nut with a somewhat caustic taste. From high trees we also got large beans, called the *baloto*, which have a sweet yellow substance not unlike cassia inside them.

We were now in the Djur country. The villages were palisaded all round to protect the inhabitants from the attacks of wild animals at night. The huts had conical roofs built so as to allow a space between the roof and the wall in order to let air circulate. A high platform was generally to be seen in front of every four or five huts, and upon this platform rested mats, utensils, and the thatching for the roofs which was placed there to dry.

In front of us, to the south-west, was now a long low hill-range, if it deserves such a name, as it was merely fifty or sixty feet high—the first undulation I had seen since leaving Abyssinia, barring one or two small isolated hills I had discerned in the distance.

The Djur were principally noticeable for their ability in working iron. They were, in fact, the blacksmiths of the district. The Djur were particularly numerous at M'bili and Cangia, where they had many furnaces and forges.

These people were in type much like the O-chiolla, with almost identical features, ornaments and language. Whether they took the name from the river Djur, flowing into the Bahr-el-Ghazal, where they inhabit,

or the river took the name from them, I could not
exactly say.

They supplied nearly all the neighbouring tribes with
spear-heads. It was quite remarkable to see how these
people could smelt iron ore and work the extracted metal
with considerable precision, notwithstanding the rudimentary tools they possessed.

Their cylindrical furnaces showed a great deal of
ingenuity in the draught arrangements in order to
obtain high temperatures. The furnace was open at
the top and possessed three apertures at the base, one
with a channel of mud acting as a chimney. The process
of smelting was shortly this. They first placed one layer
of charcoal of mahogany wood, plentiful in that region,
and upon it one layer of iron ore broken into small
pieces. Then again a small layer of coal and another
one of iron, and so on until the summit in the interior
of the furnace was reached. They set fire to the lower
layer, and in twenty-four hours extracted the molten
metal of this, then causing each superposed layer to descend and the coal to ignite. Twenty-four hours later
more molten metal was collected, and so on every
twenty-four hours until the last layer was exhausted.
The metal was then separated as much as possible from
impurities and was smelted in earthenware vessels,
the combustion of the fuel being aided by cleverly-
devised bellows made of two mud cylinders, each
with an escape channel joining into a common outlet
blowing on the fire. A loose skin was tied at the upper
ends of each of these cylinders and worked by hand,
raised and lowered, by a man standing between the two
cylinders, so as to cause a constant draught. The metal
was then worked into spear-heads, axes and knives.

Until quite lately all spear-heads possessed by the Denka were manufactured by the Djur. These people did not know how to temper steel properly. It took no less than four men to work a forge : one to do the blowing, two to hold the metal, the other one to strike with a stone hammer.

The Djur population extended in a narrow crescent from Tonj to the south-east, to some miles north of Wau.

Between Meshra and Wau could be noticed rubber vines. Malual was the first Djur village we had encountered on our westward way, the Denka practically inhabiting the country eastwards. This village was only three or four hours' journey from Wau, the capital of the Bahr-el-Ghazal province.

CHAPTER XXXII.

WAU, where I arrived in the evening of April 18th, was situated on the site of Fort Desaix, built by Marchand in a well-selected spot, slightly elevated, on volcanic ferruginous rock. The fort itself, well constructed of volcanic boulders and mud, with an outside trench and a tower able to command the country in all directions, stood on the left bank of the stream. A red-brick building, used as an arsenal and ammunition magazine, had been constructed within the walls of the fort, and behind the old fort another larger fortified enclosure had been built, with corner towers enclosing military stores, etc. Along the bank of the Djur stood in a row the meek, tumble-down residences of the *mudir,* or governor, and of the English officers, then beyond, those of the Egyptian Sudanese officers and employees.

Behind were the barracks, a good hospital, some workshops, the quarters for the soldiers' wives and friends, and a sort of market. Further away were the humble quarters of the Austrian mission.

An attempt at gardening was being made along the stream, and an experimental farm had been started under the able direction of a Polish gentleman, Mr. Skirmunt. Beyond was thick forest with valuable wood, such as ebony (*drospyrus mespiliformis*), tall *eugeniæ* and *un-*

Author's caravan arriving at Fort Desaix (Wau). (The central structure with conical roof is Marchand's fort.)

cariæ, amorphophallur, and the red-blossomed *melas-tomaceæ,* gardenia trees, *borassus* palm, and the *can-delabra-euphorbia ;* also most excellent mahogany.

In an open space, which goes by the name of " The Square," are two or three sheds for Greek traders, Angelo Capato, of Khartoum, being perhaps the best supplied and the most reasonable in his prices. By the time goods reach this point, after infinite vicissitudes, their cost becomes almost prohibitive.

My instruments registered the elevation of Wau at 1,310 feet.

At the time of my visit there were in Wau some four or five British officers, all pleasant, especially Sutherland Bey, the *mudir,* who most kindly offered the hospitality of the officers' mess and placed a house at my disposal. I, however, while thoroughly appreciating the *mudir's* kindness, was unable to accept either, as I never like to be under obligations. I make it a rule seldom to accept anything from my own countrymen, except upon payment or the giving of an equivalent. I think if this rule were generally followed, many unfair remarks about travellers imposing upon British officers in Central Africa would be avoided.

In this particular case, the local Government officials seemed, judging from a despatch I received, destitute of everything, except a newly-imported American buggy ; and it would have been wrong to accept their well-meant hospitality. Their shanties—they could hardly be called houses—were so leaky that waterproof sheets and mackintoshes had to be arranged in the interior over the beds in rainy weather.

Comparisons are always odious, but, having travelled in many non-British countries, I am always struck by the helplessness of Britishers in the matter of making themselves comfortable homes immediately upon arriving in tropical climates. It is true that the Bahr-el-Ghazal had not been opened up more than a couple of years when I was there. Still, that would give ample time to build some sort of dwellings, the roofs of which would not be a constant danger to the residents.

I have seen French, Belgian and Italian officers in similar climes make their own kilns, bake bricks, extract lime from shells (when lime was not obtainable from the soil), and make neat vegetable gardens which were a great boon to their health and happiness. In the military posts I visited in the Sudan, Wau was the only place where an attempt at gardening had been made—and that was only the keeping-up of Marchand's garden.

I put up one of my own tents some distance from the town in a most picturesque spot along the river. On one or two occasions I visited the Austrian mission, where a couple of miserable sheds were erected. The poor father in charge was pitiably ill, and to my regret I hear that he has since died of fever. These Catholic missionaries were real martyrs. They were sent out to these trying climates with no comforts of any kind, next to no food, no money, and they had to live mostly on the country. In their heavy black gowns, which they seldom changed, they went about among the sick or ailing, with no hope of a holiday when ill or dying, but always in the most critical moments resigned to their fate. Most of them succumbed, but a few with a finer physique, greater vitality and brighter mental abilities, survived, and even enjoyed life. Father Tappi, whom I had the great pleasure of meeting at Meshra, was one of them. Practical, thoughtful, unselfish, vivacious, and with great magnetic influence over the natives, this man was indeed the type of missionary one would always like to see sent out to do good work among heathens. His great ambition was to teach them trades, agriculture, and how to earn a living honestly. Religion, he said, would gradually come in afterwards, when these people were getting educated. Father Tappi knew that country probably better than any white man, and my conversations with him were most instructive.

Between Meshra and Wau many were the subdivisions of tribes to be found in the country. First, the Afuk, the Furumch and the Falli, north of our trail ; and the Min, the Luanedian, the Atok, Ayur and Sadyok, to the south. Then west of these were the Djur, Nyang, Aniar, Regnelol, Abuk and Aguok, all these tribes being east of the course of the Djur river.

Few natives were, however, to be seen along the trail itself, as they had all removed their villages to distant points where they remained undisturbed. They had no communication with the Sudan Government officials, and I was told that they had shown hostility towards individual officers on shooting expeditions in their country.

The route between Meshra-el-Rek and Wau made by the Government could not be better for local wants, and the Sudan Government should be congratulated upon endeavouring to open an easy communication between the various points of that country, and establishing a regular postal service. Trails are easily made, the land being flat and the soil hard enough in the dry season; all that is necessary is to knock down a few trees and keep the trail free from grass after the rains.

The entire distance from Meshra to Wau, according to Government measures, is 114 miles, divided thus :

MESHRA				Dug-Dug			
to Amien	..	..	11	to Deleba ..		..	5
,, Medal	..	..	6	,, Ayum ..		..	15
,, E. Mayik	..	..	5	,, Moyem ..		..	12
,, W. Mayik	..	..	5	,, Malual ..		..	12
,, Gemaiza Tree	..	..	6	,, Tombashi		..	2
,, Gedain	..	..	9	,, Malual, Djur vil-			
,, Biril Gozad ..		..	11	lage ..		..	5
,, Dug-Dug	..	..	6	,, WAU ..		..	4

With my caravan I covered the distance in six days, but I travelled briskly. Sheds have been erected at all the more important camping places.

All the men I had taken to Wau left me, and it was impossible to obtain fresh men at this place, the Government having apparently no control over the natives, even for its own use. I employed some Niam-Niam, but after having been well fed in camp for three or four days, when the moment came to depart, they did depart, truly enough—but in a different direction altogether from the one in which I wanted them to go, and I never saw them again.

At the last moment, Major Sutherland, the Governor, kindly gave me three natives, all that could be found, but they were absolutely useless, and they were more of a hindrance than a help. So with practically only one man, my faithful Somali, I packed up the baggage on April 23rd, and we two loaded the entire caravan, while the three newly-employed natives sat gracefully upon their haunches watching us. On no

Adem, the Author's faithful Somali.

account could these three men be induced to go near the donkeys. They feared them more than lions or elephants.

The heat was intense. From this moment I well grasped that we should have further. hard times in looking after the animals. My Somali and I would have to do all the running about and the trying work of recovering the loads and putting them on again every time they fell off.

We left in the middle of the day, as, come what might, I would continue. I had a sort of suspicion that obstacles were placed in my way so that I should not get on. Perhaps this was the case, perhaps not. It little mattered to me.

With my straw hat at a dangerous angle upon my head and my best blue serge suit—such as I should wear to walk down Piccadilly in summer-time—I started off, somewhat to the amazement of the British officers, making the donkeys march briskly before me with my *courbash*.

" Where are your men ? " shouted one officer.

" I do not need any men. Good-bye."

" Have you no helmet to protect your head from the sun ? "

" I need *no* protection *of any kind*, thank you."

And on we went, outside the military post, then getting into the forest, soon after leaving the part that had been cleared of trees. The country was slightly undulating, with mere corrugations, hardly more than ten feet in height. The first undulation was close to Wau, and upon it the new officers' quarters will eventually be constructed, as it is of a rocky, volcanic formation, with plenty of iron in it. The new building will be slightly healthier than the quarters which the officers have at present.

Others of these undulations, further out, were somewhat higher, possibly some twenty feet or so, and were also of red volcanic rock. There were, indeed, great patches of this ferruginous stone, and we wended our way along the good trail amid innumerable fig-trees, *lu* and *lulu*, *drospyrus mespiliformis*, *eugeniæ* and *uncariæ*.

Close to Abu Shakka, twelve miles from Wau, were three sheds. The trail ran practically due west until we got close to the last hill, where we proceeded slightly south-west.

There were plenty of fig-trees all along, and some rubber vines, acacias and wild fruit-trees, some quite deadly, others not so bad to eat, among these being a yellow elongated fruit, and the *baloto* beans, which were quite good.

There were here many Golo, who have villages in this region, and further west, especially near Kaiaongo. Another tribe inhabits further south upon the Wau river. The Golo build their houses solidly and neatly, quite unlike their neighbours, the Bellanda, who live north of the Golo tribe, upon the Wau river.

Each Golo family occupies a site upon the Chief's land, and each erects a *zeriba* of wooden pillars, with as many huts inside as the head of the family possesses wives. The huts are of wood, plastered inside, with low walls and a rectangular door, generally kept closed by a mat. Near the hut is always a granary or storehouse. Under the granary a *morraca*, or stone mill, is invariably to be found. In many of these houses are several of these *morraca*, and Father Tappi, I remember, once told me that he saw as many as three of these *morracas* in one hut.

The great regularity of construction of Golo roofs is mostly due to the bamboo rafters used. As is the case at Abu Shakka, the Golo frequently put up, round their *zeribas*, a strong palisade, which they hide behind a thatch of grass so as to deceive the enemy.

Like the Yambo, these people use a wonderful cement, which they extract from a particular clay in the river. They use it both for plastering their huts and for covering over their graves. This cement contains a good deal of iron, which is perhaps responsible for its great solidity when dried up in the great heat of the sun.

I cannot say that the Golo women were attractive, nor, indeed, the Golo men either. They most of them possessed big paunches, the legs were weak-looking and not particularly straight, with feet extraordinarily long. Young women plastered the hair in lumps with red mud and oil, but the older women matted their hair in vertical plaits upon the head, leaving spaces of exposed scalp, which gave a mangy appearance to those adopting this fashion. Some of them wore bracelets of blue beads. Most had three horizontal and three vertical cuts on each cheek, which made them quite repulsive with their huge lips and squashed noses. They nearly all had a peculiar squint, which certainly did not add to their beauty.

From the habit of constantly kneeling down to grind grain under the *morraca*, as well as from squatting upon the long logs of wood which are placed across the broad wells when drawing water, the skin of their knees was rough and wrinkled with a thick, callous growth. The

legs were under-developed, especially from the knee to
the ankle, but the ankle itself was small and rather
well formed.

Their wardrobe consisted of a small—very small—
bunch of verdure, sometimes behind, sometimes in
front. The Golo ladies seemed to have adopted all the
fashions which can make a woman repulsive to European eyes. I saw at Abu Shakka an old lady who had
stuck in her right nostril a white cylindrical bead, which
looked like half a cigarette stalk ; while another lady
had a bead of a similar size, only red instead of white,
also inserted in her nose.

Large silver and iron earrings were worn, and were
so heavy that the ears became elongated. The lobes of
the ears of this tribe were, when in their normal condition, attached and the ear itself flat and malformed,
even when not affected by ornaments hanging from it.
For some reason or other, the ears of these people
seemed absolutely desiccated, and with no life in them ;
they possessed no well-defined ridges or curves, the outer
rim being rounded over instead of curling forward, as
is usual with better-formed ears. In fact, I noticed how
that malformation was greatly responsible for the in-
ability of these people to catch accurate sounds. They
could not distinguish the difference between an " l "
and an " r," nor between an " e " and an " i," nor between " d," " t " and " b." Their hearing was altogether dull, and one required to talk to them fairly
loudly and explicitly for them to understand at all.

This is, of course, more or less general with all blacks
of tropical Africa, and many people who have had
experience with them will tell you that even one's own
servants, accustomed to European ways, do not often

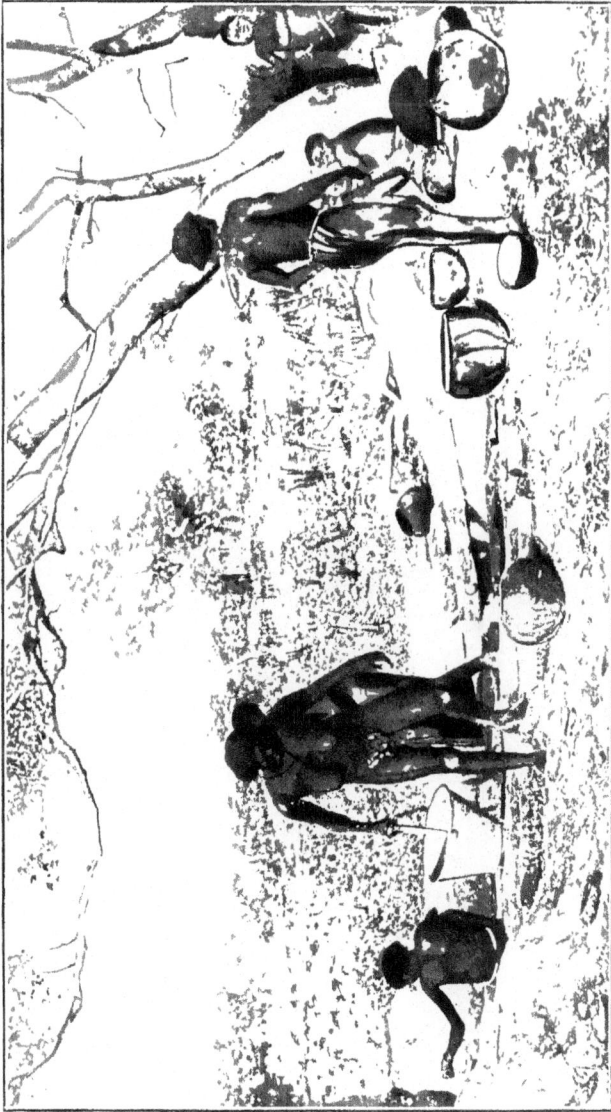

Women at a well in the western Bahr-el-Ghazal. (The bucket belonged to Author and was not a native vessel.)

hear their master speak unless they are facing him, when they will pay attention to what is said. When their back is turned, it is difficult to make them hear, as their auditory organs do not work quite so accurately as ours, or, at least, do not bring the impressions received quickly to the brain, unless when working jointly with the sight.

The eyebrows of the Golo form a double curl, and give them a frowning, dissatisfied expression, even in their brightest moments of happiness. They have a considerable development of the upper portion of the lid between the rim and the eyebrow, a development which almost amounts to a swelling. In fact, when the eye is open the lower section of the lid itself is absolutely covered, and hardly shows at all.

There was a good deal of the monkey in the movements and postures of these people. One day I saw six women in a row, squatting just like quadrumanes upon a long pole thrown across the aperture of a well some thirty feet deep. They had chimpanzee-like big paunches and delightful expressions on their faces. They pulled up water as fast as they could go in small vessels made of half gourds with a forked stick attached to the upper portion as a handle. With these they filled large earthen jars by the side of the well. These jars were decorated with dots in the upper portion, with a row of large dots at the mouth, and with a lot of smaller dots either in transversal or vertical lines covering two-thirds of the vessel from the bottom up.

The Golo women had the hair plastered down into little tresses at the side of the head. Red beads were stuck in the nostrils. The upper portion of the nose directly under the glabella was absolutely flat, and the tip of the nose had the appearance of having been pushed back, so much so that the apertures of the nostrils in a full face appeared like two circular holes.

One or two, while balanced on the unsteady, primitive bridge across the well, carried their babies in a sling from the right shoulder, the child riding astride upon his mother's left hip, on which he supported himself. The mammas had extraordinarily flat noses, particularly at the bridge, but their nasal flatness was nothing to that of their darlings. I do not think that I have ever seen babes whose lack of nose was so glaring as with these Golo youngsters.

Men and women had eyes wide apart, almost bird-like, and I believe the squint which I have mentioned above is partly due to the great distance between the two pupils, which is bound to produce a defect of sight, since in focussing objects close by they must converge at an angle.

They seem proud of the little tufts of fresh grass held—I do not know how—in front, behind, or at times in both places, and constantly renewed when getting dry. Fashions are cheap in Gololand, where an in-exhaustible dressmaking department is to be found in the nearest meadow.

Much as I like to encourage bathing among natives, I must say I was rather vexed with the Golo ladies of Abu Shakka. After they had finished filling their vessels with water, they drew water from the well and proceeded to have shower-baths, one woman pouring water on the head of another with a calabash. As they did this on the edge of the well, the water flowed in again to the place it had come from. The verdure was torn off on these occasions and renewed after the bath was over. When I scolded them they, too, were quite offended, and asked me what I was complaining of, as they were " not wasting " the water, which was scarce in the region. No, indeed, it was all flowing back into the well !

Cicatrices in sets of three vertical lines were popular among the ornamentations upon the chest, sometimes also on the back. These began directly under the shoulder-blades, and extended as far as the waist ; a waist-band of a great number of cicatrices all round the body was also to be noticed. The women had sets of cicatrices upon the breasts right down to the nipples. The breasts were extraordinarily developed and pendent.

Unlike the tribes we had seen until now, we were here among people with long bodies and short legs. Instead of square, the people had rounded shoulders, with good waists arched inward.

I was surprised to find how white the palms of the hands were in these people. The nails were light pink. The fingers were badly formed, short and square-tipped, the thumb particularly, which in more civilized people would be put down as the thumb of a highly criminal type. It was short and flattened, with a mere strip of nail much elongated sideways. Their hands seemed to obey the brain only to a slight extent, and it would be difficult to find clumsier people than these Golo when they had to do anything with their fingers.

There were two villages at Abu Shakka. They took the name from their chief, a flat-faced, pock-marked individual. The village nearer the well was the newer of the two, and comparatively tidy, within a *zeriba* of wood and high grass forming a wall over ten feet high. In the

enclosure stood the quadrangular mud house of the
chief, with its neat thatched roof and three or four
more irregular huts entirely made of reeds upon a
wooden frame.

CHAPTER XXXIII.

WE left at six the next morning on an excellent trail that went over ferruginous soil through fairly dense forest. Here began our troubles with flies of all kinds, particularly big horse-flies, the sting of which was painful. There were millions of them round us, and the mere buzzing near one's face was enough to drive anybody out of temper. The animals suffered a good deal and kicked and dashed about, rubbing themselves against trees in order to shake them off. The result was that the loads were constantly getting scattered upon the trail, and the Somali and I had to run after the demoralized animals. No sooner had we our hands occupied in lifting the loads upon the pack-saddles than our eyes, ears and faces were simply covered with flies taking advantage of our helpless condition. If you opened your mouth they flew into it, and, indeed, travelling under those circumstances was not a pleasure.

There was a tiny kind of gnat, also troublesome, which seemed to have a particular attraction to the eyes. Swarms of them dashed into one's face, and during the day I have had consecutively as many as fifty or sixty of these little brutes in my eyes. They stick at once to the moisture, and spread a highly-scented, acid liquid, which makes the eyes and lids sting acutely. Fortunately,

they are easily removable, but they cause severe in-
flammation with some people. They have a way also of
getting inside one's ears, and when they get far enough
into the channel they are difficult to get out again.

With the stifling heat, the riotous animals, the flies
big and small, sore eyes and worrying ears, with stings
itching all over one's body, the effort of lifting the loads
fifty times a day at least upon the packs—not to speak
of the running about to recapture the animals—was
indeed hard work. The Somali behaved faithfully.
Notwithstanding all, we travelled that day thirty miles to
the next camp, sometimes over open stretches near the
trail, where families of huge monkeys dashed across,
carrying their young upon their backs ; then further
among thousands of anthills from one to two feet high,
and shaped like mushrooms. There were other conical
anthills of the *termix voratrix ;* these were of great height,
although they were built by a smaller ant.

For the first few hours the trail wound considerably,
first to the north-west, then to the west, then west-
north-west ; but after passing some slight undulations
and volcanic rocks and boulders beyond a brooklet's
channel, now waterless, we arrived at 11.30 at Bisellia,
where, fortunately, we obtained plenty of water from
the Khor, bad as usual, but plentiful enough to allay the
thirst of my animals.

An abandoned village stood near the Khor in a mat-
walled *zeriba*, with a number of tumble-down huts. The
former chief's house was plastered with black polished
cement. In each hut, the Bongo, another tribe who inhabited this village, had built a quadrangular platform
some six feet long by three feet wide, raised six inches
above the ground, which they used as a bed. A fire was

made within the triangle of three stones, on which were placed the cooking vessels. In some huts I saw curious beds of black cement, with a hollow in the centre where the people lay.

There were near this place some extensive earthworks : a trench, with a bastion, which the natives said had been made by the Turks. It was, as a matter of fact, put up by Limbo's father on his return to Bisellia, after having fled from this place on the arrival of the Dervishes. He had escaped to two hills north of Dem Zebir, then to Kossinga, where Sultan Nasr Andel offered fight. He then returned to his old place where he erected the fortifications visible to this day.

Over the marsh close by, a ruined bridge was to be seen.

I had an amusing experience here. A glass of French jam I had just emptied was lying in camp. I saw a Bongo examining the glass with attention, turning it round and round in his fingers and expressing great admiration. He then put the glass down and walked away.

In this place, being near the military post of Wau, silver money is known, as the natives are paid in currency for supplies they sometimes sell to the soldiers. Presently the man returned with an Egyptian coin worth one shilling, and deposited it on my lap, taking the glass and proceeding to walk off. Whereupon I took the shilling and threw it at him. The man seemed much taken aback, picked up his money and brought back the glass to me. He departed a second time, and a few minutes later returned from his hut, and after describing three or four circles round me to discover in what mood I was, he now squatted in front of me, and in a most endearing fashion laid before me two shillings' worth of Egyptian coinage. I told him that I was no merchant, and did not care to sell anything. He took back the money, gave a leap in the air, and ejaculated some sound or other, dashing full speed to his hut. A little later I saw him cautiously approach my camp, holding something in his hand. He was looking at the sky, by which I understood he was up to some trick—as people generally are when they look innocently skyward. In fact, after pretending indifference, I saw him get nearer and nearer the glass, which he suddenly seized, throwing at me what he had in his hand, five shillings altogether, and bolted away with my glass, worth at most a halfpenny.

I collected the money and went to call upon this gentleman. He was afraid that I should take a revenge. His pleasure had no bounds when I gave him back the money and told him he could keep the glass.

In the afternoon, at 3.25, we left in a heavy shower, which only lasted a short time. We marched through forest until nearly eight o'clock, finding no water on the trail nor at the place where we camped. We, therefore, made an early start the next morning, gradually and slowly rising among semi-desiccated trees of no great beauty. Further on, where the trees had not been so burnt up, one found some hard woods, which, were transport easier, ought to be of commercial value. The fibre was extremely close and twisted, and it almost seemed as if these trees had experienced difficulty in growing through the ferruginous soil. There were mimosas, tamarind and fig trees, and trees with bark like cork.

During the whole march I only saw one solitary

bunch of flowers—small jessamines. We went fairly steadily at a rate of about three miles an hour, over slightly undulating and gradually and gently rising country. Occasionally we came to more of the typical " swellings of the earth " of volcanic rock. Near the summit these were strewn with almost spherical boulders, seemingly spluttered out when during the eruptive period the molten rock had come into contact with the colder atmosphere.

We marched steadily from five o'clock till one in the afternoon, the sun positively baking us. Then, owing to an approaching tornado, the heat became quite un- bearable. A severe thunderstorm caught us as we reached the Pongo stream, which, at the place we met it, flowed northwards, eventually, according to the natives, finding its way into the Djur river. Dirty as the water was, it seemed delicious to men and animals, and we all drank copiously. At any rate, it possessed a little more the lively taste of running water, and was more palatable than the fetid water we had been drink- ing since leaving Meshra.

There were three *tukles* here and a *rakuba* in construc- tion, with a house for a native policeman directly outside the *zeriba*. The Pongo river at this point was 1,600 feet above the sea, which showed us that we had risen 290 feet since leaving Wau, a distance of fifty-five miles.

From south to north, between lat. 7° N. to lat. 9° N., there are in this zone a good many tribes, such as the Bare, some Golo, then north of them the Bellanda, and north of these the N'dogo. We find a similar tribe of Bare slightly north-east of Limbo, where the Emdoco tribe is to be found, and another tribe of Bongo directly west of them. North we have more Golo, then another tribe of N'dogo, and, further along the Pongo river, more Bare.

The Bongo are people of fine stature, somewhat stoutly built. They are great cultivators of the land, probably the most successful agriculturists in the entire Bahr-el-Ghazal district. A few of the men have adopted cotton clothes, but the women go about absolutely naked, with the usual tuft of verdure in front and behind. They wear brass and iron bracelets; armlets, anklets and necklaces made of beads.

Their faces are greatly deformed by the *kagga* hanging from the lower lip, which consists of a straw inserted through the lip in young girls, and gradually increased in size until the little cylinder becomes as big as a large bottle cork. This fashion, as we shall find, gets more and more exaggerated as we travel towards the west. Another ornament is frequently to be seen, consisting of two straws, or sometimes of two small sticks, projecting from holes in each nostril. Both the Djur and the Bellanda tribes follow this fashion, like the Bongo.

At Kaiongo, north of the trail, the Austrian mission has a station, where it is doing good work among the natives, principally teaching them blacksmith's and agricultural work.

The country in that part is hilly, thickly wooded, and populous in parts, especially the villages of Chiefs Bakili and Malunga, the first chief of the Bellanda, the other a Golo chief. Unlike the Golo huts, those of the Bellanda are of a flimsy character, but their villages are enclosed in *zeribas* made of great chunks of wood solidly stuck into the ground.

The Bellanda are great hunters. They make large

nets, in which they drive and capture gazelles. The Bongo people, too, are fond of hunting, but they prefer to make traps. I saw some of these Bongo traps quite close to the Pongo river. They consisted of a passage-way along the trail, which was walled in with sticks on both sides for some five or six feet. The passage was closed up by a small net across, not visible at night, which when even slightly touched broke a frail piece of cane. By a series of crossed sticks at well-calculated angles just sufficient resistance was established to hold in position a heavy beam above at a dangerous angle. When released from this balanced position, the beam fell directly over the passage, crushing with its weight the unfortunate animal which had found its way there.

There were millions of mosquitoes of all sizes at Pongo, but by this time we were getting acclimatized. Although they bit us furiously, they hardly produced a swelling at all, if not disturbed during their process of suction, and caused but moderate irritation.

We left Pongo at 6.15 on April 26th. The river flowed in a tortuous channel, rocky in some parts, sandy in others. The banks were as much as ten to twelve feet high, and the river bed about thirty feet across. We found a vast grassy plain to the west of the river, and fairly open ground near the rest-houses which had been erected, but which seemed rather unpractical in their construction, owing to the absolute lack of ventilation, which made it impossible for anyone but a native to breathe when inside. The huts were thatched with grass, and the doors so low that they broke one's back every time one went in or out.

Further west we proceeded across thinly-wooded forest with hardly any undergrowth. We had gradually risen to 1,800 feet. We saw on one side of the trail a great granitic dome emerging some ten feet above the ground, with huge volcanic boulders by its side. Further on, to the west of this dome, about four hundred yards north of the trail, a high rocky hill, about one hundred feet high, was met with (1,900 feet above sea-level), and this was probably the highest hill I had seen in the Bahr-el-Ghazal, certainly the highest west of Meshra.

About an hour later on the march we met another big grey dome of granite, emerging some fifty feet above the ground. Partly owing to the great fires which are frequently caused by lightning and otherwise, the forest was thin in this portion of the country. After we had been gradually descending among lean young trees we came to another high hill, north of Ganna camping-ground, where I arrived towards noon, only to find that the well was absolutely dry, and not a drop of water was to be obtained. There was a deserted *zeriba* here, with three huts and a large shed for animals.

We were here at a slightly lower elevation, 1,750 feet. Having given my animals a short rest, I had to move on, endeavouring to find water at the next camp. The continuation of the Ganna hill formed a low hill-range of granitic rock, the general direction of which was from north-east to south-west. Here the trail went south-west. Towards sunset we had on our left another huge granitic dome, some forty feet high, and, having crossed the vein of granite, we proceeded through fairly dense forest, until we arrived at Hardeb at eight o'clock in the evening. The sheds at this station had been burnt down, but we found a small pool, some fifty yards long by five wide, with pestilential water, which, bad as it was, we were only too glad to have, as we had marched some twenty-six miles that day in intense heat across waterless country.

On the road we had met a suspicious crowd of ten or twelve men, armed to the teeth with matchlocks, spears and daggers. They seemed upset at meeting me. On being cross-examined, they professed to be looking for elephants.

This camp, called Hardeb by the natives, because of the mimosa *hardeb*, which is plentiful here and gives an edible fruit, generally goes by the name of Khor Idris or Gamus upon maps. *Lulu* trees were plentiful, with their thick, rugged bark cut up into so many neat little squares, and with bunches of large oblong leaves, thickly ribbed and fluted, in clusters generally of ten or twelve together. The *hardeb* had tiny little dark green leaves in double sets along a common stem. It was a most compact little tree, its branches shooting skyward and forming quite a thick mass.

We saw large dog-faced monkeys in abundance, which not only had a head like a dog, but also quite a canine bark.

White and white and yellow marble, not unlike Sienna marble, was to be found in this locality.

Again, we had to make a double march, this time first descending over undulating country, the slopes of which were drained by the Khor Idris; then, ascending gently in a dense forest of *lulu* trees, various acacias and mimosas and some occasional giant *hardeb*. An hour after leaving camp we saw to the south of the trail another heap of black volcanic rock. This was a great place for giant anthills; some built in domes, which I measured, were as much as eleven feet high. Near the foot of *hardeb* trees great conical accumulations of earth were frequently to be seen not less than ten feet high, formed mostly by white ants.

Among a lot of *abil* trees, with their tiny pointed leaves, we gradually descended to the Khor Gamus, a valley evidently swampy during the rains, lying between two hill-ranges with a ditch intersecting it from east to west. This ditch was now dry with the exception of two small pools not larger than four inches in diameter and three inches deep, where a small quantity of water had accumulated. As there was not sufficient to allay the thirst of my animals, I proceeded to Khor Raml, rising over a hill-range of volcanic rock, and finding a good deal of eruptive, ferruginous rock all along the way. In fact, after some ups and downs, we had to go over a lot of broken rock close to Khor Raml, which gave my animals a great deal of trouble, as there was a violent thunderstorm raging at the time and we had been overtaken by night.

We were drenched to the skin. Terrific lightning struck quite close to us, blinding us temporarily, and we lost our way. The night was so dark that it was difficult to get along.

The poor Somali and I had a great deal to do to keep the entire caravan together. The donkeys were absolutely paralyzed with fear by the deafening noise of thunder and the sudden flashes of lightning, which were useful in a way, for while the scene was brilliantly illuminated I could perceive where we were going.

Late at night we arrived at Raml, the storm still raging. We took shelter under the shed. The tornado got more and more violent, and presently I witnessed a sight, very beautiful in itself, but which made me somewhat nervous, as I had never before experienced the effects of the atmosphere being charged to such an extent with electricity. The entire sky became gloriously and incessantly lighted with a most vivid pink, almost violet, light, which was most penetrating, and produced on one's skin a similar sensation to the X-rays. The thunder became continuous overhead, and was quite deafening, like myriads of huge cannon being fired simultaneously. Incessant flashes of lightning streaked the sky in brilliant yellow, zigzag lines across the pink background, some coming so unpleasantly near that I was indeed glad when, after a couple of hours or so, I heard the thunder gradually get further and further away, and eventually we found ourselves under a brilliantly star-lit sky.

We had these storms nearly every day, but I never fancied them. Many people are killed by lightning in these regions, and in more frequented parts many Europeans have lost their lives in this manner, as white men generally carry firearms or metal objects about them which attract lightning.

The reason the storm seemed particularly bad at this place I discovered the next morning when, to the north-west of the camp, some fifty yards off, beyond a small *khor*, appeared a rocky, volcanic, ferruginous mass, which undoubtedly attracted and became charged with electricity. This mass extended northwards, where it rose some fifty feet above the *khor* at its foot.

We collected a quantity of excellent rain-water in all the vessels and buckets we possessed. I do not know that I have ever enjoyed anything so much as the good drink of clean water after the filthy stuff we had been tasting since leaving Meshra. My donkeys, too, had a great time drinking in the small pools which had been formed in large holes in the rock, these innumerable and curious large holes being caused, I am told, by lightning.

Camp Raml was at an elevation of 1,800 feet. Owing to the soaking we got the night before, and the loads being now nearly double their usual weight because of the moisture they had absorbed, not to speak of the fatigue which my animals had endured of late, I made a late departure in order to allow the donkeys to pick up some strength.

In a stroll round the camp I noticed a great many *abugani* plants, another kind of mimosa, with minute leaves. Then there were lots of *ofa*, a large fat-leaved, dark green fig-tree with whitish bark ; also *jokhan*, a large tree, with leaves not unlike those of cherry trees. Interesting was the *gorot*, a short tree, with waxy-feeling elongated leaves. The *thur* was a spiked tree, with tiny leaves, and the *ameruh* a graceful, white-stemmed tree, with most elastic branches. Perhaps the most plentiful was the *basson*, a plant growing to no greater height than ten or twelve feet, and possessing pinnate leaves two and a half inches long, with saw-like edges, these leaves growing in sets of two, like those of mimosas or acacias. The small white fruit of this plant was good to eat.

More granite domes were passed on the march, when we left at about 9.30 a.m. on April 28th, and towards 10.45 I mounted another high dome on the right of our trail, from which an extensive view was obtained over the practically flat country around. Only one high hill was visible at 15° bearings magnetic (or slightly north-north-east), some ten or fifteen miles distant. The ground seemed to be sloping from that hill towards the south-west. The top of the dome on which I stood was 1,975 feet, or twenty-five feet higher than the trail. It was of granitic formation, extending with a lower dome to the north-north-west. Many smaller domes and broken-up granitic blocks were to be seen towards the south, and extending south-west of the trail.

At 11.15 I arrived at Dem Idris, where four neat *tukles* and one open *rakuba* had been built within a *zeriba*. A few mud and thatched huts, about a hundred yards off, formed the quarters of the police. These *tukles* were kept beautifully clean by the policeman in charge. One large well had been dug, the water now no more of a white milky appearance, owing to being saturated with lime, but being instead of a thick red colour, with a strong, ferruginous taste. The well was forty feet deep. Other wells a quarter of a mile distant, only twenty feet in depth, had bad white-looking water again, such as was familiar to us.

At Dem Idris could be seen a two-storeyed mud building, with square windows in ruins, a relic of Zebir Pasha's historic days. Further down upon the trail the remains of a large mud-walled *zeriba*, said to have been made by the Turks, were also to be noticed.

Murjam Bahit, the policeman in charge of this station, was an excellent man and most helpful. In the *zeriba* was a fine *unzai* tree, under the shade of which I spent some pleasant hours.

I made a start late in the afternoon, at about four o'clock, and shortly after having descended where the old *zeriba*, now destroyed by fire, and the well used to be, we rose to a slightly higher table-land (2,150 feet), which we had observed encircling Dem Idris to the west and south-west.

I had at last found some use for one of the natives who had been given me by the Governor at Wau, and who so far had followed us at a distance. I made him the botanist of the expedition. It is quite amazing what a wonderful knowledge of botany all these natives have, and how wonderfully rich their language is in botanical terms, whereas upon any other subject, their fauna excepted, we find a corresponding poverty of expression. This man, who was an incredible idiot about anything else, was truly wonderful in his knowledge of plants. Sometimes his knowledge seemed so astonishing that I thought he was inventing the various names of trees. Time after time I checked him in various localities, but I found that, at least, as far as botany was concerned, he was truthful and learned.

We saw some high *rumm* trees and any number of *caruba*, with their large double leaves like the wings of a butterfly. Having descended into another *khor* (2,050 feet), we found a large pool of rain-water which had collected during the last storm, and which was separated by a mere undulation from another large pool of stagnant water in the marshy plain.

At night, as we were marching, a hurricane blew again with tremendous force. Black clouds collected overhead and all round us, so that it was impossible to distinguish the wet trail in the forest, and I was compelled to halt. Although the thunderstorm was fierce enough, we had no rain during the night; but in the morning, as we were leaving, heavy showers came upon us and made travelling inconvenient.

The ground was undulating, but with no great dips. We saw beautiful orchids of an electric violet colour (produced, I think, by the iron in the soil), and with a yellow centre. We were now gradually descending from an elevation of 1,950 feet, at which we had been travelling almost all along, with a granitic formation showing through in the more rocky places and volcanic, ferruginous rock visible here and there. We were as low as 1,800 feet at Khor Afifi, fifteen miles from Dem Idris.

The well at this place was thirty feet deep. There was a small village in a strongly-built *zeriba* for protection against lions, which were plentiful in this region. The country was more open and grassy. Further on our march, we still continued a gradual descent over fairly thickly-wooded country, with another huge dome of granitic formation over which our trail ascended.

I saw some huge wart-hogs, the *phacochœrus*, most plentiful in this region and generally seen in couples. The curiosity of these animals was quite entertaining ; when they saw a stranger they raised their elongated noses in a most characteristic way, partly to sniff the newcomer, partly to observe the better what his intentions were. They were stupid, and sometimes after you shot at them and missed them they would stand and look at you, and you could shoot two or three times before they ran away, if they were not killed.

I arrived at the river Kuru, ten miles further, in the afternoon, and such was the surprise which awaited me that I decided to halt for the day. The policeman in charge of the *zeriba* had actually been able to grow a huge and delicately flavoured water-melon, which was, indeed, a great treat in those thirsty regions. Luck never comes singly, and I was able to procure also fresh eggs and a chicken or two, which made quite a variation from the tinned provisions on which I had lived for some months, and of which I was beginning to be tired.

The Kuru stream, which ran in a north-easterly

direction, was a nice little rivulet, with large, deep pools full of fish, so I had plenty of choice for dinner that night. There is no doubt that when one's digestive organs are properly looked after a great step is made in the direction of happiness.

The *zeriba* at Kuru was at an elevation of 1,650 feet, the river about twenty feet lower. A rope was placed across the stream, about fifteen yards wide at the fording-place, with water only one to twelve inches deep. A kiln had been erected for baking bricks, probably with the intention of constructing a bridge.

Dem Zebir was due west of this place, but the trail made a long détour to the south-west.

During the night we had lions roaring round our camp. In fact, we had had them nearly every night, but beyond making much noise, the king of all animals seldom came near enough to be a nuisance. If they did come, it was sufficient to throw a piece of lighted wood at them, when they retreated in graceful bounds. Surely, not what people at home imagine the behaviour of the " king of all beasts " to be towards peaceful travellers ! One must, nevertheless, keep a sharp look-out on one's animals.

CHAPTER XXXIV.

WE left Kuru at 6.30 on April 30th. There was a high rocky hill to the west of the *zeriba*, but no view could be obtained from the top, as high trees stood in the way.

Between Kuru and Khor Silik we rose to an elevation of 1,800 feet. Silik itself was some fifty feet higher (1,850 feet). Further on we continued to rise to 1,950 feet, the country being in parts covered with ferruginous boulders.

We had felt the cold intensely during the moist night. The surviving little ostrich was taken ill and became unconscious. In order to save him I carried him in my arms for some miles, but towards noon the poor little thing expired.

I was fond of this little affectionate companion, and I proceeded to give him a suitable grave among picturesque volcanic boulders. For this purpose I walked away from the trail among fairly high grass looking for a convenient spot, when I almost trod on a crouching lion. I do not know which of us two was more surprised, the lion or myself. I gave a leap one way, the lion a much bigger leap in the opposite direction, and continuing to leap most gracefully, disappeared.

The notions of civilized people regarding wild animals

are curious, even ridiculously false. They imagine that wild beasts attack without provocation whenever they see you. There is no more mistaken idea than this. No wild animal, if the tiger under certain special conditions be excepted, will attack a man or woman who leaves him alone. I have seen hundreds of wild animals of all kinds at different times, and my experience is that they generally make away when they see you, or at any rate let you go by undisturbed, unless you fire at them and wound them, when, of course, in their pain and anger they may retaliate. They may, of course, attack one's animals, especially at night.

We arrived at Khor Ghanam at 12.30 in the afternoon. There was here a variety of trees. The *dorot*, a large-leafed fig-tree, much like the *lulu* ; the *sahabai*, a resinous tree, tall, with small light green leaves and bark of a burnt sienna colour. Then the *abagheud*, with bark in scales easily chipped off and tiny pointed leaves. The *viugo*, a tree producing large bunches of seeds ; the *sohk*, a long-spiked mimosa with tiny little leaves about one centimetre long, whereas the spikes were three times the length of the leaves; the *aguma*, a tree producing sets of three hard, spherical fruits, not good to eat ; the *abukadfer*, with a whitish-green bark and extremely elastic branches, with small metallic green leaves, quite rough to touch. The wood of this tree is extremely hard, mahogany-like.

The charmingly-shaped elongated little leaves of the *hemeru* are much eaten by the natives, as they possess a pungent taste which allays thirst. Then we have a hard and resinous wood in the *zawa* (*melastomaceæ*), the fire-tree, with fluted leaves rounded at the end instead of pointed. The clean-barked *jemsui* and the *kilimbah* also produce a hard wood ; the *andugulugulu* is a fine tree growing mostly along streams. On the banks of the Khor were great quantities of the *vera*, a tall shrub with small oval leaves and an intricate confusion of branches. Handsome trees were the *afoma* and the *bengheh*, the latter being quite smothered in dark green small leaves of the acacia type and producing a poisonous brown bean about two inches long. The wood of the *bengheh* was hard and resinous. The *andarap*, with long yellowish leaves resembling those of the lemon tree, was mostly remarkable for the contortion of its branches. The *amsitoro* was a clean-looking tree, with few branches shooting straight skyward. Its bark was whitish and the leaves, two to three inches long and of a long oval shape, grew tightly together. This tree produced big fruit in bunches, frequently three together, with a solitary fourth hanging below them. The *amsitoro* fruit, taken singly, was shaped like a cucumber, four to six inches long and of a yellowish-brown colour.

The *ndafu* rubber vine, of great size and strength, grew in quantities along the Khor, climbing to the top of trees in intricate masses. It ejected a white latex when incisions were made. In fact, one could see where many of these vines had been tapped by the natives ; especially at the elbows or angles of the vine, where the natives say the latex collects and can be made to flow in abundance.

Although one saw tempting fruit of all kinds in the forest, it was dangerous to try experiments. Most was poisonous, and what was eatable had neither a delicate flavour nor particular sweetness. In fact, most samples possessed an acid taste which set one's teeth on edge. The best was the long *yaguma* bean, enclosing yellow pulp like cassia. The *hameru*, a small yellow medlar, much resembles the *mespilus japonica*.

In this region we and our animals were much tormented by flies. Swarms of them buzzed round us as we were marching along. A big fly, believed by many to be the tze-tze, was plentiful here and gave men and animals vexatious stings. We had met this fly before during the last two or three days of our journey, but never in such legions as we did that day. I was badly stung in the back of the head, and it left a lump as big as half an egg for several days.

That day I saw on the trail two lions. They were not more than four or five yards away. They had a good look at me, and then pleasantly and majestically walked away, well surmising that I had no evil intentions towards them. The lions of this region, like most Central African lions, are not beautiful to look at, as they are maneless and have somewhat mangy skins with short hair. They have, however, honest expressions and dignified eyes, and a most powerful and beautiful stride.

At Khor Ghanam were two villages for the police, and a large *zeriba* in a filthy condition, with four huts and a *rakuba*. The Khor was almost dry and we only obtained a little water from two small pools. During the rainy season the drainage of the surrounding country fills the Khor. There was a roughly-made ferry boat, so long that when across it nearly touched both banks of the stream, twelve feet apart. The policeman at this place was a Niam-Niam, a first-class robber. In fact, barring one or two, nearly all these police upon the trail were impertinent scoundrels, the cream of the riff-raff of the Sudanese army.

Photograph of two maneless lions, taken by Author late one afternoon on a rainy day.

The channel of the Ghanam Khor had a direction from south-south-east to north-north-west at an elevation of 1,800 feet, with banks twelve feet high.

On April 31st we left Ghanam at 7.30 and we gently rose to 1,950 feet, from which elevation we descended through forest—not dense—and eventually arrived at Dem Zebir at 10.15. As we approached the place a beautiful wide road had been cut near the military post, the officer's house being on the highest of the two hills upon which the post is situated.

To the north was a high straight horizon-line, somewhat higher in its eastern portion than to the west. The two hills on which Dem Zebir stood, although not high, formed quite prominent points in the landscape, one at 7° bearings magnetic, the other at 4° 30', when we obtained the first view of them.

The Somali and I, convoying the entire caravan, reached Dem Zebir, 147½ miles from Wau, in shortly under eight days' marching, having kept up an average speed of eighteen and a half miles a day.

Abu Shakka	12 miles
Bisellia	13½ ,,
Khor Gombolo	10 ,,
River Pongo	20 ,,
Khor Ganna	13½ ,,
Khor Gamus	10 ,,
Khor Raml	9 ,,
Dem Idris	8 ,,
Khor Afifi	15 ,,
River Kuru	10 ,,
Khor Abanga	9½ ,,
Khor Ghanam	9 ,,
Dem Zebir	8 ,,
	147½ miles

Dem Zebir, upon a commanding position (1,990 feet), was decidedly the pleasantest-looking place in the Bahr-el-Ghazal. Near the summit of the highest hill was a fort of earth with an outer palisade at an angle, and two large thatched buildings in the interior, as well as a central tower upon which the Union Jack and the Egyptian colours flew gaily. This fort was first established by a French officer, who built it of stone. Then Bimbashi Rawson, of the Egyptian Government, reconstructed it of earth. The *mamur* continued this work and Bimbashi Comyn finished it.

Everything in Dem Zebir was extremely neat, owing to the energy of a most excellent and practical officer, Bimbashi Percival, who resided here, with a staff of intelligent Egyptians under him, such as the *mamur*, Ali Effendi Wahbi, and a Syrian doctor, who were stationed in the place.

One or two buildings, of locally-made bricks, were in course of construction, and an endeavour was made to mark out the streets of a town which will perhaps some day grow on that site, the most westerly Anglo-Egyptian post in the Bahr-el-Ghazal.

One or two Syrian traders, mostly dealing in ivory and rubber, and a Turk, had found their way to Dem Zebir. I saw magnificent elephants' tusks at this place, some weighing 134 lbs. each. Others had been obtained weighing as much as 194 lbs. The quality of the ivory in this part of the country was excellent.

The section of the Bahr-el-Ghazal between Wau and the French Congo boundary was to my mind the only portion over which I had travelled in that province which was worth developing and which had any wealth in it at all. In the northern part, near Hofrat-el-Nahas, I

am told that about one mile south of the river
Umbelacha copper mines are to be found, in shallow
pits covering about half a square mile. The ways of
communication at the time of my visit to the Western
Bahr-el-Ghazal were deficient, the best trail, besides the
road between Wau and Dem Zebir, being between
Dem Zebir and Kossinga, a distance of eighty-four miles
through thick forest and over gigantic boulders in the
bed of the river Biri.

From Kossinga the trail continued to Hofrat-el-
Nahas, two hundred miles distant, going through the
Kresh and Ferogheh tribes under Sultan Mousa. This
route first went south-west from Kossinga to Ragga,
then fairly directly in a north-westerly direction to Kafi-
Khangi, whence in great détours, and getting bad
beyond the river Adda, it proceeded north to Hofrat-el-
Nahas. There were fair camping grounds nearly all
along this route, only horse-flies and the supposed
tze-tze being plentiful and troublesome. From Ragga
to Dem Zebir the distance was eighty-seven miles.

Deleb palms stud the country in many places,
principally near Kresh villages. There was a direct
trail between Kossinga and Wau *via* Shaat and the river
Biri (locally known as the Chel), where the Denka
Sultan, Chak-Chak, had made his residence on the east
bank of the stream. Several Denka villages were in that
region, especially some tribes under the powerful Denka
chief, Agaka, a brother of Chak-Chak, in the district
called Ayak. Golo and Djur, Bari and Endogo villages
were also to be met with on this trail. The distance
between Kossinga and Wau by this direct route was
210 miles.

We were here close to the French Congo boundary

and we had a great mixture of people. Some had come
with Zebir (or Zuiber) Pasha before the time of the
Dervishes in 1880. Tribes on both sides of the boundary were restless and occasionally shifted their quarters
from one side to the other of the frontier.

The most powerful tribes were perhaps the Kresh
and the Banda, with the Ajah and the Four, the latter
lately over from French territory.

When Zebir Pasha travelled over this country Sultan
Yango, of the Banda, was on the Bibi river. Probably
frightened by the arrival of the terrible slave-dealer,
Sultan Yango and his people went over to the French
Congo ; Zebir Pasha also travelled down to the Mbomu
river in the French Congo as far as the Great Sultanate
of Bongasso.

Sultan Yango, of the Banda tribe, only returned to
the British side from the French Congo in 1903. Mousa-
Kemdego, another sultan near Dem Zebir, was a Kresh,
who also came over from the French Congo about the
year 1900.

There were other important sultans, like Nasr Andel,
the sultan of Kossinga, a man of Negogely, south of
El Fasher. The sultan lived at Kossinga, a large village
of straw *tukles* and *zeribas* with some three hundred
inhabitants, situated north of the Khor Juyu, where
the villagers got their water at the foot of a three-peaked
granitic hill. The sultan was wide awake and had good
trading instincts. The negro portion of the population
was formed of Mandalla, but the majority were a half
Arab (Baggara and Jaalin) and half Mandalla breed. In
this village were a number of Syrian and Arab traders
from Omdurman, who exchanged cloth, cotton goods, salt,
beads and wire for ivory. It was a fair market for *dhura*,

Dem Zebir fort.

sem-sem, bamia, beans (monkey nuts), etc. Nasr Andel tells of his descent from sultans in the Darfur country. He himself became a sultan when he came to Kossinga, having succeeded his uncle. He says that his grandfather (who was the first to come from Darfur) took possession of the country around Kossinga, assuming the title of sultan. Nasr Andel had under him fourteen sheikhs. This man was an inveterate drinker and levied heavy duties on the traders. There was a good market at Kossinga for donkeys, sheep and oxen. A good donkey fetched about £2 sterling, a sheep from two to four shillings, and a bull about forty shillings. Nasr Andel had for a son a fellow who rejoiced in the name of Nogolgoleh.

Many tribes were under the sultan, such as the Mangayat, the Forogheli, the Tuguyu, the Kresh, the Shaat and the Mandalla, the only occupation of most of these tribesmen being chasing elephants in order to obtain the ivory. A few possessed matchlocks, but most went in a body with their spears with which they riddled elephants with wounds.

Sultan Nasr Andel warmly welcomed the arrival of the British in the Bahr-el-Ghazal a couple of years ago. He also sent messages to the Sirdar of Khartoum before the Bahr-el-Ghazal was opened, assuring the Government of his friendship towards the British.

A similar message was sent, I believe, by the neighbouring sultan of Ragga, Mousa-Hamed, who had under him the following tribes : The Forogheh, a portion of the Mangayat tribe, a section of the Kresh population, the Shayù, the Mandalla, the Dongo, the Bornu and the Borgu, the latter being a tribe from Wadai. His district was fairly rich in rubber, but owing to the distance and difficulty of carriage little came towards Khartoum. Perhaps most of the produce found its way into the French Congo, where the natives sold it to advantage to honest and generous French commercial companies rather than to local Syrian and Armenian traders.

Mousa-Hamed's people are said to have come originally from Mecca, from which sacred spot they proceeded to Yedda, then to Khartoum, which they subsequently left to proceed to Kordofan ; eventually they moved over to Darfur and then at last came to settle at Ragga. There was a feud between Nasr Andel and Mousa-Hamed when the latter's father was made a *muduru* by the Government. When the *muduru* died some twelve or thirteen years ago, there was trouble between the two sultans, as Nasr Andel, who had acknowledged the authority of the *muduru*, refused to acknowledge that of his son who had succeeded him and who was then about eighteen years of age. Things went so far that he gathered his men and declared himself sultan, challenging Mousa-Hamed, who had not the courage to take up arms against him.

That secluded person, the sultan of Wadai, is a Borgu by birth, while our friend Sultan Mousa-Hamed is a Forogheh.

On the Bahr, or Boro river, is found Sultan Saïd-Bandas, of the Kresh-Nakka, a tribe quite apart from the Kresh proper and somewhat intermixed with the A-sandeh or Niam-Niam. He, with his people, came to settle in this region at the end of 1902. These Kresh-Nakka were mostly brought over owing to the efforts of *mamur* Ali Effendi Wahbi, as they said the Banda tribe frequently raided their country, stealing their women, *dhura*, etc. When they came over they presented the *mamur* with white beads as an emblem of the purity of their hearts. In time of peace they wore sometimes white cloth ornaments or white beads, but in time of war red beads were always displayed. Saïd-Bandas was extremely loyal. He at one time suffered severe reverses in fighting against the Dervishes and had to escape to the Banda country. His village, humble and tumble-down, was about three or four miles from Sultan Mahommed-Merikki's headquarters.

Sultan Mahommed-Merikki, of the Kresh-Aja, and also of the Banda-Uassa, came over from the French Congo in 1902. Mahommed-Merikki's father came from the banks of the Umbili river. When his father died, having learnt that Zebir Pasha had formed a post at Mudirieh, now called Dem Zebir, he came there. Under Zebir, he became a chieftain and followed him as far as Shakka. Then Zebir sent him to a place called Lawa where the Sinussi fought him. When Zebir discharged him he presented him with a hundred guns, which he afterwards gave to Suliman. His people came mostly from Lawa, a river about ten days' journey beyond Aja. When Zebir was ordered back to Egypt, Merikki became a sultan in his country.

At Kafi-Kanghi, a post north-west of Dem Zebir and probably the most westerly point of the Bahr-el-Ghazal province, where a native officer and twenty-five police were at one time stationed, was Sultan Ibrahim-Morad, a Kresh by birth. He has under him three sheikhs. His father was originally from Darfur and came to settle at Hofrat-el-Nahas. Ibrahim-Morad was by nature more or less of a robber, and managed to squeeze what he could out of the people passing through his country. He professed to be unable to prevent the trade in rifles and ivory in his country and applied for protection from the post at Kafi-Kanghi.

Ibrahim-Morad's people were members of the Kresh, Dongo, Endogo and Banda-Uassa tribes.

The Kresh tribe was the most numerous of all, and the sultan of Ragga perhaps the most important sultan in the Western Bahr-el-Ghazal. He had some six thousand men, all warriors in a sort of way. It was hard to understand why the Bahr-el-Ghazal Government found so much difficulty in obtaining carriers when such a rich source of labour could be tapped with no difficulty. Transport at least would become possible in that country. This is only one out of many sources which could be exploited in the Bahr-el-Ghazal, as the Banda also could, I think, produce a practically inexhaustible supply of men, not to count what might be obtained from minor tribes.

Types of the different tribesmen are given in illustrations in this work. Some, it will be noticed, are powerfully-built individuals, who may some day be useful not only as carriers but as fighting material. They show great fondness for soldiering, and although not particularly brave, could be trained well enough to be fair soldiers for local needs.

It was interesting to see, not only what numbers of people these sultans possessed, but also to observe how many rifles and guns had found their way into that country. True enough, most of those guns were more dangerous to the people who carried them than to those who are likely to be aimed at, but many excellent rifles have of late, I believe, been smuggled among the better people, who are paying enormous quantities of ivory

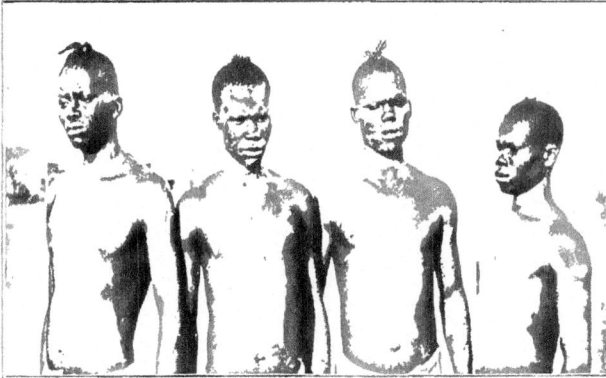

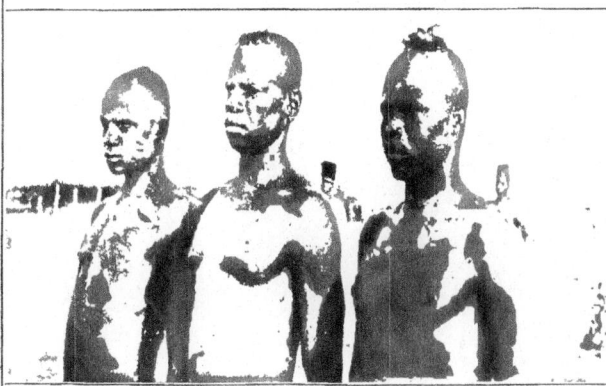

1.—Aja.   Aja.   Aja.   Aja.
2.—Aja.   Banda.   Banda.
3.—Kresh and Yango.

to obtain good weapons.   Surprises may be forthcoming in those regions some day.

I have before me figures which I think are accurate enough, and which show the number of able-bodied men under the different sultans, and the number of guns possessed by each sultan :—

Sultan Nasr Andel possesses 380 able-bodied men, with 200 good Remington and Lebel rifles.

Sultan Mousa-Hamed, 560 able-bodied men, 18 sheikhs and 200 guns.

Saïd-Bandas, 180 relations, 6 sheikhs, and 145 guns.

Sultan Mahommed-Merikki, 200 relations, 3 sheikhs, and 120 guns.

Sultan Yango, whose people are most excellent workers and easily manageable, possesses only 96 relations, about 100 able-bodied men, and 25 rifles.

Sultan Mousa-Kemdego, of the Kresh tribe, has 6 sheikhs, 120 able-bodied men, 15 guns, and only 56 relations.

There was another sultan, Sultan Ibrahim Dardug, of the Dongawi tribe, but he was extremely troublesome and had to be confined for life in the prison of El Nahud.

From Dem Zebir alone as a centre, at least six to seven hundred carriers could be supplied, and the people, I think, would be quite willing, even glad, to do the work.   In fact, they look upon the British Government as weak for not making them work.   Ragga alone could easily supply 400 men, and Yango from 100 to 150 men.

We do not find among these people the same marriage customs of purchasing a wife by handing over cattle, for the simple reason that these people possess few animals. When marrying a girl, a man must supply the girl's father with another woman in exchange. If the bridegroom has no way of fulfilling his part of the agreement, the father of the girl takes her husband to live with him and makes him work like a servant. If this arrangement does not answer—and generally some difficulty is experienced in making it run smooth—the bride's father may permit the wedding but will become the legal proprietor of the first-born child.

Since the British Government came in 1903, these picturesque arrangements have to a certain extent been put a stop to, and more civilized, as well as vulgarized, weddings have been enforced. The bridegroom must pay for his wife so many rolls of calico. Fancy, the mere idea of exchanging a wife for calico !

The Banda had similar wedding customs, but all other tribes to the north generally paid cloth and beads in order to obtain a life partner.

The manners and customs of all these tribes differ little from others we have already met.

Art and music are unknown to them.

Of religion they know but little. The Kresh believe in three deities : One who kills men, another who tries to make everybody ill, and one " good god " who endeavours to heal those who suffer. In the centre of every village a big tree is generally to be observed, and they believe that the " good god " hovers unseen under its shade. I asked a Kresh whether it was the same " good god " who lived under trees of all villages or whether each village had a separate god, but they seemed puzzled, almost perplexed, at the question. They had never thought of it before, and I could not get a definite answer. Most, however, were partial to the monopoly of a " good god " for each village.

When anybody committed a fault or else felt in bad health it was usual to take offerings of *merissa* (liquor), beans and different foods, and put them either in a hollow in the tree or else at the foot as offerings for the "good god." Soon after, however, the givers returned and drank and ate everything themselves.

With the exception of a few superstitions the tribes offered few features of general interest. Their funeral ceremonies were extraordinarily simple ; a few ululations and moans, and the dead man was buried with his head towards the east or the west, according to the tribe to which he belonged. With nearly all these tribes, the dead man's house must remain empty until it collapses. Other tribes clear the ground round the grave and repair the hut of the deceased in order to preserve it ; this especially in the case of a chief.

In their marital relations the Kresh adopt certain rules which are interesting. During the time the wife is in an interesting condition no sexual intercourse is permitted, the husband and wife generally living apart. Girls in the Kresh country can marry at the age of ten or twelve. They are then fully formed and developed quite as much as women in England and America at the age of eighteen or twenty. Although this physical development takes place at an early age few women can bear children until they are about fifteen. The treatment of the umbilical cord at birth of a child is done by a special woman, a sort of midwife, who also attends women during labour.

In case of unfaithfulness, the man who has committed adultery must hand over a slave to the offended husband, or else forty *malud*, or forty *tukkya*, pieces of locally woven cloth. A significant notion exists among Kresh that if this payment is not forthcoming to the betrayed husband, the co-respondent will become impotent and also will have ill-luck in anything he may undertake in the future, such as elephant-hunting or agricultural pursuits. Were this not sufficient punishment, his hut will be destroyed by fire or blown down by the wind. Yes, indeed, the revenge of the Kresh gods will come down in all its force upon unrepentant adulterers !

Ali Effendi Wahbi told me a curious tale of an elephant hunter called Barni who had been absent during four months. His wife had been unfaithful during his absence. The offender was fined forty pieces of *tukkya*, which he at once paid. On leaving Dem Zebir, Barni shot elephant successfully, killing five elephants in one week, this success being put down altogether to the forty pieces of cloth received in compensation for his wife's unvirtuous life.

Virgins in the Kresh country are valued in marriage contracts at the equivalent of £2 sterling ; whereas ladies somewhat more mature do not fetch more than ten shillings or so, perhaps ten-and-sixpence. Heiresses are known to have cost a bridegroom as much as eighty shillings and the daughter of a sultan from five hundred to one thousand *tukkya*, one *tukkya* being worth from three to five piastres, according to locality.

In connection with love affairs, one finds sometimes symbolical figures of rudimentary representations of sexual organs carved on trees.

lines, of sets of three cicatrices each, are to be noticed along the centre of the chest. The skull taken as a whole does not show such elongation as we find among the Ferogheh, and the brain-case, or calvaria, is fairly well formed and balanced. They shave the head, but leave sufficient hair on the top, which they then tie into two or three small tresses.

The Banda, who, in many ways, have similar characteristics to the Niam-Niam or A-sandeh, are short people, with a great development of the breasts. Some men had prominent breasts almost like women. They possessed somewhat flabby arms and big paunches, and great length of body in relation to the legs, which were in comparison more muscularly formed. The great prominence of their upper jaw gave their palate an elongated parabolic form like the letter " u," very narrow at the curve, whereas the Aja have an elliptical or horseshoe shaped palate, much broader than that of the Banda and not so long.

The Banda, like the Niam-Niam, have ill-formed hands, with square-tipped fingers and hardly any lines in the palm except the four principal ones. The thumb is extremely short, the last phalanx mean and flattened. In fact, the Banda are people of a degenerate order, with no great brain capacity ; people who will eat anything they find, no matter how repulsive and disgusting.

Their ornamentations take the shape of cicatrices, which are made in a rudimentary manner ; so rudimentary that it is difficult to define accurately what they are meant to represent. In other tribes one finds a certain geometrical regularity and precision of execution in these ornamentations, but not so at all among the Banda. They have evidently attempted to copy

some of these ornaments from the Aja and the Nogolgoleh. They attempt to reproduce a qi   with
a cross of double lines inside ; also they 1
tary attempts at a five-pointed star and tl

More interesting as a type was the Nog
in the plural becomes Nogolgoleh. The\
to say, several characteristics in common
golian type. One could trace this Mongo
any of the tri   across Africa,

The hands of these people were somewhat more delicately formed than those of the Aja, for instance, and on a very different level from those of the Banda.

The Kresh showed a great bizygomatic breadth, with well-padded zygomatic arches. The tip of the nose and the nostrils were broad and flattened, so elongated that the latter were parallel to the angular planes of the lips instead of being almost vertical, as with Europeans. The head was elongated upwards, the back of the skull flattened and forming almost a vertical line from the top of the skull to the base of the neck.

Again we found here the habit of removing the four incisor teeth. Occasionally the two central upper teeth were filed each into a sharp point, giving a ghastly expression to the face. Four vertical and three horizontal cuts on each cheek were usual among the Kresh, the four vertical cuts being each of two parallel lines. Like the Nogolgoleh, they wore small tresses upon the head.

The Kresh-Nakka were not unlike the other Kresh, except that they shaved a great portion of the hair of the head, and adorned themselves with only three large cuts on each cheek and three cuts on each temple. On the arms they had adopted a four-pointed star in double lines.

I visited some of the Kresh villages. The chief, as a rule, had built himself a square mud house, with no furniture, if we except the few pots of a spherical shape in which water was kept, and some slabs of stone or of hardened cement for grinding grain, which we found in a separate hut used as a kitchen. Holes in the ground, coated with cement, were used as mortars. Grain was stored in cylindrical baskets on piles, numerous in their villages. In the chief's house I noticed a double bed,

was raised on piles five feet high, and it had a conical thatched roof. The sultan's wife seemed scared when I suddenly appeared. She was nursing a fat child smothered all over in red and blue beads, especially on the right side of the head, upon the temples and back of the head. She herself had a huge red bead stuck in the left nostril. Her hair was plastered down in tiny tresses soaked in oil, and ending in little bullets of dirt and green vegetable oil.

The cicatrices in the Yango took the form of the wave pattern around the neck, with three vertical cuts on the temples and three horizontal slashes on each cheek. Vertical cuts were noticeable under the knees, with five or six lines of the wave pattern underneath.

At death the Kresh were buried under one of the *dhura* store-houses, which they abandoned, with its contents. The dead man's house was closed and nobody was allowed to go into it. It was then eventually destroyed. When a man died he was buried with his head towards the west, while the Kresh women were laid down with the head towards the east.

At various points west of Wau and in the forest I came across a number of stray Niam-Niam. Their country lies to the south of the Bellanda and Bongo countries. In fact, in some settlements of Niam-Niam, we find mixed with them a few Bellanda.

Although these people are called dwarfs, I did not find them so extraordinarily small. They were not tall certainly, the tallest I saw being some five feet four inches. Most adults, I should say, were about or over five feet in height.

The skin of the Niam-Niam was of a deep chocolate colour, and the hair of the usual negrito type pre-

senting a woolly, poodle-like appearance. Their bodies
were long in comparison with the limbs, particularly with
the legs, and they possessed big paunches and chests,
so developed that in many of the men the upper portion
of the anatomy appeared at first sight quite feminine.
We have already met other tribes with similar characteristics. Although this development made them appear
stoutly built they possessed comparatively little strength,
in the arms particularly. The short legs, which were
thinner and more sinewy, showed slightly more power,
but physically these people were in no way to be compared either with the tribes further north-east or with
many of the tribes to the west ; a number of tribes,
however, in their immediate neighbourhood in the forest,
the Kare, for instance, whom we shall meet later on,
closely resembled them in their physical and moral
weakness.

The almond-shaped eyes, set at a slant, like Mon-
golian eyes, were wide apart upon their broad skulls,
quite *à fleur de tête*, and almost bovine in character,
with extraordinarily heavy overlapping brows. The
eyeball was of a sallow yellowish tint, bloodshot ;
the iris deep brown, with velvety-black pupils, widely
dilated in the green light of the forest, the upper portion
of the iris much discoloured—in fact, in many cases
quite obliterated.

The nose of the A-sandeh was square and flat, the
lips heavy and drooping, the cheeks well padded, and
the chin somewhat receding but fairly broad and well
rounded. They filed the front teeth into a point, and
this gave a fierce expression to their countenances.

The head, which seemed large and heavy in proportion to the height of the individuals, was rounded and

west of this region, who perhaps are related to the A-sandeh.

Although rounded, the skull of the A-sandeh was ill-proportioned when seen in profile, being much elongated and slanting, absolutely devoid of intelligence or mental balance. Treachery and meanness and a craving to possess were the predominant features of the specimens I met, although on several occasions they astonished me with their ruses in endeavouring to obtain what they wanted. Maybe other people have found good qualities in these people. I did not. They were invariably unscrupulous, contemptible rascals, whom one felt a great desire to strangle every time one had dealings with them. Liars they were to a most tantalizing extent, even when it would pay them to be truthful; thieves, traitors, filthy in their food—they would eat any animal raw in the most advanced state of putrefaction and enjoy it! They would do the same with human beings when they had a chance. Really, I could not be attracted by these people. Dogs were relished as food by them, and they kept a breed of small, short-haired, curly-tailed, fat-paunched animals of a yellowish colour, which, after having been loved as pets, were generally eaten.

It is said that the A-sandeh are faithful to their wives, and that they will make any sacrifice—even to the loss of their lives—in trying to recover them when seized in raids by slave traders. That is surely a good quality, but perhaps the intrinsic commercial value of his better half is more to the A-sandeh than his personal devotion or affection for her.

Their marriage and burial ceremonies resemble those of the Bongo. Polygamy is practised.

The vanity of these ugly people is incredible. Entire

blades of each tribe are of a different shape and easily recognizable by experts.

Unlike their neighbours on the east, the A-sandeh possess no cattle. They have a few chickens. They are agriculturists to a certain extent. Good and evil omens and the evil eye find a ready belief in the A-sandeh country. Many detailed descriptions of these have already been given, and also of their cannibalistic feasts, for which they are world-renowned. The collection of skulls near the dwellings are sufficient proof of the desire they have for human flesh. They eat, of course, mostly their enemies, but dying friends unclaimed by their relatives may provide a good meal at a pinch. A lonely stranger dying of fever or wounds in their country would, I think, even to this day, supply them with a palatable dish, disease or putrefaction being no bar at all to their craving for human delicacies.

Perhaps a few of the less-known characteristics of their language may be of interest.

There are such curious and indisputably well-defined peculiarities in their language as lead one to repeat that these people must have degenerated from a higher standard of mental ability. However, of course, these peculiarities might be merely accidental. Whether accidental or not, we find in the A-sandeh tongue examples of deep philosophy which are not to be found in more complete languages, such as Italian, French, German, Spanish, Portuguese or English. For instance, in order to explain that some inanimate object belongs to him, such as a hut (-*kuorau*), a spear (-*basso*) . . . . the A-sandeh would use the pronoun corresponding to " my " in English—" my hut, my spear," etc. ; but in describing a part of himself or talking of people of his own blood, he will never say, " My father, my mother, my eye, my leg, my hand," but will say, " I father, I mother, I leg, I hand," etc., to denote that those people of his own blood and flesh, as well as any part of his own anatomy, are more than mere possessions. They form part of himself. This is generally done by the suffixes " *sse* " or " *rè* " or " *mi* " after the noun. My father, *Ba-mi ;* my friend, *Badia-rè ;* my eye, *Bengli-sse.*

We do not find the same accurate philosophy in many other A-sandeh expressions, although some descriptiveness is generally noticeable in many of their words, and is usually borrowed from meteorological phenomena or from the botanical world. Beard, for instance, *mainguengoua*, is nothing less when translated literally than " rain from the chin."

The hand, *ppe'be*, is the " leaf of the arm" (*ppe*, leaf; *be*, arm). A finger nail, *sissi ouil insaga* (*sissi*, bark ; *ouil insaga*, finger), means literally the "bark of one's finger." The foot, *ppe' ndoue*, is the "leaf of the leg." Perhaps the most remarkable of all is the word *de'goude*, meaning girl, but which translated literally means : *de*, woman ; *goude*, boy, or a " woman boy."

They are almost as immoderate as we are in speaking of their sensations, nothing short of death being sufficient to describe love or drunkenness. *Kpi na gnamou,* " to die of love." *Kpi na boda,* " to die of beer."

Astronomy is perhaps not the strongest point of the A-sandeh. The stars, in their language, *care courou*, are the " enemies of the sun " (*care*, enemy).

Numerals are counted, as usual with almost all African tribes, with the aid of the fingers up to five : *ssa*, one ; *iouë*, two ; *bia'ta*, three ; *biama*, four ; *bissouë*, five ; six, *bati ssa*, being " give one from the other hand " ;

EQUATORIAL AFRICA

Showing route followed by A. Henry SAVAGE-LANDOR

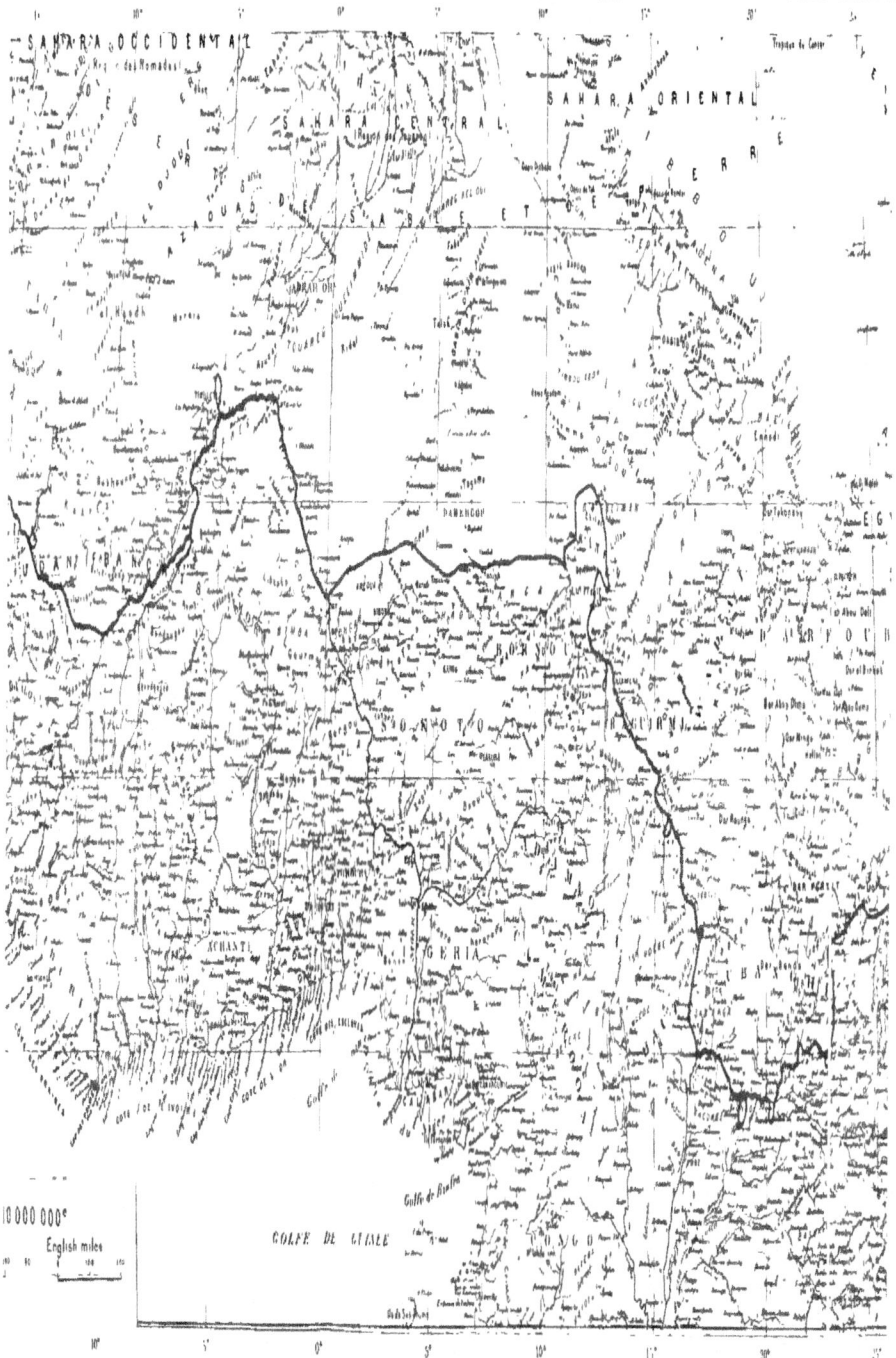

of the Geographical Society of Paris. H.Barrère Publisher.

Central Asia and Tibet:
Towards the Holy City of Lassa.
By SVEN HEDIN,

Gold Medallist of the Royal Geographical Society of Great Britain,
Author of "Through Asia," &c.

With 420 Illustrations from Drawings and Photographs, 8 Full-page
Coloured Illustrations from Paintings, and 5 Maps, mostly by the Author.
In Two Volumes, Royal 8vo. £2 2s. net.

In 1 vol., demy 8vo, profusely Illustrated. Price 10s. 6d. net.

Adventures in Tibet.

By SVEN HEDIN, Author of "Central Asia and Tibet."

In 1 vol., demy 8vo. with Illustrations. Price 16s. net.

Russia, Travels
and Studies.

By ANNETTE M. B. MEAKIN, Author of "A Ribbon of Iron," &c.

" The book gives a most interesting account of the success of German subjects of the
Tzar settled in Russia proper among less progressive neighbours."—*Pall Mall Gazette.*

" Miss Meakin has produced a most readable and informative book on Russia.
The Russia she describes is a normal Russia—not the Russia of war and revolution."—
Scotsman.

THE FIRST COMPLETE JOURNEY ACROSS AFRICA FROM
SOUTH TO NORTH.

From the Cape to Cairo.

By EWART S. GROGAN and ARTHUR H. SHARP. With Introduction
by the Right Hon. CECIL RHODES. New and Revised Edition.
In 1 vol., demy 8vo, fully Illustrated by Drawings by A. D.
McCORMICK (from Sketches by E. S. GROGAN) ; Original Drawings
by E. S. GROGAN ; Photographs and Photogravure Portraits of the
Authors, and two Maps. Price 7s. 6d. net.

" 'From the Cape to Cairo' is essentially a work of high importance, and it is
no small boast for a traveller of Mr. Grogan's years to have been the first to accomplish
a task which no one had previously brought to a successful issue."—*Daily Telegraph.*

Beautifully Illustrated from Drawings by A. J. ENGEL TERZI. 1 vol.,
demy 8vo. Price 10s. 6d. net.

The Voice of the South.

By GILBERT WATSON, Author of "Three Rolling Stones in Japan."

The Egyptian Campaigns, 1882-85.

New and Revised Edition continued to 1899. By CHARLES ROYLE,
late R.N. ; Barrister-at-Law, Judge of the Egyptian Court of Appeal,
Cairo. In 1 vol., demy 8vo, extra cloth, Illustrated by numerous
Maps and Plans. Price 12s. net.

" A comprehensive narrative of the Mahdist and Arabist movements, including the
story of the English intervention in Egypt."—*Daily News.*

In 1 vol., demy 8vo, with numerous Illustrations reproduced from Photographs taken on the journey. Price 10s. 6d. net.

In Remotest Barotseland.

From the Victoria Falls to the Source of the Zambesi. By Col.
COLIN HARDING, C.M.G., Acting Administrator for Barotseland.

1 vol., medium 8vo, with over 200 Illustrations from Photographs specially
taken for this work. Five Maps. Price 18s. net.

Antarctica.

Two Years among the Ice of the South Pole.

By Dr. OTTO NORDENSKÖLD.

In 1 vol., royal 4to, containing numerous Illustrations in Colour, and in Black
and White, from Drawings and Photographs by the Author and
others. Several Maps, Diagrams, &c. Price 25s. net.

The Tanganyika Problem.

An Account of the Researches undertaken concerning the Existence
of Marine Animals in Central Africa. By J. E. S. MOORE, F.R.G.S.,
Author of " To the Mountains of the Moon," &c.

The present work contains the only illustrated description of the fishes and
other animals which inhabit the Great African Lakes.

UNIVERSITY OF CALIFORNIA LIBRARY

Los Angeles

This book is DUE on the last date

UC SOUTHERN REGIONAL LIBRARY FACILITY

A   000 480 850   7

9 781314 641738

CPSIA information can be obtained at www.ICGtesting.com
Printed in the USA
LVOW04s1840290415

436496LV00041BA/492/P

9 781314 641738